W9-CKR-046

People of
provide for the common defen
and establish this Constitution
Artic
Powers herein granted shall be
Representatives shall be compose
ations requisite for Electors of the m
presentative who shall not have
an Inhabitant of that State in w
Taxes shall be apportioned amon
ed. by adding to the whole Numbe
Persons. The actual Enumerati

TO CREATE A NATION

THE LINK PRESS PRESENTS

Marjorie Ashworth

TO CREATE A NATION

THE CONSTITUTIONAL CONVENTION *of* 1787

Marjorie Ashworth

Copyright © Marjorie Ashworth

All rights reserved
including the right to reproduce this book
or portions thereof in any form.

Manufactured in the United States of America

First edition

Library of Congress Catalogue Number 87-82007
ISBN 0-912991-05-4

TABLE OF CONTENTS

FOREWORD

As I REVIEW YET AGAIN, during these Bicentennial years, those remarkable debates of the 1787 Constitutional Convention in Philadelphia, I am struck by how often the delegates refer to "the people," and how they ponder whether to accept the new government document being drafted.

One of the momentous chapters in world history is the writing and ratifying of the Constitution of the United States. The Constitution has long been rooted so deeply in American life and/or American life rooted so deeply in it — that the drama of its origin is often overlooked.

And so it is fitting and proper now as we approach the 200th anniversary of its birth that we commemorate and celebrate it. One way to celebrate and commemorate is to acquire and read the splendid text written by Marjorie Ashworth.

Yes, the delegates who framed our Constitution held in their minds constantly the body of citizens beyond the State House. There was an important reason for this. The newly-independent Americans had a keen interest in politics and a sharp eye on their leaders. Visitors from Europe were astounded that the general public of the young nation was so aware and knowledgeable in the governmental arena. As the author of this book aptly comments, citizens looked with derision upon those among them who were ignorant or indifferent to their government and how it functioned. The 18th-century taverns and marketplaces and homes were alive with discussion about the nature of law and the rights and duties of human beings in society. They understood there is a pact between government and citizens, each accountable to the other.

As the 200th anniversary of our U.S. Constitution approaches, it came to me that one of the great rewards of living two centuries with this remarkable document could be the opportunity for a time of renewal.

Once more — in the context of the 20th and 21st centuries — we could rediscover our roots, the foundation of law upon which we stand. We could reaffirm, if we examined our Constitution and subsequent amendments, the guarantees and responsibilities it outlines. We could also understand the ways this body of law offers growth and change as we confront the manifold problems of today.

Our legislature, executive branch, and judiciary system all need us as we need them — government cannot sustain the well-being of society without an active, thinking public. And neither government nor public can afford to be ignorant or contemptuous of the other and risk peril to ourselves and future generations.

I see these Bicentennial years as a time of learning and debate as were those fateful days in 1787 when 55 men struggled with new concepts of law and self-government, and an enlightened public was able to understand, support — and then finally to add those crucial first ten amendments, the Bill of Rights, to the document.

I invite all Americans to find ways — by reading the Constitution and books about it such as this one, by participating in discussions with friends and children — to become the kind of informed public which helped set our country upon its glorious path.

And I would be remiss if I did not invite all Americans to be proud of our Nation's flag and of our Capitol, a magnificent edifice in stone, which stands as a symbol of the success of our Republic.

I recall with humility and pride what a former Member of Congress, Rufus Choate, once said: "We have built no national temples but the Capitol. We consult no common oracle but the Constitution."

Fred Schwengel

FRED SCHWENGEL, *President*
The U.S. Capitol Historical Society

INTRODUCTION

Where would we be, those of us trying to make real the spirit and flavor of Philadelphia summer 1787, if we lacked the helping hand of that remarkable delegate from Virginia, James Madison?

Among the first arrivals in Philadelphia, head stuffed with countless government theories of the ages, Madison had the fixed goal of bringing to the 13 states a viable form of rule that would bind them into a nation. For years he had been preparing for this Convention; now he was ready with a plan, and a mind sharpened to defend it.

On top of this, he added yet another task—one which has been all-important to us in understanding what went on during that memorable summer. Madison undertook to keep a running diary of the Convention, quoting the delegates as they rose day after day to speak their minds. He missed not one single session, using his own shorthand which he transcribed later. As the debates were secret, we would be lost without this precious journal. It must stand as one of the great documents of history, a gift to posterity that cannot be measured.

Nevertheless, one finds many books about the Constitutional Convention paraphrase what he wrote, or offer judgments about delegates and their performance without letting us read Madison's account. And so, Franklin may be termed "wise" by one and "a mere figurehead" by another; Gouverneur Morris "elegant and bombastic" by one and "a gifted stylist" by another.

It seemed to me that the reader should have a chance to measure the delegates himself and decide how certain decisions were reached.

To do this, there was no better way than to offer extensive segments of Madison's notes. How else can one comprehend fully the frustration, the break-throughs, the fears, the triumphs of reason during those four hot months within the Philadelphia State House?

The Convention must certainly be our nation's great drama. And so, those chapters of this book dealing directly with it are termed Acts One, Two and Three. In them, the Madison journal is used liberally, as he wrote it, except for the misspelling of delegates' names. Madison repeatedly wrote Nathaniel Gorham of Massachusetts as "Ghorum"; Oliver Ellsworth of Connecticut as "Elseworth"; Charles Cotesworth Pinckney of South Carolina as "Mr. Pinkney", and so on. These have been corrected. But Madison's other idiosyncrasies have been left intact. Sometimes he slides from direct to indirect quotation, abbreviates and misspells words. And so the "Honble" gentlemen "negative" motions, "animadvert" on each other's pet theories, describe their "painful feelings" while "descanting" on issues.

I am grateful to Dr. Herman Belz, Department of History, University of Maryland, for his thoughtful comments and corrections of this book in manuscript form. And I am deeply indebted to Mss. Ruth Traurig and Claire Murray for their informed suggestions both in content and syntax. All have added enormously to what I hope is a glimpse, dispelling the curtain of years, at the crucial moment in our nation's history.

Now, let the curtain rise.

Washington, D.C. • Summer 1987 Marjorie Ashworth

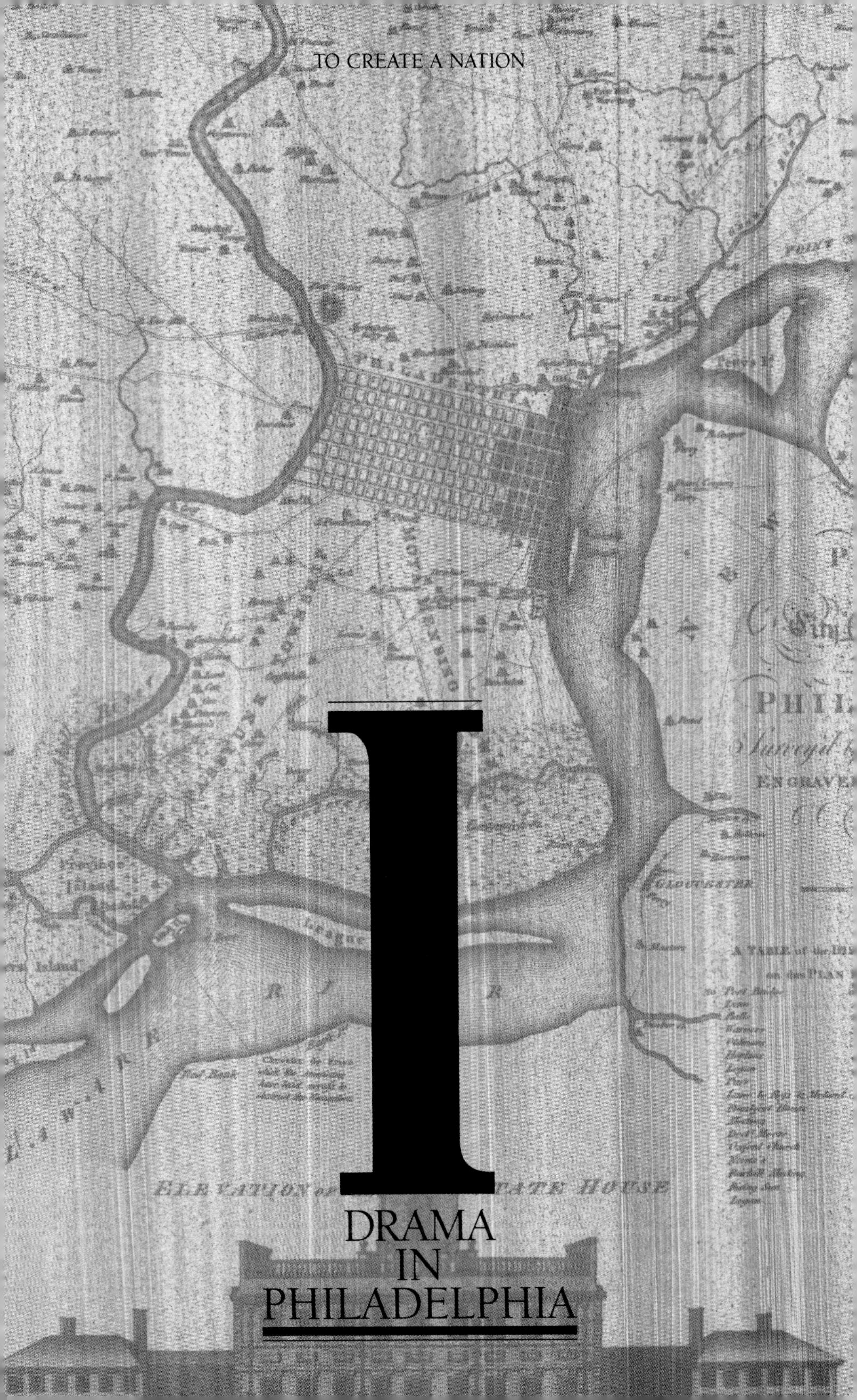

I

DRAMA IN PHILADELPHIA

I

DRAMA IN PHILADELPHIA

PHILADELPHIA
MOYAMENSING TOWNSHIP
PASSYUNK TOWNSHIP
League Island
Province Island
R I V E R
Red Bank
Chevaux de Frise which the Americans have laid across to obstruct the Navigation
GLOUCESTER
Petty's Id.
POINT N
Fair Mount
Fair Hill Meeting
Gunner's Run
Road to Frankfort
Hollanders Creek
Schuylkill River
Mud Id.
Bush Hill
Springettsbury
Gov. Penns
Sugar House
Schuylkill Ferry
Gardner
Masters
Gloucester Point
Timber Cr.
Newton Cr.
PHIL
Survey'd by
ENGRAVE
ELEVATION OF THE STATE HOUSE
A TABLE of the DIS
on this PLAN b
To Pool Bridge
Lynn
Balls
Warners
Oldmans
Hopkins
Logan
Parr
Lane to Ross & Moland
Frankfort House
Meeting
Doct. Moore
Oxford Church
Norris's
Fairhill Meeting
Rising Sun
Logan

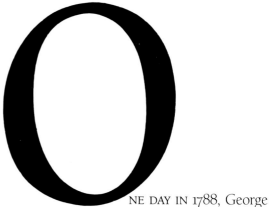

TO CREATE A NATION

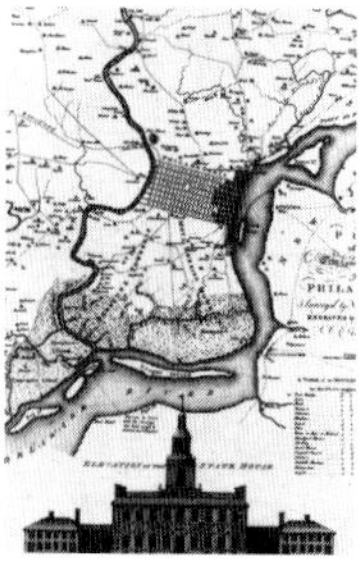

A Plan of the City and Environs of Philadelphia, engraving by William Faden after N. Scull and G. Heap, 1777. Courtesy of the Historical Society of Philadelphia.

ONE DAY IN 1788, George Washington wrote in a letter: ". . . a greater Drama is now acting on this Theatre than has heretofore been brought on the American stage, or any other in the World. We exhibit at present the Novel and astonishing Spectacle of a whole People deliberating calmly on what form of government will be most conducive to their happiness; and deciding with an unexpected degree of unanimity in favour of a System which they conceive calculated to answer the purpose." Washington was, of course, writing about the ratifying of the U.S. Constitution which had been written one year earlier in Philadelphia. It was there that the curtain rose on the great drama to which he referred.

Its forerunners had been many. Urged forward in a way that seemed like the persistent pressure of Destiny's hand, America had moved through its colonial period and the beginnings of self-government to a Convention called at last to form a way of regulating an independent society in a New World.

The country's first attempt at self-government after independence had produced the dangerously inadequate Articles of Confederation. Under the Articles, signs of discontent and weakness became ever more alarming. Foreign powers were poised, waiting for the breakup of the fragile union, while within the country the small population scattered over a large area acted in terms of individual states rather than as a whole. A re-examination of the government was coming none too soon.

Luckily, the young nation had among its population a remarkable number of politically-concerned people who saw government and politics as tools to create a healthy society, and felt a duty to do just that. They had experience in looking at what works in a government; what makes citizens rebellious; what inspires harmony and progress. And while these remarkable men were believers in the importance of the material things of life, they knew that if the country was to become all it was possible for it to be, a higher inspiration was not only morally desirable but a practical necessity.

Urged forward by the carrot of creating a great nation, and driven by the stick of internal and outside dangers, they met in Philadelphia to search for a new, better, government structure. Opinionated, high-principled, they fought for their particular ideas as fiercely as any maneuvers on a battlefield. But somehow they managed to modify their personal goals and make compromises with colleagues who differed with them. The result was the unique governing document by which we now live.

Although we can recognize today how great was their achievement, at that time they were not particularly happy with their handiwork. Because they were not satisfied, they built into the document two invaluable elements: methods for its modification, and portions written in deliberately general terms.

Many of the delegates had wished for a second convention so that revisions could be made forthwith. And some of the state ratifying conventions half-expected that another assembly would take place to smooth out their own criticisms. To take care of such change or reform, the delegates had written into the document clear provisions for amendment. The early passage of the Bill of Rights showed that the new document was fluid and responsive to the desires of the people.

In many places, the Constitution also was intentionally written in vague language. The delegates knew they could not divine the future, and therefore left many parts of their work loosely worded, expecting future generations to interpret it as new situations arose. We have, then, a constitution which has been amended or interpreted to meet new conditions as they have arisen — a document that may be re-examined at any time, and, with due deliberation, changed.

. . . the Constitutional Convention was, in its most creative aspects, less a forum of debate than experimental laboratory in which a group of men educated each other to work out together such a government as existed nowhere in the past or present of the world.
— JAMES THOMAS FLEXNER

I. DRAMA IN PHILADELPHIA

The Constitutional Convention of 1787 is an often-told tale, and it may be hard—after the crust of repetition—to see the wonderful event in a fresh light.

But let us try. For the experience of seeing it as it must have been, helps us to know why our society is the way it is, even why we are the kind of persons we are—our prejudices, our inquiring spirits, our provincialism, our openness, our materialistic streak, our acceptance of life's great possibilities.

When we read the debates of that Convention, we read about ourselves and recognize our own traits. The inspiring element is to see how these persons with sharply disparate views managed to find a path which overcame most of the negative directions of the individuals there.

More than anything else, the Convention seems like a strange and wonderful drama planned by Fate, a kind of pageant being enacted in secrecy in a small, hot room in Philadelphia. The players acted an almost sacred ritual spun out from the interaction of human minds. We welcome the times when these actors were petty, confused, selfish, crass. For then we know they were human. Their actions make it possible for us to accept in them—and in us—the times when they were noble and farseeing.

II

THE PLAYBILL: WHAT CAME BEFORE

Don't give up the Ship

TO CREATE A NATION

Fourth of July in Center Square (Philadelphia) by J.L. Krimmel, 1819. Courtesy of the Historical Society of Philadelphia.

RARELY DOES A GREAT IDEA or discovery burst full-blown upon the world without earlier, unrealized attempts at the same thing. The Constitutional Convention which met in the summer of 1787 in Philadelphia did not come miraculously into being without its own background of growing, changing documents which prepared people's minds for the brave undertaking.

Its precursors stretch all the way back to one of the first settlements in America. Before stepping ashore on the rocky New England coast, male passengers on board the little ship *Mayflower* first signed an agreement — the famous Mayflower Compact — that they would follow the will of the majority in whatever government regulations the Pilgrim colony in Massachusetts agreed upon. Even then, in 1620, Americans felt the need for some kind of written contract to control and regulate government.

During the Colonial period a whole series of intercolonial bodies took shape, planned by the British or with their full cooperation. Generally, they were loose associations to protect the colonies from French, Spanish, Dutch or Indian attack. The United Colonies of New England was an early league of this kind, formed of Massachusetts Bay, Plymouth, Connecticut and New Haven. It was active in mutual assistance from 1643 to 1684. An intercolonial Congress from 1689 to 1691, which included New York, Massachusetts, Plymouth and Connecticut, was a military league serving the same purpose. Another similar union from 1698 to 1701 stretched from New Jersey north along the Eastern seaboard to include New Hampshire and Rhode Island.

As time went on, these rudimentary associations for protection — under the aegis of the Crown — were enlarged to include more governmental duties. The so-called "Hamilton's Plan" of 1699, offered by the Deputy Governor of Pennsylvania, included an intercolonial assembly for frontier defense. And a whole spate of plans surfaced in England about this time—one, the "Earl of Stairs Plan of 1721," proposed that the American colonies be united with the British West Indies under a governor-in-chief appointed by the Crown. To aid him, an advisory council was to be formed of two members chosen from each colony.

Two proposals went even further. An anonymous "Virginian's Plan of Union," published in London in 1701, asked for an intercolonial congress with a governor general. And "Daniel Cox's Plan" of 1722, also appearing in London, suggested one governor over all the area with a lieutenant representing him in each colony. A "Great Council" of two delegates from each colony was to advise the governor and to handle many aspects of colonial defense.

Cox's plan was an enlargement of the colonial government system already existing. In all the colonies there were separate councils. The people were accustomed to the idea of individual "state" governments with written constitution-like documents by which they lived. Each colony had a governor appointed by the Crown (only Connecticut had the right to elect its governor), and each of them (except Pennsylvania) had legislatures composed of two houses, as in England. The council, or upper house, acted with the governor as a supreme court of appeals in civil cases and many of the governor's acts required the council's approval. As it did in so many parts of the world, England was planting the seeds of self-government, without ever intending they should grow to independence. In America's colonial assemblies, men were learning the art of self-government, preparing for a future time of freedom from British control without realizing how imminent it was.

Benjamin Franklin now enters the picture with the Kennedy-Franklin Plan of 1751, published by Archibald Kennedy, the Receiver-General of New York. In this proposal a superintendent would be assigned to the colonies by commissioners representing the colonial assemblies.

Thirteen sovereignties pulling against each other and all tugging at the federal head will soon bring ruin on the whole, whereas a liberal and energetic constitution, well guarded and closely watched to prevent encroachments, might restore us to that degree of respectability and consequence to which we had a fair claim and the brightest prospect of attaining.
— GEORGE WASHINGTON TO JAMES MADISON

Franklin refined and enlarged his plan and in 1754 offered it to an Albany Congress assembled to consider the danger of French-Indian collaboration. The Congress had been called by the British to negotiate with the Iroquois in hopes of getting their support against the French who were edging into areas the British considered were theirs. Commissioners arrived from New York, Massachusetts, Rhode Island, Connecticut, Pennsylvania, New Hampshire and Maryland, and in the course of discussions urged that there be closer ties with each other. Franklin's plan was then offered. It provided for a grand council of delegates chosen by the legislature of each colony, each member to hold office for three years. The council would have powers of taxation and legislation. An executive was to be the president or governor-general, appointed and paid by the Crown, with the right of nominating all military officers and a veto on all acts of the grand council. The Albany Congress liked the plan and adopted it. Had it gone into effect it would have changed our history. But it was not to be. England felt it would surely encroach on the royal prerogative, and, after consideration, the colonies themselves thought it would not give them enough independence.

The Albany Plan was followed by the Stamp Act Congress of 1765, called by the House of Representatives of Massachusetts to protest England's Stamp Act requiring stamps to be bought and used on all legal and commercial papers, pamphlets, newspapers, and so on. This move on the part of the Crown was a systematic plan to impose tight imperial control upon the internal life of the colonies. Nine colonies responded to Massachusetts' call. Twenty-seven delegates met in October in New York's City Hall to prepare "rights and grievances," petitioning England to repeal the legislation. The Congress accomplished its purpose. More importantly, it helped unify the budding states and made them aware of their power when acting together.

Committees of Correspondence put the colonists in touch with each other, cementing their common desire for independence. Political thinkers began examining the possibilities of independent government and speaking their minds. An astute political observer, James Otis of Massachusetts, had a strong influence well beyond his own community.

The same year as the Stamp Act Congress, he published "The Rights of the British Colonies Asserted and Proved," and set many people thinking about taxes, their own lack of political independence and the nature of government in general. Otis wrote that if laws passed by the English Parliament were arbitrary and unconstitutional, it was the duty of the English courts to nullify them. In a governmental system, he saw the legislative and executive branches controlling the growth of power through a plan of checks and balances.

One of the persons deeply affected by Otis' concepts was John Adams. In 1775, he wrote his own ideas in "Thoughts on Government" which circulated among colonial leaders. Adams set forth a blueprint for what he considered would be an effective, representative government. His plan called for a republic ruled by laws and not men, with a representative assembly elected from the people at large and a second smaller, more deliberative body. A governor would be selected by the two legislative bodies, while the upper house would be chosen by the lower. To prevent a dangerous growth of power, annual elections would be held.

Having grown bolder, the colonies convened their First Continental Congress in September 1774, to form mutual agreements against products coming from England and the British West Indies. Its delegates were chosen by revolutionary committees and other bodies considered illegal by the Crown.

This Congress called its successor into session and with the gathering of the Second Continental Congress in Philadelphia in May 1775, a real movement toward government began taking shape. The Philadelphia body asked the colonies to organize as states and form their own constitutions.

New Hampshire was the first to draft its document; Virginia came next. In the latter state, the framers went back to Adams' ideas of government, even using today's terms of "Senate" and "House" for their legislative bodies. The first portion of the Constitution was a Bill of Rights and the Preamble, written by George Mason, states that "all men are by nature equally free and independent." Passed in 1776, Virginia's Constitution was a model for the constitutions of many of the other states. The Massachusetts Constitution of

As to the future grandeur of America, and its being a rising empire under one head, whether republican or monarchial, it is one of the idlest and most visionary notions that was ever conceived even by a writer of romance. . . . The mutual antipathies and clashing interests of the Americans, their difference of government, habitudes, and manners, indicate that they have no centre of union and no common interests. They can never be united into one compact empire under any species of government whatever, a disunited people till the end of time, suspicious and distrustful of each other, they will be divided and subdivided into little commonwealths, or principalities. . . .

— DEAN OF GLOUCESTER CATHEDRAL *(after the Treaty of Paris)*

1780 established the principle of submitting such a document to the people for ratification.

The Second Continental Congress also appointed two important committees, the first to frame a declaration of independence and the second to prepare some kind of articles of union.

The latter committee, headed by John Dickinson of Delaware and consisting of one delegate from each state, considered various governmental plans, and submitted a document they had drafted as the "Articles of Confederation and Perpetual Union."

When the Congress adjourned in February 1781, these Articles were the governing instrument of the country. Adopted in November 1777, it became the law of the land when all 13 states adopted it in 1781. In its final form, the new government had neither executive branch nor national judiciary. Congress consisted of a single body representing the several states, each with one vote. It could declare war, make peace and form treaties with foreign countries—but its ability to require the states to abide by these actions was questionable. Domestically, Congress lacked power over tariffs, interstate commerce and disputes between the states. And it had no taxing power.

The document underscored the power of the states: "Each state retains its sovereignty, freedom and independence, and every Power, Jurisdiction and right, which is not by this confederation expressly delegated to the United States, in Congress assembled."

This was the governmental structure the country lived by in the early 1780s. At first, life under the Articles of Confederation must have seemed relatively similar to that under English rule, minus the irritating interference in internal affairs. And at the end of the Revolutionary War it seemed as though the country was in fairly good condition. It was an illusion. Actually it was a boom time, brought on by a heavy influx of manufactured goods from overseas, not available during the war. Afterward came depression and all kinds of economic difficulties.

Signs of financial trouble appeared when, in 1782, officers of the Continental Army drafted a message to Congress asking for pay on behalf of themselves and their men—and there was no money to reimburse them. As noted before, the government had no power to collect taxes from the states and soon the money it issued was "not worth a Continental." Individual states started issuing their own money. The Confederation's finance minister, Robert Morris, resigned in despair in 1783, unable to cope with his powerless situation. Requisitioning funds from the various states was, he said, "like preaching to the dead." That same year, a more dangerous threat came when officers and men considered refusing to disband until they were paid. Only Washington's moving appeal for patriotism caused the trouble to subside. Later in 1783, some of the Continental troops marched to Philadelphia's State House to demand their pay while a frightened Congress fled. James Madison commented later that the threat of fiscal chaos "contributed more to that uneasiness which produced the Constitution, and prepared the public mind for a general reform" than political weakness of the government structure.

Our affairs seem to lead to some crisis, some revolution — something that I cannot foresee or conjecture. I am uneasy and aprehensive; more so than during the war. . . .
— JOHN JAY TO GEORGE WASHINGTON

But certainly its other weaknesses were formidable, and uncontrolled trade was one of them. Interstate arguments abounded. New York, for example, set its own entrance and clearance fees for ships to New Jersey or Connecticut. At one time, New Jersey became so angered it taxed the lighthouse on Sandy Hook.

In foreign policy, Congress could not speak with one voice for the nation, and a uniform trade policy with other countries could not be regulated either. Each state made its own arrangements and European countries watched with interest to see how far order would deteriorate. Britain kept its military posts within the northwestern territory. Lord Sheffield in 1783 wrote: "Our great national object is to raise as many sailors and as much shipping as possible. Parliament should endeavour to divert the whole Anglo-American trade to English bottoms. America cannot retaliate. It will not be an easy matter to bring the American states to act as a nation." Spain, France, the Indians were also poised for dismemberment of the fragile new union.

Conflicts between the states over boundary lines caused more mischief. The population — only some three million, about 20 percent of whom were slaves—were scattered over a vast expanse of land which stretched east and west from the

Atlantic to the Mississippi River, and north and south from British Canada to Spanish Florida. State boundaries were uncertain. A number of times, shooting warfare broke out over disputed claims—and Congress was unable to solve the problems. As people began to perceive how ineffectual their national government was, some of the states did not even bother to send delegates to Congress. Absenteeism was common.

In 1783, George Washington wrote in his diary that he wished "a convention of the people" would form a federal constitution that would leave local matters to the states, but "when superior considerations preponderate in favor of the whole, their [the states'] voices should be heard no more."

It was during these years that Washington, withdrawing officially from public life, began building on an earlier dream he had had of expanding a system of inland waterways. In the fall of 1784, on a trip as far west as what is now Pittsburgh, he became aware of a situation potentially dangerous to the young nation. The Ohio-Mississippi river system, a vast artery of trade, began in British territory and ended in French Louisiana. Some day, he believed, it would become the most desirable way for American settlers beyond the Alleghenies to transport their goods. If they became tied economically to foreign nations these Americans might be pulled away from an allegiance to their own country.

Washington concluded that a combination of wagon roads and the Potomac River (if made more navigable) could draw trade from the west to the east and dissolve one danger of foreign encroachment. Earlier, Washington had obtained approval from the Virginia legislature to develop a stock company for the project. Maryland controlled the Potomac's north bank, so he secured that state's approval as well, and a Potomac Canal Company was chartered by both Maryland and Virginia. Pennsylvania was approached for building a road and an agreement not to collect tolls on its connecting waters. The possible use of the waters of the Elizabeth and Roanoke Rivers was then discussed with North Carolina.

Besides these interconnections, Maryland and Virginia had continuing issues to discuss together on navigation of the Potomac below where the canal would end. The many problems involved made it advisable for them to select persons to meet and consider how the waterway should be administered. Maryland and Virginia delegates were chosen and met first in Alexandria in March 1785, then moved to Mount Vernon, with Washington presiding at their meetings. In only eight days this Mount Vernon Conference solved many troubling commercial difficulties and the representatives decided to recommend that such meetings take place every year for similar discussions.

The French charge d'affaires at New York cannily observed, in a report to his government, that the Annapolis Convention was never intended to be anything more than a stalking horse for a federal convention.
— SAMUEL ELIOT MORISON AND HENRY STEELE COMMAGER

When the Maryland legislature considered the Conference report, it proposed the meeting next year, in 1786, be expanded to include the States of Pennsylvania and Delaware for a general discussion of the commercial interests of the several states. Virginia wanted to enlarge the next gathering even further: It proposed a conference of all of the 13 states "to consider how far a uniform system in their commercial regulations may be necessary to their common interest and their permanent harmony."

The delegates met in September 1786 in Annapolis, Maryland, a fairly central location for the participants. The representation was not very significant — nine states appointed delegates but only those from New York, New Jersey, Delaware, Virginia and Pennsylvania came. Maryland's House of Delegates had nominated people, but their Senate ruled that such a convention would infringe on Congress' powers. Consequently, the meeting took place not in the State House but in George Mann's Tavern. The *Maryland Gazette* took note of the historic meeting with a small item: "Several gentlemen, members of the proposed commercial convention, are arrived in this city."

But there were "several gentlemen" present who would figure prominently in the future of the young nation — John Dickinson from Delaware, chairman; delegates James Madison and Edmund Randolph from Virginia, and Alexander Hamilton from New York.

As the delegates pondered the fate of their infant government and its weaknesses, Abraham Clark of New Jersey let it be known that his state was ready to discuss not only commercial problems but also others not being dealt with by Congress. Tench Coxe of Pennsylvania went further expressing interest in standardized commercial laws and a "blending of interests" to "cement the Union of the States."

Edmund Randolph drafted a resolution for the states and for Congress, which Hamilton rewrote, calling for a convention in 1787 where delegates from all 13 states would meet "to devise such further provisions as shall appear to them necessary to render the Constitution of the federal government adequate to the exigencies of the Union."

That very same month of September 1786, another important event was taking place in New England: The Governor of Massachusetts issued a proclamation against unlawful assemblies and called out the militia to quell the famous Shays' Rebellion.

The story of Shays' Rebellion is a confused one. It hinged on the desperate money problems which were common to all parts of the country. In many places, barter was the only sure thing; often in cities, you paid with two or three kinds of money — English coins, paper money of the national government or of your own state. More and more, states failed to send to the national treasury the amounts they owed. Money issued by Congress had less and less value, while paper money from the states depreciated equally rapidly.

Western and Central Massachusetts were particularly hard hit. Small property owners and debtors were losing their possessions or being sent to jail when they could not pay their taxes or their debts. In town meetings and conventions the people petitioned for lighter taxes, and reform of the courts, which seemed to be siding with landlords, lawyers and propertied men. They asked for a revision of the state constitution, for many of the petitioners could not meet the property qualifications to vote.

Appeals were sent to the Massachusetts legislature which procrastinated and finally adjourned in July 1786 without responding to the petitions. Bands of unruly men then moved from petitions to threats. They found a leader, Daniel Shays, former Captain in the Revolutionary Army and a local officeholder of Pelham. He and his followers marched to Springfield and demanded that the Massachusetts Supreme Court help protect them from ruin. The Court adjourned. The men then marched on the federal arsenal. It was then that the Governor called out the troops. An agreement was reached with the militia, and Shays and his men dispersed.

But the rebellion was not over. In January 1787, Shays and his men returned to Springfield for supplies from the arsenal. The state appealed to Congress for help, but Congress was shown to be powerless. Evidently private individuals raised $20,000 for state troops and some 4,000 soldiers were put into the field. After government troops opened fire on the protestors, the rebellion collapsed: Shays escaped to Vermont and eventually he and some of his fellows were pardoned; amnesty generally was granted and reforms were made. An old Massachusetts ballad runs:

My name is Shays; in former days
In Pelham I did dwell, Sir.
But now I'm forced to leave the place
Because I did rebell, Sir.

While the uprising was relatively small and resulted in only a minor amount of disruption for the country as a whole, it frightened every state government and its leaders. To them, it indicated that the union was close to slipping into anarchy while people abroad watched and waited to take advantage of a weak, struggling country.

Washington wrote about Shays' Rebellion: "I am mortified beyond expression that we [Americans] should by our conduct verify the predictions of our transatlantic foes and render ourselves ridiculous and contemptible in the eyes of all Europe." And Alexander Hamilton thought there was "something . . . contemptible in the prospect of a number of petty states, with the appearance only of union, jarring, jealous and perverse . . . weak and insignificant in the eyes of other nations."

If Congress needed something to make it act on the proposal from the Annapolis Convention, Shays' Rebellion was it. The same month that the rebellion fell apart, February 1787, Congress — after the states themselves had acted — got on the bandwagon and invited the 13 states to send delegates to Philadelphia in May "for the sole and express purpose of revising the Articles of Confederation," to "render the federal constitution adequate to the exigencies of government, and the preservation of the Union."

The stage was set. It was time to choose the cast of characters for the most important drama of our history.

It was common rumor that a son of George III was to be invited to come over, and there is reason to believe that only a few months before the Convention met Prince Henry of Prussia was approached by prominent people in this country to see if he could be induced to accept the headship of the States, that is, to become king of the United States.

— MAX FARRAND

III

THE CAST OF CHARACTERS

DELEGATES WHO ATTENDED THE CONSTITUTIONAL CONVENTION OF 1787

III

THE CAST OF CHARACTERS

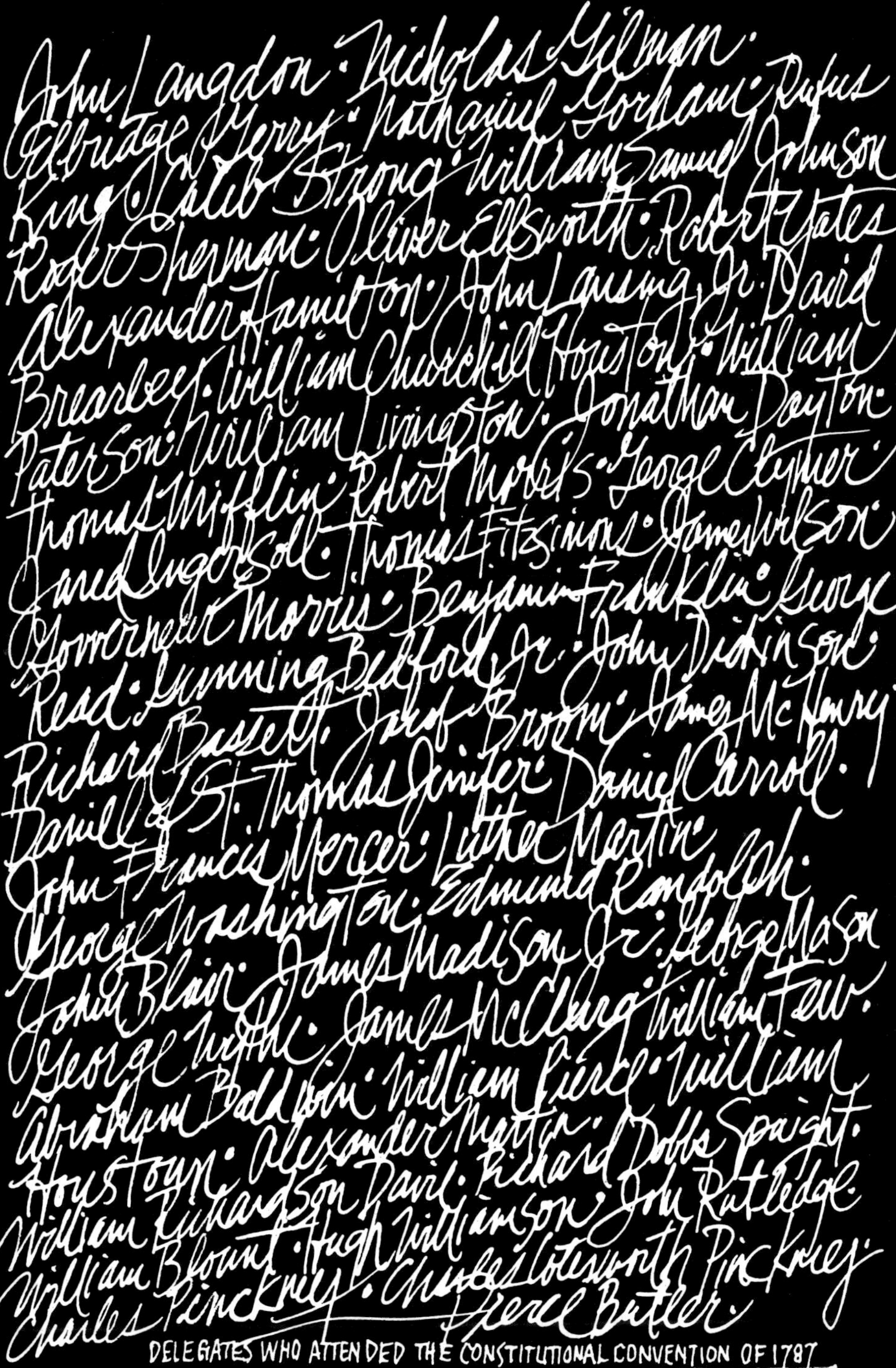
John Langdon · Nicholas Gilman · Nathaniel Gorham · Rufus King · Elbridge Gerry · Caleb Strong · William Samuel Johnson
Roger Sherman · Oliver Ellsworth · Robert Yates
Alexander Hamilton · John Lansing Jr. · David Brearley · William Churchill Houston · William Paterson · William Livingston · Jonathan Dayton
Thomas Mifflin · Robert Morris · George Clymer
Jared Ingersoll · Thomas Fitzsimons · James Wilson
Gouverneur Morris · Benjamin Franklin · George Read · Gunning Bedford Jr. · John Dickinson
Richard Bassett · Jacob Broom · James McHenry
Daniel of St. Thomas Jenifer · Daniel Carroll
John Francis Mercer · Luther Martin · Edmund Randolph
George Washington · James Madison Jr. · George Mason
John Blair · James McClurg · William Few
George Wythe · William Pierce · William Houstoun · Abraham Baldwin · Alexander Martin · Richard Dobbs Spaight
William Richardson Davie · Hugh Williamson · John Rutledge
William Blount · Charles Cotesworth Pinckney
Charles Pinckney · Pierce Butler
DELEGATES WHO ATTENDED THE CONSTITUTIONAL CONVENTION OF 1787

TO CREATE A NATION

WHO WERE THESE MEN, chosen by their peers, who came together in Philadelphia to create the government that affects every day of our lives? It was a very remarkable collection of personalities — farmers, scholars, shippers, statesmen — all vitally involved in the life of their country and the functioning of their state and national governments.

Congress set no limit to the number of delegates and 74 were named, but 19 of them failed to attend. Delaware sent five delegates while New Jersey and Massachusetts sent only four each. The actual number of delegates was 55; they came and went, sometimes leaving for family reasons and sometimes because of frustration with the Convention itself. Of them, 31 had gone to college, two had even been college presidents (William Samuel Johnson of Connecticut and Abraham Baldwin of Georgia). Three of them were or had been professors (James Wilson of Pennsylvania, George Wythe of Virginia and William Houstoun of Georgia) and at least a dozen of them had taught school. Four had read law at the Inns of Court in London; nine were foreign-born. Twenty-eight had served in Congress and most of the others in state legislatures. At least 30 had served in the Revolutionary War. It was a very young group — five were under 30 years of age and only four had reached or passed 60. The oldest member, Benjamin Franklin, was 81.

Several important men of the nation were not present: John Jay had his hands full with the foreign relations of the Confederation. John Adams and Thomas Jefferson were abroad on foreign missions, Adams in London and Jefferson in Paris. Others elected not to attend. The states' rights firebrand, Patrick Henry, said "I smell a rat," and stayed home in Virginia; the Revolutionary War patriot, Samuel Adams, remained in Massachusetts.

Most notable member of the cast of characters was of course George Washington, his fame undiminished even though he had returned to private life. So much has been written about this individual, truth and legend, that it is hard to conceive of him as a living, breathing person. One of Washington's most thoughtful biographers, James Thomas Flexner, tells how difficult it was for him to see the man afresh without the layers of legend and preconceived notions. "Beginning thus, as it were anew, I found a fallible human being made of flesh and blood and spirit — not a statue of marble and wood. And inevitably — for that was the fact — I found a great and good man. In all history few men who possessed unassailable power have used that power so gently and self-effacingly for what their best instincts told them was the welfare of their neighbors and all mankind."

> ***Send me my blue coat with the crimson collar and one of those made of the cloth sent me by the Spanish minister, to wit that without lapels and lined with white silk, as I see no end to my staying here [at the Convention].***
> — GEORGE WASHINGTON TO HIS NEPHEW

Physically tall and commanding in appearance with gray eyes and a broad nose, Washington invariably impressed his contemporaries with his remarkable self-control, his natural dignity and courteousness. He was not a great speaker, often addressing others with slow or careful words, and with a surprising sense of humility. Because he was a man of few words, with a well-earned reputation for integrity and civility, he was an ideal person to preside at a Convention such as this one was to be — a delegation of brilliant men, often caught up in the passion of their particular ideas.

Before the Convention, when he was asked to lead the Virginia delegation to Philadelphia, Washington was worried and unsure. Apparently he was able to set himself apart from his towering reputation and consider objectively how his influence could be used best for the country's good. Without a doubt the Convention appeared to be a chancy thing at the outset. What if he put his influence behind it and it failed? The prestige that he could offer the country would have dissipated and there would be less to give a second time.

From his Revolutionary War experiences of living with and leading men from all the colonies, Washington's thinking had changed. No longer merely a Virginian, he saw himself as

Gouverneur Morris, Pennsylvania.
Courtesy of the American
Philosophical Society.

Alexander Hamilton, New York,
by Charles Willson Peale. Courtesy of the
Independence National Historic Park Collection.

George Mason, Virginia.
Courtesy of the Independence National
Historic Park Collection.

Roger Sherman, Connecticut.
Courtesy of the
American Philosophical Society.

George Washington, Virginia, by
Charles Willson Peale. Courtesy of the
Pennsylvania Academy of Fine Arts.

Charles Cotesworth Pinckney,
South Carolina, by Cornelius Tiebout
after Jeremiah Paul, Jr. Courtesy
of the Smithsonian Institution.

Edmund Randolph, Virginia. Courtesy of the American Philosophical Society.

James Madison, Virginia, by James Sharples, Sr. Courtesy of the Independence National Historic Park Collection.

Elbridge Gerry, Massachusetts. Courtesy of the American Philosophical Society.

Benjamin Franklin, Pennsylvania, by Charles Willson Peale. Courtesy of the Pennsylvania Academy of Fine Arts.

James Wilson, Pennsylvania. Courtesy of the American Philosophical Society.

William Paterson, New Jersey. Courtesy of the Supreme Court of the United States.

DELEGATES WHO ATTENDED THE CONSTITUTIONAL CONVENTION OF 1787

NEW HAMPSHIRE
*John Langdon
*Nicholas Gilman

MASSACHUSETTS
**Elbridge Gerry
*Nathaniel Gorham
*Rufus King
Caleb Strong

RHODE ISLAND
(no delegates)

CONNECTICUT
*William Samuel Johnson
*Roger Sherman
Oliver Ellsworth

NEW YORK
Robert Yates
*Alexander Hamilton
John Lansing, Jr.

NEW JERSEY
*David Brearley
William Churchill Houston
*William Paterson
*William Livingston
*Jonathan Dayton

PENNSYLVANIA
*Thomas Mifflin
*Robert Morris
*George Clymer
*Jared Ingersoll
*Thomas Fitzsimons
*James Wilson
*Gouverneur Morris
*Benjamin Franklin

DELAWARE
*George Read
*Gunning Bedford, Jr.
*John Dickinson
*Richard Bassett
*Jacob Broom

MARYLAND
*James McHenry
*Daniel of St. Thomas Jenifer
*Daniel Carroll
John Francis Mercer
Luther Martin

VIRGINIA
*George Washington
**Edmund Randolph
*John Blair
*James Madison, Jr.
**George Mason
George Wythe
James McClurg

GEORGIA
*William Few
*Abraham Baldwin
William Pierce
William Houstoun

NORTH CAROLINA
Alexander Martin
William Richardson Davie
*Richard Dobbs Spaight
*William Blount
*Hugh Williamson

SOUTH CAROLINA
*John Rutledge
*Charles Pinckney
*Charles Cotesworth Pinckney
*Pierce Butler

**Delegates present and signing the Constitution, September 17, 1787*
***Delegates present and refusing to sign*
Remaining delegates not present when the Constitution was signed

an American involved with the people of the whole country. And with that had come the abiding wish to see some form of government which would give cohesion to the independent-minded states, one which would limit the power of the states to local problems. From his writings we know he was very worried about the condition of the country under the Articles of Confederation. He wrote: "We have probably had too good an opinion of human nature in forming our confederation. . . . I do not conceive we can exist long as a nation without having lodged somewhere a power which will pervade the whole Union."

The amazing thing about the Constitution is that it is as good as it is — that so subtle and complete a document emerged from that long debate. Most of the Framers, obviously, were second-rate men; before and after their session they accomplished nothing in the world. Yet during that session they made an almost perfect job of the work in hand.
— H. L. MENCKEN

During the time he had been trying to make up his mind about attending the Convention, Washington was not well and followed his work at Mount Vernon in a preoccupied fashion. As his indecision continued, his rheumatism returned — so severely he could scarcely move in bed. Gone was the joy he had first felt when he returned to his home and retired — he thought — from public life. It was at that time he wrote to Lafayette: "I am not only retired from all public employments, but I am retiring within myself. . . . Envious of none, I am determined to be pleased with all, and this, my dear friend, being the order of my march, I will move gently down the stream of life until I sleep with my fathers."

And there was another of Washington's worries: He had declared that he was leaving public life forever; how would friends and enemies perceive his return to the political scene, leading the Virginia delegation to the Philadelphia conference?

It appears, however, that once he decided to go to Philadelphia, his rheumatism abated and his determination became firm. He made the journey without physical difficulty, continuing in good health during the whole Convention. As a presence at that gathering, he can hardly be overestimated both in the role of presiding officer and in the prestige he brought to the Convention in the eyes of the general public. Excluded from the debates taking place in the Philadelphia State House, the average citizen was alerted to the importance of the deliberations by the very fact that George Washington was there.

Another illustrious personality at the Convention was one of Philadelphia's own sons, Benjamin Franklin, the 81-

year-old elder statesman. And, like Washington, the very fact of his presence was a great part of the influence he exerted there. Not entirely, though, for Franklin was a man of wide experience and master of diplomacy. On a number of occasions he cleverly timed a rambling, whimsical speech when tempers flared, or pointed out with great humility the value of compromise. These were moments when the Convention delegates had time to collect their thoughts and catch their breath. It is probable that some young delegates listened to him with impatience, but the sheer magnitude of his accomplishments compelled them to hear him out.

Delegates also knew that Franklin had been working on various governmental plans for years. As we have seen, he had been involved in the Kennedy-Franklin Plan, the Albany Plan, and the Articles of Confederation. He had also taken part in the shaping of the Declaration of Independence.

Franklin was a true cosmopolitan, another gift he could offer to the Convention scene. Boston-born, 15th son of a soapmaker, he became a printer in Philadelphia at the age of 22 and was soon making a name for himself as a journalist. His Almanac became famous world-wide, even when it was criticized for some of its Yankee-trader maxims. His scientific work alone would have given him a well-deserved reputation, particularly in his experiments with electricity. His lightning rods, Franklin stoves, bifocal spectacles, and maps of the Gulf Stream were testimonials to his brilliant, inquiring mind that turned scientific research into practical use.

During the Revolutionary War when the colonies needed someone in Paris to win France to their side, Franklin was the ideal candidate. A shrewd diplomat, he charmed the ladies and brought to bear a whole arsenal of wit, philosophy and scientific knowledge to captivate French society and government officials. The French statesman Turgot said of his accomplishments as a scientist and statesman, "He seized the lightning from the sky and the scepter from tyrants."

Following the war, he acted as the country's peace commissioner to England. Franklin had experienced the culture of England as a youth. When in his teens, he visited that country to learn the printer's trade. Years later, he was there for an extended period when he became acquainted with such notable figures as chemist Joseph Priestley and

William Strahan, publisher of Dr. Johnson's Dictionary. He was so much at home in England that for a time he even considered staying permanently.

The many years that Franklin spent abroad helped him bridge the Atlantic and offer the Convention the benefit of his tolerant, wide-ranging view of the world. He was an astringent antidote — even as he is today — for America's tendency toward provincialism and self-righteousness.

The men who founded your republic had an uncommonly clear grasp of the general ideas that they wanted to put in here, then left the working out of the details to later interpreters, which has been, on the whole, remarkably successful. I know of only three times in the Western world when statesman consciously took control of historic destinies: Pericles' Athens, Rome under Augustus, and the founding of your American republic.
— ALFRED NORTH WHITEHEAD

And finally, no one can estimate the importance of Franklin's "open house" during the Convention. As President (Governor) of Pennsylvania, he assumed the entertaining of the delegates in his home where they might discuss in an informal atmosphere the debates of the day. His house was only a short distance from the State House. One reached it through an arched passage to Franklin Court. There, the space opened into a garden famous for its large mulberry tree where Franklin's daughter served tea.

Manasseh Cutler, a Massachusetts clergyman and agent for a company involved in western settlement, has left us a vignette of these afternoon get-togethers in Franklin's garden during that summer of 1787: "We found him in his Garden, sitting upon a grass plat under a very large Mulberry, with several other gentlemen and two or three ladies. There was no curiosity in Philadelphia which I felt so anxious to see as this great man, who has been the wonder of Europe as well as the glory of America. . . . In short, when I entered his house, I felt as if I was going to be introduced to the presence of an European Monarch. But how were my ideas changed, when I saw a short, fat, trunched old man, in a plain Quaker dress, bald pate, and short white locks, sitting without his hat under the tree, and, as Mr. Gerry [a Convention delegate from Massachusetts] introduced me, rose from his chair, took me by the hand, expressed his joy to see me, welcomed me to the city, and begged me to seat myself close to him. His voice was low, but his countenance open, frank, and pleasing." Cutler noted that most of the other men present were delegates to the Convention who "were swallowed up with politics. . . ."

When Washington arrived in Philadelphia, the first person he went to visit was Benjamin Franklin. They had met briefly on earlier occasions; theirs was a warm relationship of mutual respect. And they held in common a deep wish to see some form of national government. Franklin, in particular, had always held to a faith in people. "God grant," he wrote to a friend, "that not only the love of liberty but a thorough knowledge of the rights of man may pervade all the nations of the earth, so that a philosopher may set his foot anywhere on its surface and say, 'This is my country.'"

Undoubtedly the third most important figure at the Philadelphia Convention was James Madison. Although he was almost 20 years younger than Washington, they were close and the latter leaned on him for depth of perception into the nature of governments and political thinking. A principal figure in Congress from Virginia, a key person at the Potomac and Annapolis conclaves which had brought about the Convention, Madison came well-prepared to play a major role in the proceedings. Earlier, when he recognized the drift of the country as it lived precariously under the Confederation, he wrote to Jefferson in Paris asking for books which "may throw light on the general constitution and *droit public* of the several confederacies which have existed."

Jefferson took him at his word and loaded him with scores of volumes on political history, laws of nations, biographies, political memoirs. After long and exhaustive study, he wrote an essay comparing various governments, and included a critique of them and the governmental system in his own country. He advocated a national government and judiciary which would have authority over the states in measures relating to national issues. In letters and discussions, Madison pushed his views, aware—perhaps more than any other person present at the Convention—of the long road to be traveled if the country's governmental system was to be changed. He wrote: "The necessity of gaining the concurrence of the Convention in some system that will answer the purpose, the subsequent approbation of Congress, and the final sanction of the states, presents a series of chances which would inspire despair in any case where the alternative was less formidable." Probably it is because he saw so clearly the difficulties ahead that he advocated constitutional ratification by only nine states rather than unanimous approval as had been necessary for approval of the Articles of Confederation.

At Convention time Madison was 37 years old and a bachelor. Although he was a small man with a soft voice, he was witty and effective in intimate groups and incredibly tenacious in debate. Throughout his life he was an omniverous reader and made up for his insignificant appearance with his keen, analytical mind. His dress was usually black and in personality he has been described as modest and retiring, a man of quick movements and energetic step. A graduate of the College of New Jersey where he studied constitutional law, he had long been an important figure in his state's political history. He had been a member of the convention which framed the state's constitution of 1776. Repeatedly he had been returned to Virginia's House of Burgesses before going on to Congress.

> ***. . . there was seldom, if ever, a people — certainly never a people scattered over so wide a territory — who knew so much about government as did this controlling element of the people of the United States.***
> — MAX FARRAND

At the Convention, when the day came for presenting the plan worked out by Madison and the Virginia delegation, it was Edmund Randolph who offered the resolutions to the assembly. Randolph, Governor of Virginia, was handsome, had a resounding voice and imposing presence. While he read the outline of a new government to the delegates, Madison sat quietly, ready to take part in the long proceedings ahead. Randolph, an important figure at the Convention, was undoubtedly pulled back and forth between the strong-willed members of the Virginia delegation, Madison and George Mason. He also was under political pressure from the states' rights advocates at home and had difficulty making up his mind about which direction he should take. As the debates went on, he gradually sided with Mason and the views of those supporting the rights of the states. Later, however, when the Constitution was up for ratification, he gave his support.

A consistent supporter of strong central government was James Wilson, next to Franklin the leading delegate from Pennsylvania. Wilson was one of the most effective members of the Convention. Many historians consider him the ablest constitutional lawyer present, and often during the proceedings he rephrased or summarized the problem at hand with a clarity that brought the debate back again on track. Strangely, in his personal financial affairs he was known as a reckless land speculator who later suffered heavy financial reverses.

Wilson had come to the colonies from Scotland, after studying at Edinburgh and Saint Andrew's Universities. He was a signer of the Declaration of Independence and saw as an ideal government separate states which would be independent yet connected under one rule.

He was 44 at the time of the Convention, a rather studious-looking person wearing steel-rimmed spectacles and a powdered wig. His speech went with his looks — unemotional and factual, but the brilliance of his perceptions led Franklin to call him "my learned colleague." In the debates, he joined Madison in the relentless pursuit of a government which would supersede the states in national matters.

Another foreign-born delegate who was to make his mark at the Convention, and especially during the New York ratification process, was Alexander Hamilton. Along with Madison he had turned the Annapolis Convention into a prelude to the Philadelphia gathering. Although the two differed in their views of government, they were united in recognizing America's danger if the political process was not reformed. Madison was in favor of a government with numerous checks and restraints. Hamilton greatly admired the British form of rule and advocated a more centralized and sovereign government with the rights of states reduced to a minimum. But both men believed passionately in the need for union to prevent a drift to anarchy.

Hamilton's views of the kind of government needed by America were also sharply at odds with most of the other delegates. Yet when the Constitution developed along lines different from his own concept, he was able to see beyond his preconceived ideas and in his writings and speeches support ratification with unmatched brilliance and cunning.

Hamilton was born in the West Indies and was a dashing figure never wholly accepted by his colleagues because he had a "foreign" quality about him. Mercurial, elegant, sometimes arrogant, yet capable of warm affection, he was only 32 when he was a member of the New York delegation. His life was cut short in his forties, in a duel with Aaron Burr.

While many of his peers distrusted him, Washington saw his brilliance and intense commitment to a united country. His genius also was later recognized by such disparate persons as Lord Bryce, Talleyrand and Theodore

Roosevelt; but the New Englander, John Adams, characterized him as "the bastard brat of a Scotch pedlar."

At the opposite pole from Hamilton was one of Virginia's famous delegates, George Mason, who had written his state's important Bill of Rights. Mason seemed torn on many occasions between his beliefs and their practical application. Himself a slave owner, he spoke with fervor against the custom of slavery that had taken hold in the Southern states. A firm believer in the rights of the states, he nevertheless recognized that a stronger national government was needed. Mason was a large landholder, a friend and neighbor of Washington's. Above all, he brought to the Convention a faith in the common people. He has been called the conscience of the Convention because of his forthright views on slavery and his recognition of the importance of the rights of man.

If the American colonist had come out of [the Revolution] with a single idea etched across his consciousness, it was a profound, abiding distrust of power and a determination to keep its exercise as fragmented and minimal and close to home as possible.
— BRUCE CATTON

Mason's serious approach to the business at hand was sometimes offset by a big brilliant man who loved to joke and talk — Gouverneur Morris from Pennsylvania. Graduate of King's College (Columbia) in New York where he early developed a reputation as a ladies' man, Morris lost none of his zest for life even after one of his legs was amputated as a result of a driving accident. With a quick mind, he spoke often at the Convention, leading the debates into new territory. Morris was for a strong central government and believed in an aristocracy of the intelligent. He was irritated by the support for the rights of the states and looked ahead to succeeding generations when people would think of themselves as Americans.

Probably Morris' greatest contribution to the Convention was his principal role, as a member of the Committee on Style, in rephrasing the Constitution into the clear, elegant language we know today.

To see how disparate the representatives of the young country might be, we have only to turn from Gouverneur Morris to Roger Sherman, a shoemaker's son from Connecticut. Age 66, he was tall, angular, with large hands and feet, honest and plain-spoken — the epitome of a dignified rural Yankee. He was a signer of the Declaration of Independence and the Articles of Confederation. Jefferson once said of him that he "never said a foolish thing in his life." After being apprenticed to his shoemaker father, Sherman farmed, was a shopkeeper, studied law, rose in political life and held as his motto: "When you are in a minority, talk; when you are in a majority, vote." At the Convention, he did not hesitate to speak in forthright terms, quickly winning the respect of his colleagues. Interestingly, he advocated a compromise fully a month before it actually was accepted; his proposal, a representational compromise, helped save the Convention from disbanding. Courageously standing somewhat aloof from those who strongly supported one position or another, Sherman was able to contribute a mediating influence which brought a practical solution.

New Jersey delegate William Paterson, another influential figure at the Convention, led the struggle to keep the general structure of the Articles of Confederation. He mistrusted a strong central government and gathered around him those who feared that, under such a government, small states would be overwhelmed by the power of the larger states.

Paterson was small in stature, only five feet two, with an impressive head and piercing eyes. He was an effective lawyer and led the opposition through weeks of debate until a compromise was reached.

One of his supporters and gadfly of the Convention was Elbridge Gerry, Harvard graduate and successful businessman of Massachusetts. Gerry's faith in the common people was severely limited. Throughout the Convention, the tenor of Gerry's speeches showed the profound effect of Shays' Rebellion upon his thinking. His fear of "the mob" was always near the surface and he had little patience or understanding for the reasons behind its existence.

However, he had long been active in the country's political life. He was a signer of the Declaration of Independence and Articles of Confederation, was a member of Congress and had been outspoken, along with Samuel Adams, since the early '70s in the struggle for independence. He was a small, thin man, energetic and easily offended, often confused in his thinking, but valuable to the Convention when he brought up nagging worries and hidden feelings that others were sometimes too reticent to express.

Gerry opposed the Constitution in its final form, and

would not sign it; however, later he was a supporter of the new government.

These "dissenters" — including John Dickinson of Delaware, Dr. William Samuel Johnson and Oliver Ellsworth of Connecticut and Luther Martin of Maryland — made an important contribution in a special way. In spite of their often dramatic differences from their colleagues which threatened to tear the Convention apart, by opposing the original Virginia plan, they helped bring the final document back to a better balance, making its ratification more possible.

There were many other delegates of distinction — Rufus King of Massachusetts, able supporter of the Federalist concept; the South Carolina orator and Revolutionary War leader John Rutledge; Pennsylvania's Robert Morris; Charles Cotesworth Pinckney, advocate of strong national government, and his 24-year-old cousin Charles Pinckney, both representatives from South Carolina. They, and many others who spent the long days in Philadelphia's State House, were leaders of their time — and beyond.

Curiously, there were four delegates who sat through the long debates the whole hot, turbulent summer without uttering a word. And yet, when the time came for signing the new Constitution, John Blair of Virginia, Nicholas Gilman of New Hampshire, Richard Bassett of Delaware, and William Few of Georgia, all stood up and added their names to the historic document.

. . . probably the American colonies had the highest level of literacy in the whole world at that time. And the eighteenth century was a very political century. Everybody in America talked politics. European travelers were flabbergasted by the fact that ordinary colonials could talk about politics intelligently.
— RICHARD B. MORRIS

IV

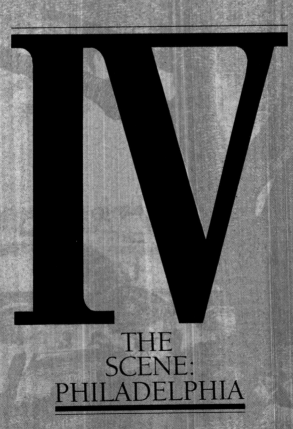

THE SCENE: PHILADELPHIA

The City and Port of Philadelphia, on the River Delaware from Kensington by William Russell Birch, 1800. Courtesy of the Library Company of Philadelphia.

WILLIAM PENN'S TOWN WAS THE PLACE where the delegates met. Of all the places in the young country, with possibly the exception of Boston, Philadelphia was the most important political and cultural center. Stronghold of the Quakers, it had developed stability and ethical standards—and had been especially attractive to small business and overseas trade. In the 18th century, a number of innovative social and cultural ideas were being tried out in the city. And, of course, its State House had been the focal point for the nation's most historic moments of all. These events had given the city unparalleled prestige, and its population of some 43,000 persons was well aware of the position it held. It was not surprising that various organizations of the nation held their meetings and conventions here, or came to marvel at its urban ways. During the summer when the Constitutional Convention was being held, Presbyterians were having their own convention, along with the prestigious Society of the Cincinnati whose membership was composed of Revolutionary War officers.

While some of the Convention delegates looked forward to seeing Philadelphia for the first time, others had come here before. George Washington was not new to the place. This time he came by carriage from his home at Mount Vernon on the Potomac and was met at Chester, Pennsylvania, by a delegation of his former officers. After dining together, the party crossed the Schuylkill River at Gray's Ferry where a floating bridge had been constructed by the British when they occupied Philadelphia. At the ferry, prominent citizens and the city's handsome Light Horse Troop met him and escorted him into town. Bells pealed a greeting, cannon fired a 13-gun salute and residents came out on the streets to cheer their most famous leader. It was the second welcome the city had given Washington. The first was in 1781 after the surrender of Cornwallis when the General had passed through from Yorktown.

Other delegates drifted in. Transportation was so slow and different from ours today that it is hard for us to picture what it meant to have your carriage mired in mud for hours, the shoe lost from your horse's hoof, or to share your bed with two other travelers at a wayside tavern. Some delegates arrived on horseback; others rode the stage lines. Philadelphia was becoming the center of a growing network of communications. A stage line between the city and New York was begun around the mid-1700s, with the first lap of the journey on a stageboat from the wharf below Philadelphia's Chestnut Street to Bordentown, New Jersey. Then an overland stage continued to Perth Amboy where the travelers were transported by water to New York. If the weather was good, the trip took three days. Another line went by way of Trenton to New York. In 1766, a stage, proudly named the "Flying Machine," made the trip to New York in two days.

Other parts of the eastern seaboard were more inaccessible. A journey from Georgia to Philadelphia could take as long as 19 days; from New Hampshire it would take about two weeks. Many of the conveyances at that time were stage wagons — vehicles predating the stagecoach — which were simply glorified wagons with a canvas top and benches on each side with the entrance from the front. Women usually were offered the courtesy of sitting in the rear seat, for this bench was the only one with a backrest.

Washington had made arrangements to stay at a boardinghouse run by a Mrs. Mary House near the place where the delegates were to meet. But Robert Morris and his wife urged him to accept an invitation to stay with them. He finally acceded and had his baggage moved to their home on High Street. Built in 1761, the house during the war had been occupied by both General Sir William Howe and General Benedict Arnold during their military commands of Philadelphia. It was considered one of the most impressive dwellings in the city, complete with icehouse, hothouse and a stable for 12 horses.

The mechanic arts are those which we have occasion for in a young country as yet simple and not far advanced in luxury. I must study politics and war, that my sons may have liberty to study mathematics and philosophy, geography, natural history and naval architecture, navigation, commerce and agriculture, in order to give their children a right to study painting, poetry, music, architecture, statuary, tapestry and porcelain.

— JOHN ADAMS TO HIS WIFE

Philadelphia homes at that time generally were of red brick Georgian design, refurbished after their generally dilapidated state at the war's end. The early Quakers had believed in planting trees along streets and walks and soon people began calling Philadelphia the "green city" with its rows of buttonwood, willows and Lombardy poplars. Even the famous old roads leading into the city were tree bordered.

Row houses were common, with white doorsteps and iron doorscrapers. Often the owners had their shops on the ground floor which usually opened directly onto the street. Living quarters were above. Occasionally courtyards or little gardens broke up the rows.

Streets were paved with cobblestones or pebbles and the side or center gutters generally served as sewers. At this time, the city was only about nine blocks extending north and south along the Delaware River and to the west, just beyond the State House. Then came a wooded area stretching to the Schuylkill. As the delegates wandered about the city in their free time, they found that William Penn had planned Philadelphia within a rectangular space with narrow streets — as if there had not been limitless land all around him. A system of alleys ran behind the streets. On them, particularly some of those extending westward from the Delaware and just north of Market Street, people of more moderate means had small two-story houses with attics.

There also were boardinghouses and taverns, and if the delegates did not stay with friends, as Washington was doing, those were sought out. Many liked the convivial atmosphere of the City Tavern, or perhaps the Black Horse Tavern. Probably the favorite was the Indian Queen, and even though rooms were often shared with another person, this particular tavern became a rendezvous for the delegates that summer.

Staying in Philadelphia at this time could be expensive for a visitor. Many of the delegates ran into debt. The state budgets were small and the representatives were issued limited sums of money to tide them over the summer. In addition, the various kinds of money had varying degrees of value. Once in awhile, shillings and pence from Britain were seen; even an occasional Spanish coin or a silver dollar made an appearance. Dollars from time to time were cut into halves or quarters to make change. Sometimes gold or silver coins had their edges clipped off; when these were used, merchants weighed each coin.

A number of delegates had to borrow in order to make the trip. George Mason, owner of large plantation lands, borrowed 60 pounds from Edmund Randolph in order to come to the Convention. Others were involved in western land speculation which could reduce a wealthy man to poverty almost overnight. Robert Morris, the Philadelphian with whom Washington was staying and also a delegate, was known as the richest man in the city, yet later, land speculation sent him into bankruptcy and even a debtors' prison for three years.

There never was a people upon earth . . . who were in less hazard than the people of this country, of an aristocracy's prevailing — or anything like it, dangerous to liberty.
— JONATHAN JACKSON (*Thoughts upon the Political Situation of the United States*)

Benjamin Franklin lived not far from the Morris residence. Oliver Wendell Holmes once quipped that Franklin was a Bostonian who spent some time in Philadelphia. Of course the truth was that at every turn, Franklin's mark was upon the city. The canny old Quaker had a knack for seeing ways good new ideas could be put to use. In London he had observed their firefighting system, came home and helped found a similar one in which insurance companies were responsible for fighting fires and paying for damage. The Philadelphia Contributionship, established in 1752, became the oldest fire-insurance company in America. Firemarks — medallions made of iron or lead — were mounted on the front wall of the houses which were insured. Buildings of stone or brick, largely wood inside and highly vulnerable to fire, were safer than those in any of the other American towns.

The first subscription library was formed in Philadelphia by Franklin in 1731 when several of his friends joined with him to circulate books among themselves. The idea of pooling private book collections caught on and by 1750 there were several local societies offering the lending of books for a small fee.

One of Franklin's important contributions to the country as a whole was the founding of the American Philosophical Society which was for many years the source of information for the young country, and later, for the early years of the new national government. Officials depended upon the Society for important information about their native country and looked to it for continuing scientific studies and

East View of Gray's Ferry on the River Schuylkill by Charles Willson Peale, engraving by James Trenchard, 1787. Courtesy of the Library Company of Philadelphia.

exchange of knowledge. In 1785, the Pennsylvania Assembly voted to give the Society a plot of ground within the State House Yard and the Society's hall was built just behind the State House—a meeting place of doctors, lawyers, clergymen and merchants interested in the sciences. Self-taught individuals were also members along with such notables as Washington, Jefferson, Hamilton, Madison, Thomas Paine, Benjamin Rush and John Marshall. Even distinguished Europeans were included. Their studies were wide-ranging and included science and technology particularly helpful to the economic independence of the young country.

It was, therefore, to the home of "Mr. Philadelphia" that Washington went on his first visit in the city. Upon his return from Paris, Franklin had made a number of additions. A three-story wing had been added to the east side of the house which gave Franklin more space and made possible a large new dining room seating 24 persons. Here he could entertain and hold regular meetings of the American Philosophical Society. Above the dining room was his extensive library where he liked to amuse visitors by showing them the "arm-extender" he had invented to lift books from the top shelves. His middle-aged daughter Sally kept house and took care of him; he called her the "comfort of my declining years."

Besides being entertained by Franklin, the delegates often dined with other Philadelphians who had the reputation of being generous and friendly. Robert Morris was a frequent host; Elbridge Gerry brought his wife and young son down from Massachusetts and rented a house where they, too, entertained delegates from the State House. Guests enjoyed copious meals which included all varieties of seafood, tripe, duck, rabbit, ham, Spanish buns, trifle, flummery, floating island, tarts, creams and custards.

On Wednesday and Saturday mornings, housewives and servants visited the city market which stretched down Market Street to the Delaware where fresh fish, vegetables and fruit were displayed alongside more exotic items such as raccoon, oppossum and bear bacon.

Besides doing the marketing and cooking and caring for the family, housewives took care of rabbits and fowl; cleaned and washed; combed, carded and spinned, sewed and knitted; put up pickles, jams and jellies. A visitor to the city

The Artist in his Museum by Charles Willson Peale, 1822.
Courtesy of the Pennsylvania Academy of Fine Arts.

observed that the ladies had breakfast at half-past five. Elbridge Gerry's young wife followed the custom of very early rising as "conducive to her health" and said that it was "the practice of the best families in Philadelphia."

A French visitor noted that pretty girls at fifteen were "faded at twenty-three, old at thirty-five, decrepit at forty or forty-five." Foreigners often found Philadelphia society stiff and formal, with somewhat harsh moral codes. The women were plain and natural in their appearance and shy or prim in their relationships with the opposite sex. While these visitors saw life in Philadelphia as provincial and usually dull, some of the delegates thought the opposite. George Mason of Virginia wrote to his son that he was getting "heartily tired of the etiquette and nonsense so fashionable in this city."

In the evenings, the delegates often spent the time together at taverns talking, consuming large amounts of Madeira and port and discussing events of the day at the Convention or making plans for the next morning. No doubt some of the most important work of the summer was done in this way — just as today a great amount of Congress' work is done in hallways, on the phone and at social functions where the atmosphere is relaxed.

Once in a while a concert was offered at the "Opera House." Poetry readings and comic opera were well attended. On rare free days, some of the delegates liked to fish; Washington often spent spare time fishing for perch or trout. Philadelphia was noted for its bookshops and the Library Company had its books in Carpenters' Hall, a block from the State House, where mechanical tools such as plows and harrows were on display. The country's First Continental Congress of 1774 had met in this Hall. There were chapbooks, or "penny histories" — paper-covered books to be bought for daughters and sons back home. Sold by the thousands, they told of medieval romance, fairy tales and Indian legends.

Also to buy were a flood of Oriental goods and knick-knacks as gifts to take back home. The voyage of the *Empress of China* to Java and Canton a few years earlier had awakened Philadelphians to an array of Far Eastern items. Robert Morris was part owner of the vessel. He already had negotiated a monopoly on all American tobacco sold to France. Philadelphia's trade in 1787 was much higher than it had been in the best days before the Revolutionary War. Scandinavian mercantile houses were represented in the city and goods from Holland and Germany competed with British imports. And to continue the Far Eastern trade, just a year before the Convention, Captain Thomas Truxtun, who brought Benjamin Franklin home on his ship the *London Packet*, refurbished the vessel, renamed her the *Canton* and sailed off for the Orient.

The tyranny of Philadelphia may be like the tyranny of George III.
— PATRICK HENRY.

And there were newspapers to read. The arrival of delegates and whatever crumbs of information that could be learned about the deliberations of the Convention were embroidered and reported. In political leanings, the *Independent Gazetteer*, the *Federal Gazette*, the *Pennsylvania Packet* and the *General Advertiser* all were said to range from lukewarm to actively against a strong national government. They were proud, however, that their city was host to such an important Convention and lost no opportunity to do a bit of civic boasting.

The year before the Convention, James Trenchard, a local engraver, began publishing the *Columbian Magazine, a Monthly Miscellany* and asked Charles Willson Peale to provide illustrations. In the July 1787 issue, Peale began a series of views of Philadelphia and its environs. Delegates no doubt sought copies of the first one which printed "A N.W. View of the State House." The accompanying text for the engraving described the State House as "a building which will, perhaps, become more interesting in the history of the world, than any of the celebrated fabrics of Greece or Rome."

It was Peale who probably offered the most interesting diversion for visitors to the city — a "Repository for Natural Curiosities," a forerunner of the museums we have today. Peale was a man of many talents — a painter of portraits, which formed the nucleus of his Gallery of Great Men; an engraver, a taxidermist and, finally, the creator of a museum.

In Peale's time, the idea of a museum was unusual; the British Museum had opened only a few decades earlier. The concept developed from the request of a Hessian physician for drawings of mastodon bones found at Big Bone Lick in Kentucky. The bones were brought to Peale's painting gallery to make the drawings. Crowds came to see them. Peale then decided to collect various other curios which might be of interest. The skylighted painting gallery became a museum. Friends made contributions, sea captains brought back exotic animals which Peale learned to preserve. Washington was on Peale's annual subscription list and contributed two golden pheasants. (Peale wrote to Washington in February 1787: "Your obliging favor of the Body of the Golden Pheasant I have received in good condition although by a stage two Days after the receipt of your Letter, the delay was vexatious yet I was richly paid in being able to preserve so much beauty. . . . When you have the misfortune of loosing the others if the weather should be warm be pleased to order the Bowels to be taken out and some pepper put into the Body. But no salt which would injure the feathers.") In techniques far advanced for his time, Peale surrounded his displays with stones and other natural objects. Painted backdrops of his own design were added to place the creatures in lifelike scenes.

And so the delegates spent their time, when away from the debates of the Convention, discovering 18th-century Philadelphia and no doubt wishing the meeting would be over so they could get back to their businesses, tend their crops and be with loved ones at home. Probably what most of them remembered most vividly about that Philadelphia summer—aside from the Convention itself—was the climate. That particular summer has been recorded as an unusually hot one with few cooling breaks. Convention members must really have suffered in the stifling room of the State House where privacy demanded that door and windows be tightly shut. Elsewhere, flies and mosquitoes were buzzing about and it was a choice at night either to close the bedroom windows and suffer the heat, or open them and be besieged by mosquitoes. Adding to the disagreeable sultry atmosphere were the outdoor privies, occasional dead animals in the streets and casual emptying of slop buckets. While much of this was normal for an 18th-century American town, the persistence and heaviness of the heat made conditions particularly unpleasant.

On happier days, however, perhaps they remembered the bells of the city which rang in the evening to announce next morning's market, or the watchman who called the time and weather during the night.

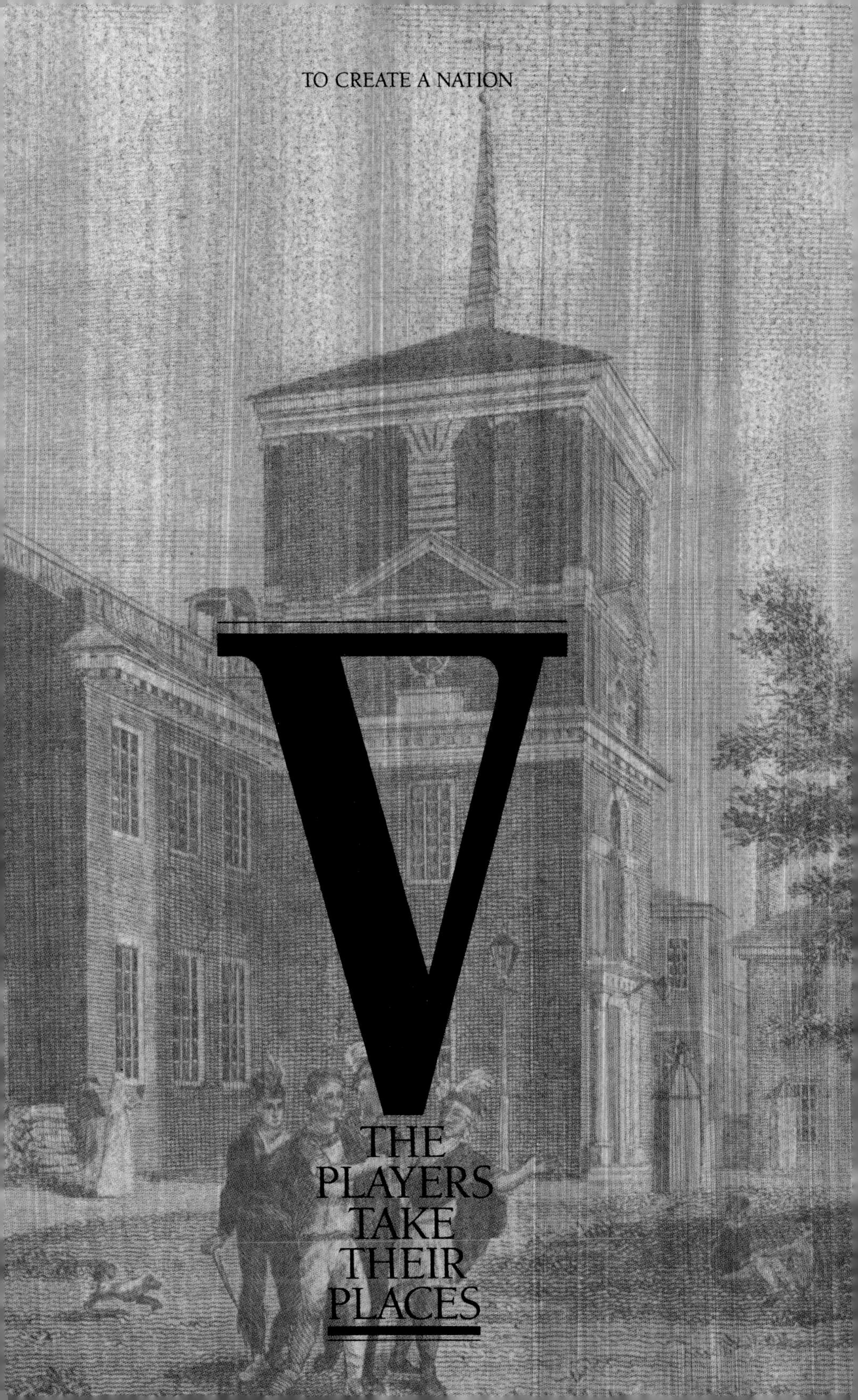

V

THE PLAYERS TAKE THEIR PLACES

V

THE PLAYERS TAKE THEIR PLACES

Back of the State House, Philadelphia by William Russell Birch, 1789-99. Courtesy of the Library Company of Philadelphia.

On May 14, 1787, the scheduled opening day for the Convention, only Pennsylvania and Virginia delegations had arrived. Washington and others fretted, while Madison busied himself on a plan to offer to the expected delegates.

Finally, by Friday, May 25, the minimum number of members needed to begin the meeting had arrived to present their credentials and settle into nearby lodgings. On that morning, the delegates—some walking along the cobblestone streets, others arriving on horseback or in carriages — gathered at Philadelphia's State House between 5th and 6th Streets, fronting on Chestnut Street. As they entered the red brick building they were in a hallway; to their right was the State Courtroom, used from colonial times onward; to their left, their own designated Assembly Room. Here, George Washington had been selected to lead the Continental Army against the British forces. And it was of course here that men had signed their names to the Declaration of Independence, placing their very lives at risk. The room was—and is—one of America's most important historical shrines.

Eleven years after the Declaration had been signed, many of the same people were here again, this time to see if, building on that bold, earlier act, they could create a more perfect Union.

On this spring day, the various state delegates gradually took their places at chairs and tables arranged in arcs to face the speaker's chair and desk at the east end of the room. This desk, on a low platform, was the very one upon which the Declaration of Independence had been signed. Two fireplaces flanked the platform, while six large, many-paned windows were on either side — three looked north to Chestnut Street and the other three south upon the square where on July 8, 1776, the Declaration of Independence was first read to a gathering of people. These were surely solemn, intimidating surroundings in which to meet.

By now, many of the delegates had greeted each other, but they were not well acquainted. There must have been cautious glances exchanged as they sized each other up. A number were famous by reputation. Benjamin Franklin had expected to place Washington in nomination for president to preside over the Convention during the weeks to come. Since Franklin was ill that first day, Robert Morris nominated Washington and he was chosen unanimously.

Washington was then escorted to the president's chair. Once again, the country was reaching out for his stability and integrity to guide it through a new bewildering phase of its history. For us, he was the director of this long-ago drama which gave us the political principles we live by today.

Standing before the gathered delegates, Washington made a little speech of acceptance which was a mixture of formality and disarming humility. He thanked the men for their confidence in him. One delegate wrote in his notes that Washington "declared that as he never had been in such a situation he felt himself embarrassed, that he hoped his errors, as they would be unintentional, would be excused. He lamented his want of qualifications."

Next a secretary was chosen, Major William Jackson of South Carolina who had been for two years Assistant Secretary of War. This done, he read the credentials which nine states had sent with their delegates — the Commonwealths of Massachusetts, Pennsylvania and Virginia; the states of New York, New Jersey, Delaware, North Carolina, South Carolina and Georgia. (The Maryland, Connecticut and New Hampshire delegations had not yet arrived.)

The wordage of the state credentials showed a sense of the importance which each individual state assumed, and the seemingly small feeling for national unity. It was a signal that most of the states and their delegates would not part with their sovereignty easily. Delaware had even forbidden her representatives to consider any change in Article V of the

The body of delegates which met in Philadelphia in 1787 was the most important convention that ever sat in the United States.
— MAX FARRAND

Confederation, which gave each state one vote in Congress. Even Virginia's credentials were ambiguous on whether or not the Convention could scrap the Articles of Confederation and produce a new form of government. Probably most members were only vaguely aware of the far-reaching plans that Madison and a few others were hoping to bring before the Convention. And as those men, hoping for a strong national government, listened to the tenor of the state delegation credentials intoned by Major Jackson, they must have wondered how it would be possible to prevail.

A messenger and doorkeeper next were appointed. A committee to set forth rules of order for the Convention was named — George Wythe of Virginia, Charles Pinckney of South Carolina and Hamilton of New York — and the first meeting adjourned until the following Monday.

By then more delegates had arrived, along with Franklin who came in his famous sedan chair which he had brought back from France. Philadelphians gathered to watch as four prisoners from the Walnut Street jail carried their famous resident the short distance from his home to the State House. Pennsylvania's delegation was now the largest one at the Convention.

Business began this morning with a report from the Rules Committee of which Wythe was chairman. The rules insisted on courteous behavior toward the chair and toward each other: "Every member, rising to speak, shall address the President; and whilst he shall be speaking, none shall pass between them, or hold discourse with another, or read a book, pamphlet or paper, printed or manuscript. . . . When the House shall adjourn, every member shall stand in his place until the President pass him. . . ." Members were not to speak oftener than twice on the same question except by special permission and not the second time until all other delegates had expressed their views.

Several very important rules were to become a part of the proceedings: Any subject might be reconsidered even though passed on by the majority, if cause was shown. This made it possible for delegates to reconsider their positions and reevaluate what had formerly been discussed. To further encourage rethinking of positions, yeas and nays on a vote would not be called for, nor would the way in which a delegate was voting be recorded. Thus, no delegate need be embarrassed by a recorded fact that he had voted one day a certain way and on the next had changed his position.

In order for a question to be reconsidered, a delegate must ask that day for review, and unanimous agreement must come from his colleagues. Then a motion for reconsidering would be made later, and if the Convention agreed, a future time would be set.

It also was decided that seven states should make up a quorum and that a delegate should not be absent without leave unless his state could have representation without him.

. . . these men had simply lived in what may have been the most self-conscious, thoughtful, participatory generation that ever existed.
— BRUCE CATTON

An important rules decision in those opening days which made it possible for the Convention to succeed was the adoption of the parliamentary procedure called the "Committee of the Whole." When called for, this device turned the whole delegation into a committee with committee rules applying. Thus, whenever the members wished to discuss their ideas without being held to any specific view, or wished to change their minds or go back to some earlier position, in committee it was perfectly normal to do so. This made it possible for members to absorb the candid thinking of one another and consider new ideas which emerged. Georgia delegates, for example, might hear for the first time the views of their Massachusetts colleagues; those from New Jersey could listen to Virginians as they outlined fresh approaches to government. And acting in committee, no one was bound to decisions. The Convention resorted to the Committee of the Whole for a large part of its proceedings.

Another very important ground rule was that of secrecy. In today's world, where diplomats and heads of state are besieged by the media before, during and after meetings, it is hard to comprehend a four-month-long meeting where individuals met to resolve the fate of their compatriots, yet kept deliberations and decisions to themselves. The rule states that "no copy be taken of any entry on the journal during the sitting of the House without the leave of the House. That members only be permitted to inspect the journal. That nothing spoken in the House be printed, or otherwise published, or communicated without leave."

There were many views pro and con on this decision even at the time. Jefferson in Paris lamented the fact that public discussion would not be possible. But Madison firmly supported the decision even many years later on the grounds that it made it possible for the delegates to change their minds and rethink their earlier-held positions without being accused of indecision and lack of conviction. Ideas and new directions were being considered and it was crucial that the delegates not be bound to their first responses.

The rule of secrecy was adhered to with strict concern, so much so that the official journal which had been kept by Major Jackson was not published until 1819. Very little seems to have been leaked, perhaps because of an incident which made a strong impression upon the members. William Pierce recounts in his notes that one afternoon someone dropped a page of proceedings on the floor. The paper was turned over to Washington. Next day, when debate was over and adjournment called for, Washington rose. "'Gentlemen!' he said. 'I am sorry to find that some one member of this body has been so neglectful of the secrets of the Convention as to drop in the State House a copy of their proceedings, which by accident was picked up and delivered to me this morning. I must entreat gentlemen to be more careful, lest our transactions get into the newspapers and disturb the public repose by premature speculations. I know not whose paper it is, but there it is (and he tossed it on the table), let him who owns it take it.'

"At the same time he bowed, picked up his hat and quitted the room with a dignity so severe that every person seemed alarmed; for my part I was extremely so, for putting my hand in my pocket I missed my copy of the same paper, but advancing up to the table my fears soon dissipated; I found it to be in the hand-writing of another person. When I went to my lodgings at the Indian Queen, I found my copy in a coat pocket which I had pulled off that morning. It is something remarkable that no person ever owned the paper."

Luckily for posterity, Madison took it upon himself to take copious notes on the proceedings, or we today would know little or nothing about what happened. Other members took notes — Hamilton, Yates and Lansing of New York;

McHenry of Maryland, Paterson of New Jersey, King of Massachusetts, Pierce of Georgia and Mason of Virginia—but they were not always present, and their notes were sketchy. Madison, on the other hand, took a seat in the front row near the president's desk and took down everything that transpired. He wrote, "I chose a seat in front of the presiding member, with the other members on my right and left hand. In this favorable position for hearing all that passed, I noted in terms legible and in abbreviations and marks intelligible to myself what was read from the Chair or spoken by the members; and losing not a moment unnecessarily between the adjournment and reassembling of the Convention I was enabled to write out my daily notes during the session or within a few finishing days after its close in the extent and form preserved in my own hand on my files. . . . I was not absent a single day, nor more than a casual fraction of an hour in any day, so that I could not have lost a single speech, unless a very short one." It is to James Madison that we turn first to learn what occurred during the momentous summer.

[The Constitution is] a triple-headed monster, as deep and wicked a conspiracy as ever was invented in the darkest ages against the liberties of a free people.
— JOHN LANSING, *delegate from New York*

After Convention rules were agreed upon, Gouverneur Morris rose to read a letter "from sundry persons of the State of Rhode Island" and signed by 13 merchants in Providence. Of all the states only one — Rhode Island — chose not to be represented at the Convention, a situation deplored by the signers of the letter. They sent best wishes for a favorable outcome of the Philadelphia meeting. The state's legislature had voted against participating. According to historian Francis Newton Thorpe, "The minority in Rhode Island greatly desired to have delegates chosen, but the majority, who represented the faction in the state wholly devoted to its paper-money system and opposed to imparting energy to the federal Union, and as the merchants and statesmen of the state declared, 'not representing its real character,' refused to allow the state to be represented."

It is interesting to note that Rhode Island did not ratify the Constitution until May 29, 1790. But we are getting ahead of ourselves by learning of Rhode Island's final decision. Our drama has not yet been played. The actors are in their places, the director has been chosen and the rules have been set. Now let the play itself begin.

TO CREATE A NATION

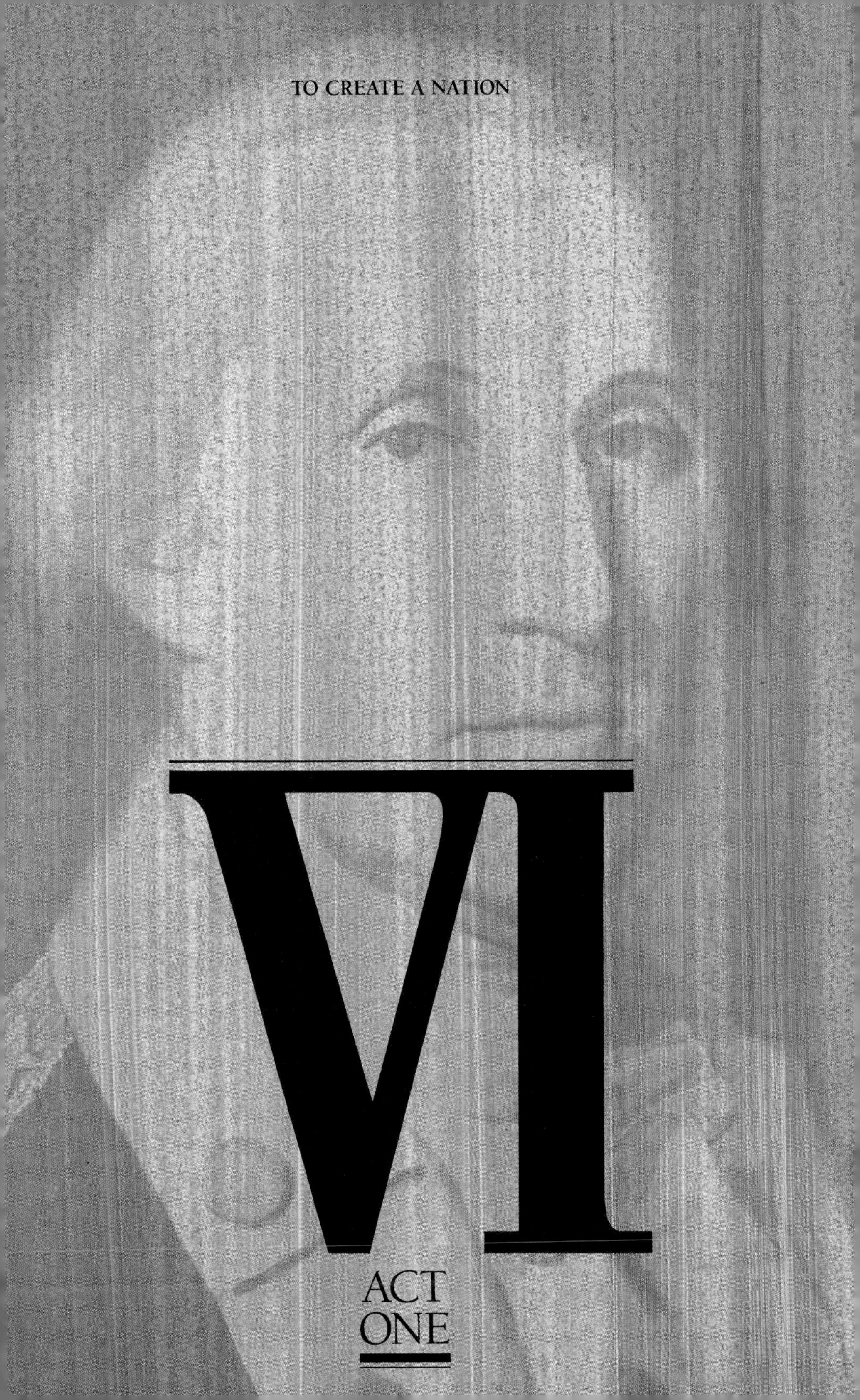

VI

ACT ONE

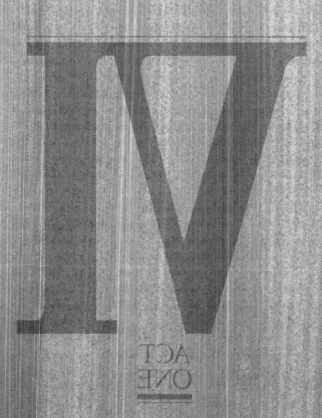

George Washington by Charles Willson Peale, 1787. Courtesy of the Pennsylvania Academy of Fine Arts.

TUESDAY MORNING, MAY 29, CAME, and according to Madison's notes "Mr. Randolph then opened the main business."

This was the Virginia Resolves or the Virginia Plan, probably shaped during those early days of May before the other delegates had arrived and Madison had been so busy working and consulting with the other Virginia members. It did not surprise the delegates that Virginia should begin the proceedings, for it had been a prime mover in bringing the Convention about. They undoubtedly expected that state would have suggestions to offer, some kind of framework to allow the Convention to get started on the business at hand.

Governor Edmund Randolph began with tactful modesty, alluding to his youth and inexperience; then he described some of the defects of the Articles of Confederation and the reasons why the delegates had gathered. He reminded them of the critical conditions in the country, the danger that the goals of the Revolution might be lost through dissension among the states and the weakness of the Articles as a governing document.

Then, with careful understatement, Randolph outlined a new kind of government which could help prevent disagreements within the country; which would give the 13 states protection against outside attack; would offer a harmonious climate for trade and general economic life, and would protect the interests of the states yet be superior to them in power.

There were 15 points to the Virginia proposal which took some three or four hours to lay before the meeting. Immediately after Randolph spoke, Charles Pinckney of South Carolina rose to express his own thoughts about a new form of government. His plan was somewhat similar but lacked the broad vision of the Virginia Plan, and Pinckney evidently had not formulated it together with the other South Carolina delegates. As the day had dragged on for many hours in the presentation of the two plans, there was no discussion of either of them, and the Pinckney proposal got little recognition then or later.

Before the assembly adjourned, it agreed to resolve itself into a Committee of the Whole to consider the Virginia Plan. The Convention had begun in earnest.

Wednesday May 30

When the Convention met in Committee of the Whole, Washington abandoned the chair and joined his Virginia colleagues on the floor. To take his place, Nathaniel Gorham of Massachusetts was chosen by ballot. The first action to be taken startled the assembly: Governor Randolph wished to amend the Virginia Resolves put forth the day before. He proposed not a union of states but "a *national* government, consisting of a *supreme* Legislative, Executive & Judicial." It was the characterization of the government as "supreme" which jolted the delegates. So long accustomed to the power of the individual states, they could hardly conceive of a national government which would have authority over them, telling them what they could and could not do.

In the stunned silence following Randolph's proposal, Chancellor Wythe of Virginia said, "From the silence of the House, I presume that gentlemen are prepared to pass on the resolution?"

Wythe's question broke the spell. Butler of South Carolina said that a national government was necessary to the continuance of the states. Pinckney wanted to know if the proposal meant the state governments would be abolished altogether. Elbridge Gerry of Massachusetts was not sure of the distinction between a federal and a national government. Dickinson of Delaware felt the country already was a nation. Through the interchange came the understanding that, while the Articles of Confederation were defective as a governing device, *federal* and *national* were confusing terms and therefore to be held under considerable suspicion.

Gouverneur Morris of Pennsylvania sought to clarify the terms. He insisted that, at the present time, the United States did not have a federal government. It was not federal because it did not have "a right to compel every part to do its duty." When the powers of the national government clash with the states, only then must the states yield, he said, and brought on a barrage of questions about where power would lie and how it would be enforced. He replied that "we had better take a supreme government now than a despot 20 years hence, for come he must."

For us today it is hard to understand how revolutionary these ideas were. The colonies had hardened their minds against central power, having lived under faraway British rule which seemed so indifferent to their needs and wishes. With independence, the states had become little countries unto themselves. Now, to be confronted with the idea of a central power which would curb the rights of the individual states was deeply disturbing. And practically, many of the delegates could not visualize how such a system would work without stripping the states of their hard-won local power.

Nor was there an example in some other country to which they could turn. Theirs was a unique situation—a vast stretch of territory, only a small population and 13 states with disparate goals and concerns. Federal . . . national. The terms really were confusing to the assembly. Randolph continued the task of defining their meaning by saying that "a union merely federal will not accomplish the objects proposed" while Madison went on to say that while a federal government operates with states, a national government reaches out to individuals.

The Committee of the Whole then took an enormous first step toward creating the Constitution which we have today. It resolved "that it is the opinion of this Committee that a national government ought to be established consisting of a supreme Legislature, Judiciary and Executive." The votes were Sherman of Connecticut nay, New York divided, Massachusetts, Pennsylvania, Delaware, Virginia, North and South Carolina aye.

Almost immediately, however, the delegates moved into the thorniest problem which they must face and the one which almost wrecked the Convention several times during that summer: how the individual states were to be represented in this new national government. Randolph referred to the second of the Virginia Resolves "that the rights of suffrage in the national legislature ought to be proportioned to the Quotas of contributions, or to the number of free inhabitants, as the one or the other rule may seem best in different cases."

Hamilton thought representation should be based on the number of free inhabitants. Madison moved and was seconded that "the equality of suffrage established by the Articles of Confederation ought not to prevail in the national Legislature, and that an equitable ratio of representation ought to be submitted." This of course ran directly into opposition from Delaware whose delegates had been committed by that state to make no change in voting rights. They reminded the Convention that they would have to leave should such a change be made.

No one wanted to see a state withdraw from the meeting, especially at so early a time. The whole matter of one-state one-vote rule was postponed as the assembly adjourned. The delegates must have returned to their lodgings with forebodings of the difficulties to come.

Thursday May 31

Having postponed the problem of representation, the delegates went on to the next item in the Virginia Plan and agreed that the national legislature would have two branches. In most of the states this was the rule and thus it offered no startling new idea.

But the next resolution was that "the members of the first branch of the National Legislature ought to be elected by the people of the several States." Roger Sherman declared the people "should have as little to do as may be about the Government. They want information and are constantly liable to be misled." Businessman Elbridge Gerry of Massachusetts added that "the evils we experience flow from the excess of democracy. The people do not want virtue, but are the dupes of pretended patriots." He was undoubtedly thinking of Shays' Rebellion of which we learned earlier. Gerry commented that he had been "too republican heretofore" but had been taught by experience the danger of the levilling spirit."

Once again the meaning of words plagued the delegates, and we are reminded how important it is to understand the *meaning* of words used then and now. Democracy in those days meant a kind of anarchy, if it was not curbed.

But George Mason of Virginia was not put off by the thought of giving common people the vote. He insisted that by turning away from too much democracy, the country could go to the opposite extreme. "We ought to attend to the rights of every class of the people," he said, urging that the delegates "provide no less carefully for the . . . happiness of the lowest than of the highest orders of Citizens." The first branch of the legislature "was to be the grand depository of the democratic principle of the Government. . . . It ought to know and sympathize with every part of the community." He asked, "Will not our children in a short time be among the general mass?"

Wilson of Pennsylvania supported Mason's views by contending "strenuously for drawing the most numerous branch of the Legislature immediately from the people" and thought it would be "wrong to increase the weight of the State Legislatures by making them the electors of the national Legislature." Madison went along with Wilson's reasoning adding that if the people were the electors for the first branch they would be more likely to give the national government more attention and support.

Six states voted for the resolution for popular election of the first branch of the legislature. Connecticut and Delaware were divided and New Jersey and South Carolina voted nay. New York voted aye along with Massachusetts, Pennsylvania, Virginia, North Carolina and Georgia.

It was time to move on to the fifth resolution of the Virginia Plan "that the members of the second branch of the national legislature ought to be elected by those of the first." When the discussion broke into a myriad of opinions, the Committee of the Whole turned to portions of the sixth resolution and unanimously agreed "that each branch ought to possess the right of originating acts," and "that the national legislature ought to be empowered to enjoy the legislative rights vested in Congress by the confederation." Nine states agreed that the national legislature could "legislate in all cases, to which the separate States are incompetent, or in which the harmony of the united States may be interrupted by the exercise of individual legislation."

As for the last clause of the sixth Virginia resolution, "to call forth the force of the Union against any member of the Union failing to fulfill its duty under the articles," Madison himself asked for a postponement. He commented that he felt it impractical to use force against a state, that it would look "more like a declaration of war than an infliction of punishment, and would probably be considered by the party attacked as a dissolution of all previous compacts by which it might be bound."

Delegates seemed to be aware immediately that punishment of a state would imply that all the citizens of the state were guilty—an impossible assumption. In its final form, the Constitution makes no mention of a national army being called forth against a state or a section of the country, but rather deals with the problem by declaring that the Constitution is the supreme law of the land. The delegates agreed with Madison and the Convention adjourned for the day.

Already a few dim outlines of the government structure they were building could be seen. But there were many weeks ahead, many problems to be resolved. No doubt at this stage the individual players were busily turning over in their minds new ideas and new combinations of power which would go into the making of that structure.

Friday June 1

The members moved on to the seventh Virginia resolution "that a national executive be instituted." Here was a delicate decision for the assembly. Fresh in every mind was the idea of a king ruling over subjects and "national executive" must have sounded suspiciously like just that. Pinckney put their thoughts into words when he urged a "vigorous executive" and Wilson further defined it by moving that the executive be a single person.

Madison called the silence that followed "a considerable pause." Franklin wished "gentlemen" would deliver their sentiments. Wilson broadened his statement by explaining that he felt vigor and dispatch would best be found in a single person. He feared delays and failed responsibility if the executive branch was represented by several persons. He

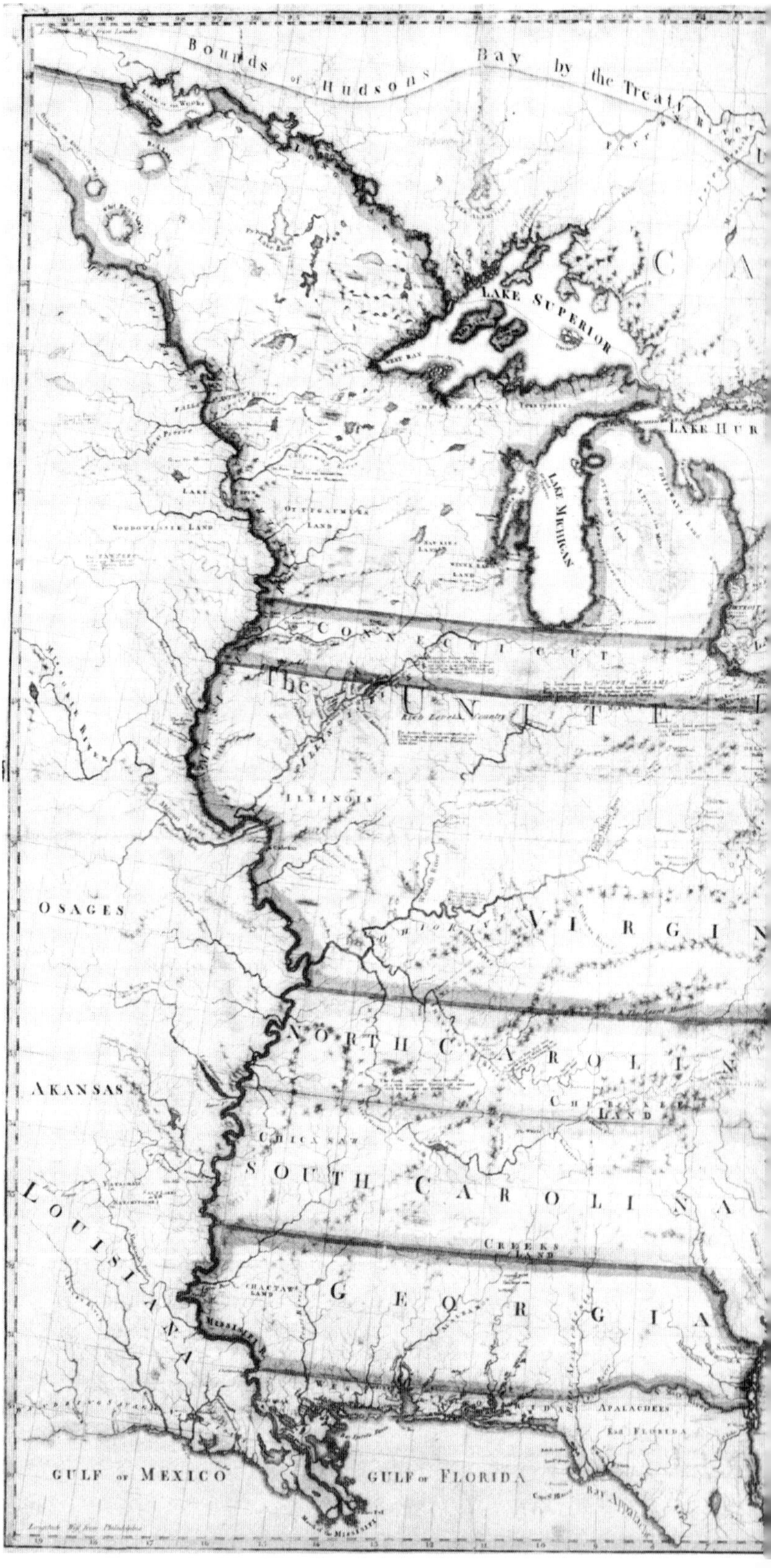

A New and correct Map of the United States of North America by Abel Buell, 1784. Courtesy of the New Jersey Historical Society.

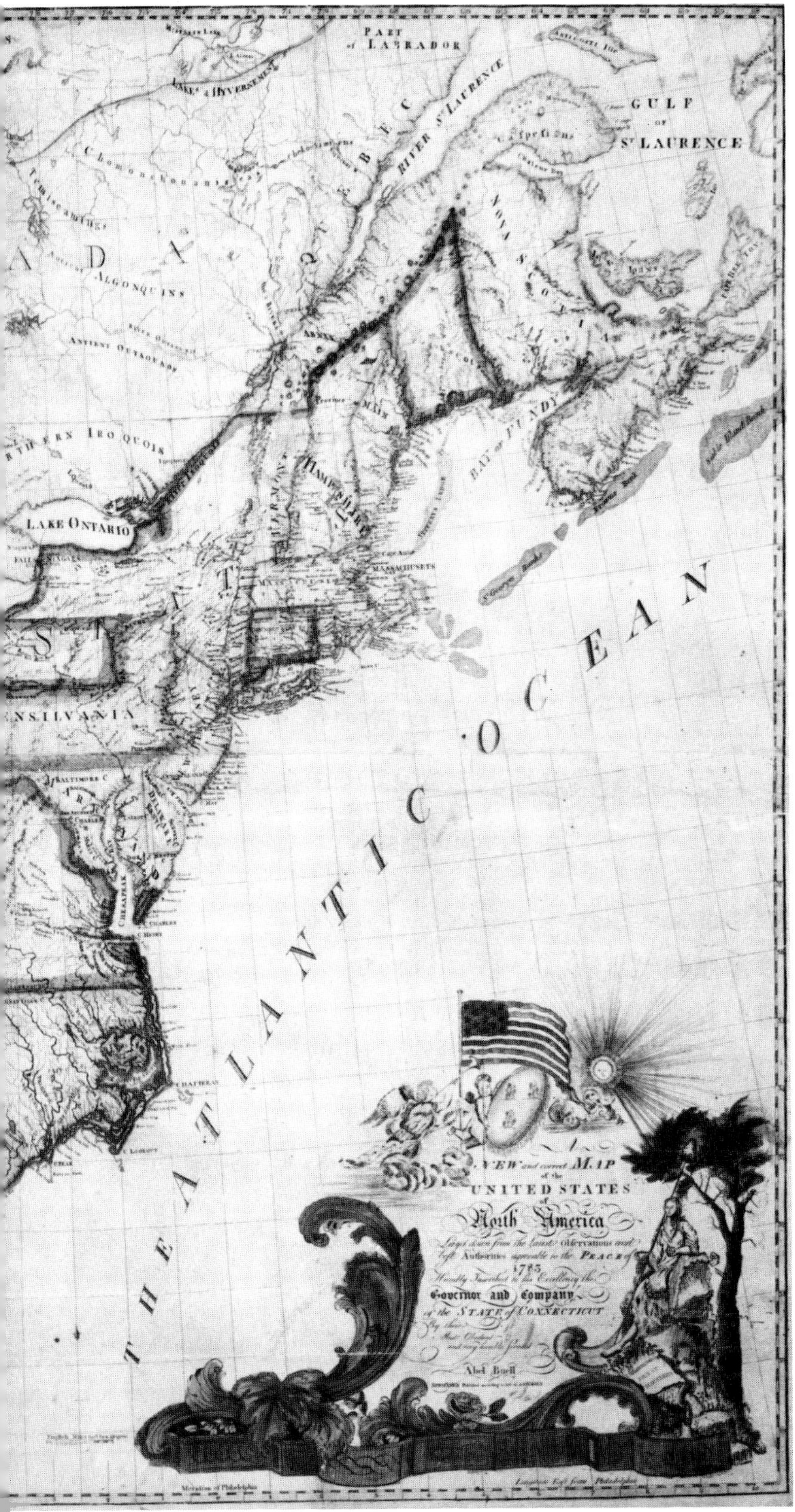

PART of LABRADOR
GULF OF ST LAURENCE
RIVER ST LAURENCE
NOVA SCOTIA
BAY of FUNDY
ALGONQUINS
LAKE ONTARIO
HAMPSHIRE
MASSACHUSETTS
NSILVANIA
THE ATLANTIC OCEAN
NEW and correct MAP
of the
UNITED STATES
of
North America
Abel Buell

believed both in a strong central government and in the sovereignty of the people.

There were of course other members who felt the danger of a lone, powerful figure. Sherman saw the executive branch as having far less power, an arm of the government which would be "nothing more than an institution for carrying the will of the legislature into effect . . . the person or persons ought to be appointed by and accountable to the Legislature only, which was the depository of the supreme will of the Society." It was clear in his comments that he did not conceive of an executive directly accountable to the people. The Convention's thinking had not gone far enough to consider the way in which the executive would be chosen.

Randolph also was fearful of a single executive. He could not see why Wilson's requirements of "vigor, dispatch & responsibility" could not be found in three men as well as in one man. He felt that Wilson looked toward "the British government as our prototype. The fixed genius of the people of America requires a different form of government."

Wilson came back with the argument that his proposal would be the best safeguard against tyranny. He called to mind the 30 tyrants of Athens and the 10 decemvirs of Rome. He rejected the idea that America was bound by the British example. "We must consider two points of importance existing in our country . . . the extent and manners of the United States." A country of America's size "seems to require the vigor of monarchy" but "the manners are against a king, and are purely republican."

It is interesting that the delegates bridled at the idea of using the British government as a model, yet it was very natural that they look to that governmental structure. They had grown up and lived under the British form of government; many of them had studied in and visited the British Isles. Wilson of course had been born in Scotland.

The discussion broke into polite disputation, with Randolph reaffirming his position of wanting a troika executive. He saw this as more representative of the country since its members could be brought from three different areas, while Butler of South Carolina noted that in Holland, several military heads had been disadvantageous to the country when it was threatened by invasion.

Unable to come to a decision on having one or more persons as the executive, the Committee of the Whole agreed only that there should be a national executive.

The discussion now ranged over the executive's powers, the length of his term of office, his salary. The delegates only agreed that the executive should have power "to carry into execution the national laws" and "to appoint to offices in cases not otherwise provided for." Considerable discussion went into term of office from three years, with an opportunity for re-election, to seven years with no re-election. A seven-year term was passed in Committee.

Saturday June 2

And how was this seven-year executive to be chosen? Wilson felt that he should be chosen by the people. He expanded on his arguments with the idea that the states be divided into districts. Voters who chose the first branch of the national legislature would choose electors in each district who would select the national executive. This, of course, was the first appearance of that formula which exists even today—the electoral college. At that time the Convention believed the states would be supporting their favorite sons and this would be a way to winnow out the large number of candidates. National parties, the Democrats and Republicans, were unknown at that time.

When that part of Resolve 7, "a fixed compensation for the services rendered," was reached, Wilson read a paper on the subject prepared by Franklin who was too infirm to stand for long. Franklin began with the thought that he had "borne a good will" to the Virginia Plan and "in general wished it success" but he could not agree to salaries for the executive. "Sir, there are two passions which have a powerful influence on the affairs of men. These are ambition and avarice; the love of power, and the love of money. Separately each of these has a great force in prompting men to action; but when united in view of the same object, they have in many minds the most violent effects. Place before the eyes of such men, a post of *honour* that shall be at the same time a place of *profit,* and they will move heaven and earth to obtain it. . . .

"And of what kind are the men that will strive for this profitable preeminence, through all the bustle of cabal, the heat of contention, the infinite mutual abuse of parties, tearing to pieces the best of characters? It will not be the wise and moderate, the lovers of peace and good order, the men fittest for the trust. It will be the bold and the violent, the men of strong passions and defatigable activity in their selfish pursuits. These will thrust themselves into your Government and be your rulers. — And these too will be mistaken in the expected happiness of their situation: For their vanquished competitors of the same spirit, and from the same motives will perpetually be endeavouring to distress their administration, thwart their measures, and render them odious to the people. . . . I am apprehensive . . . perhaps too apprehensive, that the Government of these States, may in future times, end in a Monarchy. But this Catastrophe I think may be long delayed, if in our proposed System we do not sow the seeds of contention, faction & tumult, by making our posts of honour, places of profit."

Franklin said that this might be deemed a "Utopian Idea" but there were many examples to the contrary. He cited the service of the Quakers and the "General of our armies executed for eight years together without the smallest salary, by a Patriot whom I will not now offend by any other praise; and this through fatigues and distresses in common with the other brave men his military friends & Companions. . . ." Although of course he did not mention it, Franklin himself gave away his salary as President of the State of Pennsylvania, did not patent his invention of the lightning rod or his Franklin stove.

Evidently the delegates felt it was an impractical proposal, but according to Madison's notes, "No debate ensued, and the proposition was postponed for the consideration of the members. It was treated with great respect, but rather for the author of it than from any apparent conviction of its expediency or practicability."

The discussion moved on to how the executive might be removed from office, the delegates finally agreeing only that the executive would be ineligible for re-election after his seven-year term and would "be removeable on impeachment & conviction of mal-practice or neglect of duty." The members could not agree as to whether the state legislatures or the national legislature would have the power to remove the executive, or even whether the executive should be one or more persons.

Monday June 4

Back again they went to the question of whether the executive would be one or more persons. Wilson noted that "all of the 13 States tho agreeing in scarce any other instance, agree in placing a single magistrate at the head of the Government. The idea of three heads has taken place in none." Among three equal members he thought there would be "uncontrouled, continued & violent animosities; which would not only interrupt the public administration; but diffuse their poison thro' the other branches of Govt. thro' the States, and at length thro' the people at large." A majority of the states were persuaded to his thinking, and in Committee of the Whole, a single executive was agreed to.

Delegates now turned to Virginia Resolve No. 8: "That the Executive and a convenient number of the National Judiciary, ought to compose a Council of revision with authority to examine every act of the National Legislature before it shall operate, & every act of a particular Legislature before a Negative thereon shall be final; and that the dissent of the said Council shall amount to a rejection, unless the Act of the National Legislature be again passed, or that of a particular Legislature be again negatived by ________ of the members of each branch."

The executive veto of legislative acts was first to be considered. The delegates were uneasy about joining the judiciary with the executive in veto powers: Gerry, after giving his objections to the involvement of the judiciary, proposed "that the National Executive shall have a right to negative any Legislative act which shall not be afterwards passed by ________ parts of each branch of the national Legislature," to which the delegates agreed.

Mason, who had been out of the room when the vote was taken, then voiced an uneasiness which seemed ever present. He asked: "Do gentlemen mean to pave the way to hereditary Monarchy? Do they flatter themselves that the people will ever consent to such an innovation? If they do, I venture to tell them, they are mistaken." He was considering the danger to the country should the people reject the

Constitution now being written. "And do gentlemen look forward to the dangerous interval between the extinction of an old, and the establishment of a new Government and to the scenes of confusion which may ensue. He hoped that nothing like a Monarchy will ever be attempted in this Country. A hatred to its oppressions carried the people through the late Revolution. . . . He never could agree to give up all the rights of the people to a single Magistrate." The executive must be more than one person; greater powers could then be entrusted to that branch.

Nevertheless, the delegates were willing to give the single executive veto power, but they wanted the legislature to have the power to overrule that veto.

Near the end of the day's session, they began consideration of Virginia Resolve Number 9: "That a National Judiciary be established to consist of one or more supreme tribunals, and of inferior tribunals to be chosen by the National Legislature. . . ."

The delegates quickly agreed to establish a national judiciary consisting of one supreme tribunal and one or more inferior tribunals.

Tuesday June 5

This was one of those mornings when the members had not settled things in their minds. They could not deal right away with how the judges would be chosen. After back and forth discussion and little accomplishment with the rest of Resolve Number 9, they moved on to Virginia Resolve Number 10: "That provision ought to be made for the admission of States lawfully arising within the limits of the United States, whether from a voluntary junction of Government & Territory or otherwise, with the consent of a number of voices in the National legislature less than the whole."

Without discussion the Resolve was passed. There were a number of potential states waiting to be recognized — Vermont, Tennessee (then called the independent State of Franklin), Kentucky and all the Western territories which were being explored and populated. All this large area would be affected by the resolution.

Then quickly, they moved on to Virginia Resolve Number 11: "That a Republican Government & the territory of each State, except in the instance of a voluntary junction of Government and territory, ought to be guaranteed by the United States to each State."

This would guarantee a republican government to all states, but Paterson felt the question of representation should be decided first. He was a "small state" supporter and watched for any decisions which would compromise their power.

The Resolve was therefore postponed. The delegates now took up discussion of Virginia Resolve Number 12: "That provision ought to be made for the continuance of Congress and their authorities and privileges, until a given day after the reform of the articles of Union shall be adopted, and for the completion of all their engagements."

This Resolve, guaranteeing that the country should not be without a government until the people decided whether or not to accept the new Constitution, was passed quickly and "produced no debate."

Then came Virginia Resolve Number 13: "That provision ought to be made for the amendment of the Articles of Union whensoever it shall seem necessary, and that the assent of the National Legislature ought not to be required thereto."

This Resolve allowed the new Constitution to be amended without the assent of Congress. Pinckney "doubted the propriety or necessity of it" while Gerry favored it.

This Resolve was also postponed, as was Virginia Resolve Number 14: "That the Legislative, Executive & Judiciary powers within the several States ought to be bound by oath to support the articles of Union."

And finally, Virginia Resolve Number 15: "That the amendments which shall be offered to the Confederation, by the Convention ought at a proper time, or times, after the approbation of Congress to be submitted to an assembly or assemblies of Representatives, recommended by the several Legislatures to be expressly chosen by the people, to consider & decide thereon."

The method of presenting the new Constitution to the country was, as all the delegates knew, a very important decision. Madison was strongly for bringing the decision to the people; that it be ratified "by the supreme authority of the people themselves." Sherman thought "popular ratification unnecessary," and Gerry, as noted before still remembering Shays' Rebellion, also was opposed, saying that people in the New England states had "the wildest ideas of Government in the world." It was necessary, therefore, to postpone a decision on the Resolve.

The discussion now swung back to a reconsideration of the clause for establishing the inferior tribunals of Resolve Number 9. According to the Resolve, these tribunals were to be chosen by the national legislature. Rutledge argued that the state courts "might and ought to be left in all cases to decide in the first instance the right of appeal" to the supreme court. He believed federal lower courts would take away some of the rights of the states. However, Madison felt that these lower courts should have final decision in many cases or there would be appeals "to a most oppressive degree." He commented that an effective judiciary was as important as an effective executive. Butler warned that "the States will revolt at such encroachments. . . . We must follow the example of Solon who gave the Athenians not the best Government he could devise; but the best they would receive." Wilson and Madison moved "that the National Legislature be empowered to institute inferior tribunals" be added to Resolve Number 9. They felt some kind of provision must be made for having lower courts, hoping the method of choice would be worked out later. The motion passed.

Wednesday June 6

When the Committee of the Whole gathered this morning they undoubtedly must have sensed a climax to their debates was approaching. They had moved through all 15 of the Virginia Resolves; now they must go back to what had shown itself to be one of the greatest differences: how the national legislature was to be elected. They were returning to Resolve Number Four — how should the members of the House of Representatives be chosen?

Pinckney began the discussion by moving "that the first branch of the national Legislature be elected by the State Legislatures, not by the people." He felt "the people were less fit Judges in such a case, and that the Legislatures would be less likely to promote the adoption of the new Government, if they were to be excluded from all share in it."

Gerry agreed with Pinckney, yet he worried about the people not having enough direct representation, remarking that he was "as much principled as ever against aristocracy and monarchy." He thought it was necessary "that the people should appoint one branch of the government in order to inspire them with the necessary confidence," but wondered if the people could not first nominate certain persons from their districts who would do the final appointing.

Sherman thought "if the State Governments are to be continued, it is necessary in order to preserve harmony between the National & State Governments that the elections to the former should be made by the latter."

Mason, on the other hand, felt that "under the existing Confederacy, Congress represent the *States* not the *people* of the States: their acts operate on the *States*, not on the individuals. The case will be changed in the new plan of Government. The people will be represented; they ought therefore to choose the Representatives."

Madison quickly added that one branch of the Legislature at least should be chosen by the people. He talked long and earnestly about the failings of other governmental systems, and observed that "the lesson we are to draw from the whole is that where a majority are united by a common sentiment, and have an opportunity, the rights of the minor party become insecure. In a Republican Government the Majority if united have always an opportunity. The only remedy is to enlarge the sphere, & thereby divide the community into so great a number of interests & parties, that in the first place a majority will not be likely at the same moment to have a common interest separate from that of the whole or of the minority; and in the second place, that in case they should have such an interest, they may not be apt to unite in the pursuit of it. It is incumbent on us then to try this remedy, and with that view to frame a republican system on such a scale & in such a form as will controul all the evils which have been experienced."

Dickinson thought that it was "essential that one branch of the Legislature should be drawn immediately from the people; and as expedient that the other should be chosen by the Legislatures of the States" because it was "as politic as it was unavoidable."

Read went to the other extreme, expressing the thought that perhaps state governments should be abandoned in favor of a national government — an idea rejected by Wilson who believed state and national government could work in harmony provided the state governments were "restrained to certain local purposes." He said that in all earlier confederated systems the central government eventually was gradually destroyed by the parts composing it.

The delegates then voted against having the first branch of the national legislature elected by the states.

At this point the discussion returned to whether or not the judiciary should be excluded from a share in the revision of the laws, but in spite of a long statement from Madison and support from others that "the utility of annexing the wisdom and weight of the Judiciary to the Executive seems incontestable," the assembly voted against combining the two in a council of revision "with authority to examine every act of the National Legislature before it shall operate. . . ."

It is interesting that in our own day, some students of government see the failed passage of this point as unfortunate. They cite the fact that long delays are sometimes possible until a law is declared unconstitutional by the Supreme Court. Had the council of revision been created, such laws would be declared unconstitutional long before they went into effect.

Thursday June 7

Back the delegates went to further discussion of the National Legislature, for they realized this segment of government was of crucial importance. The exchange of views began with a motion that the second branch of the legislature be chosen by the state legislatures.

Dickinson made the motion, he said, because he felt "the sense of the States would be better collected through their Governments than immediately from the people at large" and because he "wished the Senate to consist of the most distinguished characters, distinguished for their rank in life and their weight of property, and bearing as strong a likeness to the British House of Lords as possible." He believed that "such characters more likely to be selected by the State Legislatures, than in any other mode." He had no objection to a large Senate for it would then balance the other branch. It is interesting that the Convention had begun using the term "Senate"—the terms "Senate" and "House" were in the Virginia Constitution.

Wilson presented a different view: "If we are to establish a national Government, that Government ought to flow from the people at large. If one branch of it should be chosen by the Legislatures, and the other by the people, the two branches will rest on different foundations, and dissensions will naturally arise between them." He wanted the Senate "to be elected by the people as well as the other branch, and the people might be divided into proper districts for the purpose. . . ."

Madison then rose. He considered "the use of the Senate is to consist in its proceeding with more coolness, with more system & with more wisdom, than the popular branch. Enlarge their number and you communicate to them the vices which they are meant to correct." He cited the Roman Tribunes, saying that "they lost their influence and power in proportion as their number was augmented." If the Senate representation was proportional it would end up being very large, which was undesirable.

Gerry's thoughts represented the commercial outlook of his state, favoring election by the state legislatures: "The elections being carried thro' this refinement, will be most likely to provide some check in favor of the commercial interest against the landed; without which oppression will take place, and no free Government can last long when that is the case."

It is important for us to remember that these men saw property and its relationship to the character of a person in a different light from the way we do today. The delegates were people who owned property; many state constitutions required voters to own property. The Governor of Massachusetts, for example, had to own property amounting to a thousand pounds, while in South Carolina he must have "a settled plantation or freehold of the value of at least ten thousand pounds." In this young nation where land and opportunity were everywhere, owning property generally indicated that an individual was thrifty, industrious, enterprising—in short, a worthwhile citizen. Many of the delegates saw the property-less person as one who would have no real stake in the welfare of the country; property was not for the privileged few, but available to the many who would then be willing to fight for it. The fact that the colonists had used as their revolutionary cry, "taxation without representation is tyranny," was an indication of how important the owning of property was to these busy, independent people.

Wilson commented that he could not understand how "the landed interest would be rendered less predominant in the Senate, by an election through the medium of the Legislatures than by the people themselves. If the Legislatures . . . sacrificed the commercial to the landed interest, what reason was there to expect such a choice from them as would defeat their own views."

Gerry repeated his insistence that the "commercial & monied interest would be more secure in the hands of the State Legislatures, than of the people at large. The former have more sense of character, and will be restrained by that from injustice." He thought elections by districts impractical.

Finally came the vote: In favor of Senators being appointed by the state legislatures — one of the many examples of how the delegates would later change their minds, and the great value of these first meetings as a Committee of the Whole where change was possible.

Friday June 8

The relationship of state power to that of the national government came up for further clarification when the delegates reconsidered the clause giving the national legislature a veto on state laws enacted contrary to the national constitution or to treaties with foreign nations.

While Pinckney and Madison wanted the national legislature to have the power to veto state laws, Williamson was against it and Gerry and Sherman thought the cases in which the veto would apply would need to be defined. However, after further intense partisanship, the vote was in the negative and did not pass, indicating that the delegates still were unclear in their minds as to the kind of government they were shaping—was it to be another federation of states as they presently had under the Articles of Confederation or were they about to break new political ground?

Saturday June 9

This session of the Convention led off with the views of Gerry who advocated the choosing of the executive by the state governors. Randolph flatly disagreed; and another proposal went down in defeat.

Now they returned to that thorny question of how the country would be represented in the national legislature. As the discussion went on it became ever clearer that the "large" states — Massachusetts, Pennsylvania and Virginia — were ranged against the "small" states — Delaware, New Jersey, New York, Maryland, Connecticut and New Hampshire.

Early in the Convention's meetings, Read of Delaware noted that the small states must "keep a strict watch upon the movements and propositions from the larger States, who will probably combine to swallow up the smaller ones. . . ." And from the beginning, the larger states (so-called because of their larger population) questioned whether the small states should have an equal vote with them.

Brearley spoke up with the point that much discussion went on when the confederation was formed and was "rightly settled by allowing to each sovereign State an equal vote. Otherwise the smaller States must have been destroyed instead of being saved." While a ratio seemed fair on the face of it, "on a deeper examination was unfair and unjust." Virginia would have 16 votes, Georgia only one. The three large states will "carry every thing before them." He suggested the radical idea of erasing all present boundaries and repartitioning the area into 13 equal parts.

Paterson followed up on Brearley's objections with remarks on the nature and structure and powers of the Convention: "The Convention was formed in pursuance of an Act of Congress that this act was recited in several of the Commissions, particularly that of Massachusetts. . . ." He asked that the Massachusetts Commission be read again which stated that the Articles of the Confederation was the proper basis of all the proceedings of the Convention.

After this was read, Paterson warned: "We ought to keep within its limits, or we should be charged by our Constituents with usurpation, that the people of America were sharp-sighted and not to be deceived." In addition, he went on, "the Commissions under which we acted were not only the measure of our power, they denoted also the sentiments of the States on the subject of our deliberation. The idea of a national Government as contradistinguished from a federal one, never entered into the mind of any of them, and to the public mind we must accommodate ourselves. We have no power to go beyond the federal scheme, and if we had the people are not ripe for any other. We must follow the people, the people will not follow us."

Paterson's words of warning must have filled the delegates with great unease, for it was clear now that the debates had been carrying the Convention farther and farther from a simple revision of the Articles of Confederation. There was not the slightest doubt that if they continued in their present direction, they would be creating a completely new form of government.

Paterson continued with the argument that "the proposition for a proportional representation as striking at the existence of the lesser States," and thought the Convention needed to use the Articles of Confederation as the basis of its proceedings. He differentiated between a national government and a federal one and said the former "never entered into the mind" of any of those who had sent the delegates to Philadelphia in the first place. "A confederacy supposes sovereignty in the members composing it & sovereignty supposes equality. If we are to be considered as a nation, all State distinctions must be abolished, the whole must be thrown into hotchpot. . . ." He said the small states would never agree to giving up equality of representation. He continued with the thought that "there was no more reason that a great individual state contributing much, should have more votes than a small one contributing little, than that a rich individual citizen should have more votes than an indigent one."

Paterson went on even more firmly, referring to an earlier remark made that the large states might need to confederate if the smaller states did not come around. "Let them unite if they please, but let them remember that they have no authority to compel the others to unite. N. Jersey will never confederate on the plan before the Committee. She would be swallowed up." He would, he said, "rather submit to a monarch, to a despot, than to such a fate" and "would not

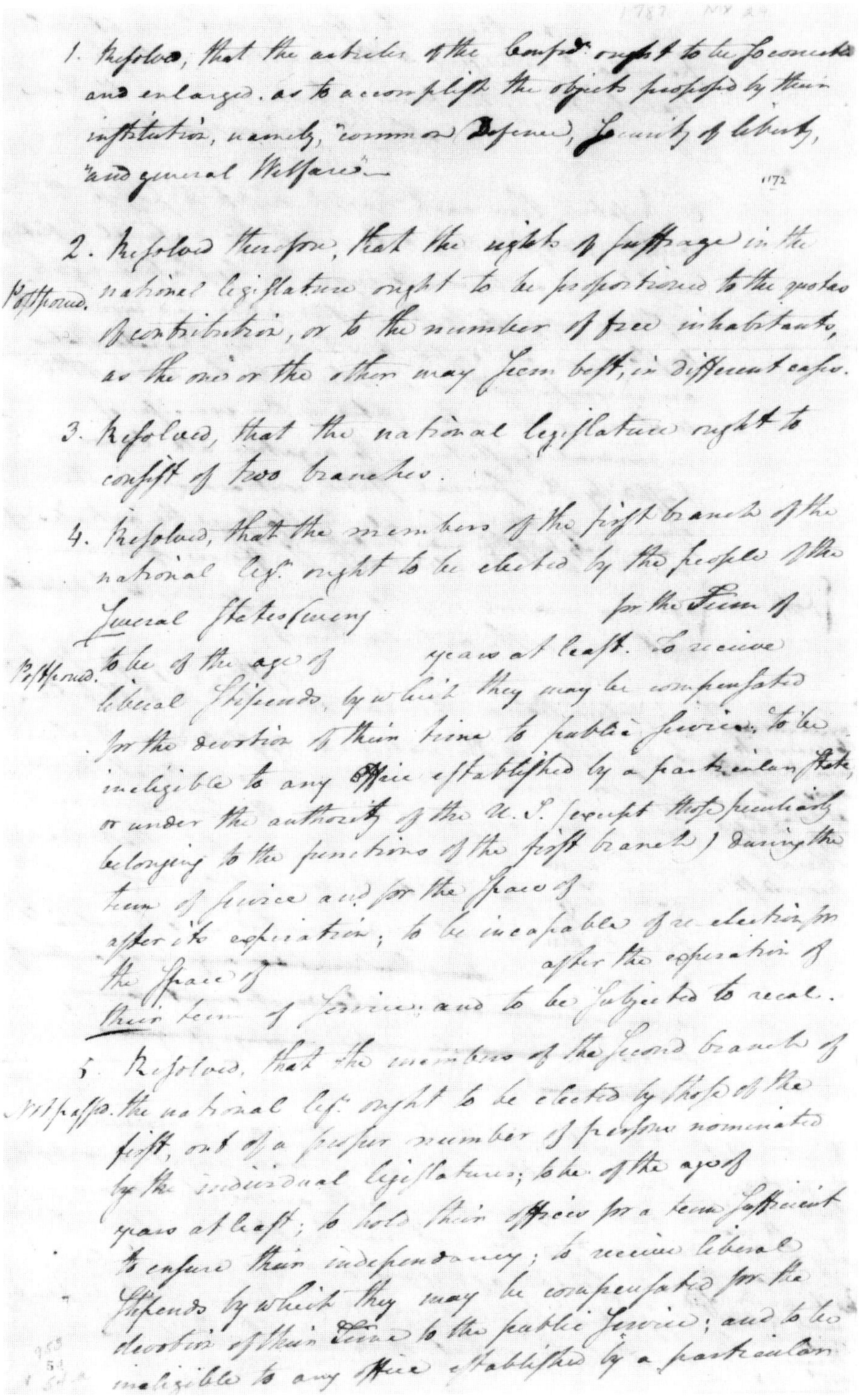

1. Resolved, that the articles of the Confedn. ought to be so corrected and enlarged as to accomplish the objects proposed by their institution, namely, "common Defence, Security of liberty, "and general Welfare.

1172

Postponed. 2. Resolved therefore, that the rights of suffrage in the national legislature ought to be proportioned to the quotas of contribution, or to the number of free inhabitants, as the one or the other may seem best, in different cases.

3. Resolved, that the national legislature ought to consist of two branches.

Postponed. 4. Resolved, that the members of the first branch of the national legr. ought to be elected by the people of the several States every for the Term of to be of the age of years at least. to receive liberal stipends, by which they may be compensated for the devotion of their time to public service; to be ineligible to any Office established by a particular State, or under the authority of the U. S. (except those peculiarly belonging to the functions of the first branch) during the term of service and for the space of after its expiration; to be incapable of re-election for the space of after the expiration of their term of service; and to be subjected to recal.

Not passed. 5. Resolved, that the members of the second branch of the national legr. ought to be elected by those of the first, out of a proper number of persons nominated by the individual legislatures; to be of the age of years at least; to hold their offices for a term sufficient to ensure their independency; to receive liberal stipends by which they may be compensated for the devotion of their time to the public service; and to be ineligible to any office established by a particular

The Virginia Plan in the hand of William Paterson, ca. May 29, 1787.
Courtesy of the Library of Congress.

only oppose the plan here" but on his return home "do everything in his power to defeat it there."

These were some of the strongest, most defiant words so far expressed. It was Wilson, one of the keenest minds in the hall, who rose to defend the direction the Convention was now taking. He began with a detailed explanation of proportional representation: "as all authority was derived from the people, equal numbers of people ought to have an equal number of representatives, and different numbers of people different numbers of representatives," and went on to ask: "Are not the Citizens of Pennsylvania equal to those of N. Jersey? does it require 150 of the former to balance 50 of the latter? . . . We have been told that each State being sovereign, all are equal. So each man is naturally a sovereign over himself, and all men are therefore naturally equal. Can he retain this equality when he becomes a member of Civil Government? He can not. As little can a Sovereign State, when it becomes a member of a federal Government. If N.J. will not part with her Sovereignty it is in vain to talk of Government."

The House adjourned shortly afterward and it can be guessed that the discussions were long and heated that weekend at the Indian Queen. For us, it is interesting to consider how these problems apply in our own time to the United Nations and how it functions.

Monday June 11

Again the subject was how the national legislature was to be chosen, with Sherman suggesting a compromise "that the proportion of suffrage in the 1st branch should be according to the respective numbers of free inhabitants; and that in the second branch or Senate, each State should have one vote and no more." He continued, "as the States would remain possessed of certain individual rights, each state ought to be able to protect itself: otherwise a few large States will rule the rest. The House of Lords in England he observed had certain particular rights under the Constitution, and hence they have an equal vote with the House of Commons that they may be able to defend their rights."

At an earlier time, Dickinson had proposed that the states be equal in representation in one of the legislative branches, but it was Sherman who made the important suggestion that such equality be in the Senate. After more discussion, Franklin asked that his thoughts be read by Wilson before the question was put to a vote.

Franklin wrote: "It has given me great pleasure to observe that till this point, the proportion of representation, came before us, our debates were carried on with great coolness & temper. If any thing of a contrary kind, has on this occasion appeared, I hope it will not be repeated, for we are sent here to *consult,* not to *contend,* with each other; and declarations of a fixed opinion, and of determined resolution, never to change it, neither enlighten nor convince us. Positiveness and warmth on one side, naturally beget their like on the other; and tend to create and augment discord & division in a great concern, wherein harmony & Union are extremely necessary to give weight to our Councils, and render them effectual in promoting & securing the common good.

"I must own that I was originally of opinion it would be better if every member of Congress, or our national Council, were to consider himself rather as a representative of the whole, than as an Agent for the interests of a particular State; in which case the proportion of members for each State would be of less consequence, & it would not be very material whether they voted by States or individually. But as I find this is not to be expected, I now think the number of Representatives should bear some proportion to the number of the Represented; and that the decisions should be by the majority of members, not by the majority of States. This is objected to from an apprehension that the greater States would then swallow up the smaller. I do not at present clearly see what advantage the greater States could propose to themselves by swallowing the smaller, and therefore I do not apprehend they would attempt it. I recollect that in the beginning of this Century, when the Union was proposed of the two Kingdoms, England & Scotland, the Scotch Patriots were full of fears that unless they had an equal number of Representatives in Parliament, they should be ruined by the superiority of the English. They finally agreed however that the different proportions of importance in the Union, of the two Nations should be attended to, whereby they were to have only forty members in the House of Commons, and only sixteen in the House of Lords; A very great inferiority of numbers! And yet to this day I do not recollect that any thing has been done in the Parliament of Great Britain to the prejudice of Scotland; and whoever looks over the lists of public officers, Civil & military of that nation will find I believe that the North Britons enjoy at least their full proportion of emolument."

Again Franklin defused a situation that was growing tense. In his long remarks and anecdotes there usually was something to make his listeners smile while at the same time pointing out a fact or solution to a problem; in these comments he reminded the delegates of how Scotland had managed to acquire probably more than its share of offices.

The delegates then passed in the affirmative a motion stating that there should be "some equitable ratio of representation in proportion to the whole number of white & other free Citizens & inhabitants of every age, sex & condition including those bound to servitude for a term of years and three fifths of all other persons not comprehended in the foregoing description, except Indians not paying taxes, in each State."

(This rule was in the Act of Congress agreed to by 11 states for apportioning quotas of revenue for the states. The "other persons" were slaves; this three fifths rule was law until the Fourteenth Amendment of 1868.)

It is hard for us today to understand the approach of the delegates to the problem of slavery; we need to remember that they were forming a document acceptable to the society of the times. New England shipowners profited by the slave trade; the Southern states' economy had been shaped on the premise of slave holdings. A number of the delegates were uneasy with the problem, particularly Mason of Virginia. It was to recur in full force in later deliberations. At this time, it was seen as part of the proportional-representation question. And the question bounced back and forth among the delegates without resolution.

Finally, they returned to agree unanimously to a reworded form of Virginia Resolve Number 11 which had been previously postponed: that a republican Constitution, and its existing laws, ought to be guaranteed to each State. And then went on to approve Virginia Resolve Number 13, also previously postponed: that provision ought to be made for the amendment of the articles of Union, whensoever it shall seem necessary, tabling decision on the words "without requiring the consent of the National Legislature."

Virginia Resolve Number 14 met with more discussion; it required oaths from the members of the state governments to observe the National Constitution and laws. Sherman opposed it as unneccessarily intruding into the state jurisdictions while Randolph thought it necessary to prevent competition between state and national laws. After further discussion, the Resolve passed finally, six to five.

Tuesday June 12

The Committee of the Whole went on this morning with the Virginia Resolves, reaching, at last, Number 15 which dealt with how the Constitution would be ratified. The delegates agreed that "after the approbation of Congress to be submitted to an assembly or assemblies of Representatives, recommended by the several Legislatures to be expressly chosen by the people, to consider & decide thereon."

Other fine points of earlier Resolves were considered or reconsidered. For example, in Resolve Number 4, how often should members of the first branch of the legislature be elected? Gerry was for annual elections saying, "The people of New England will never give up the point of annual elections, they know of the transition made in England from triennial to septennial elections, and will consider such an innovation here as the prelude to a like usurpation." Annual elections were "the only defence of the people against tyranny."

Madison replied that "if the opinions of the people were to be our guide, it would be difficult to say what course we ought to take. No member of the Convention could say what the opinions of his Constituents were at this time; much less could he say what they would think if possessed of the information & lights possessed by the members here; & still less what would be their way of thinking 6 or 12 months hence. We ought to consider what was right & necessary in itself for the attainment of a proper Government. . . . The respectability of this convention will give weight to their recommendation of it. Experience will be constantly urging the adoption of it, and all the most enlightened & respectable citizens will be its advocates." At that time, the delegates voted for a three-year term.

Also on the agenda were compensation for legislators, their eligibility, length of office for Senators. This last point was argued for some time with Madison favoring a seven year term, which was adopted.

Wednesday June 13

The delegates continued to review the Virginia Resolves they had passed, now filling in blank spaces or refining phrases. The source of money bills was a ticklish question. Gerry did not want the Senate to originate them, while Butler noted that "both Houses are appointed by the people, and both ought to be equally trusted" and the delegates voted down Gerry's proposal.

And on this day, June 13, the chairman, Nathaniel Gorham of Massachusetts, announced that the Committee of the Whole was ready with its report. The delegates had been meeting long hot hours since May 29, starting at first with fumbling beginnings, later with more sureness as their document took shape. They also knew each other better, the strengths and weaknesses of each one. As Gorham made his announcement, the assembly realized that the amended Virginia Resolves were now ready to be presented to the Convention for an official vote. The vote was to take place the next day "to give an opportunity for other plans to be proposed."

Gorham stood and read the Committee's resolutions which had grown from Randolph's document of 15 items to 19. When he had finished, he laid the fledgling charter on the table where members could make copies of it and take it home with them for overnight consideration in preparation for the important vote next day. What they now had was the first form of the Constitution as we know it today; it was somewhat like the work of a sculptor who has first chiseled away outer surfaces revealing the faint outlines of the figure which eventually will emerge.

Thursday June 14

On this fateful morning, Paterson rose to announce to the Convention that is was the wish of "several deputations, particularly that of N. Jersey, that further time might be allowed them to contemplate the plan reported from the Committee of the Whole, and to digest one purely federal, and contradistinguished from the reported plan." Paterson hoped to have "such an one ready by tomorrow to be laid before the Convention." Madison drily stated "And the Convention adjourned that leisure might be given for the purpose."

It can be imagined the stir of excitement among the delegates that day and that evening when they gathered at the Indian Queen to ponder how far they had come and where they might be going. By now all of them were aware of the differences that divided the "small" and "large" states.

To us today it seems quite strange to think of New York as "small" in comparison with, say, Virginia; or New Jersey as "small" in comparison with Massachusetts. The differences actually were much more complex than that. Undoubtedly there was resentment among the delegates when they arrived at Philadelphia to find that Virginia had a well thought-through proposal to present to the Convention — and that they were almost forced into acting upon it. Yes, they knew it was logical for Virginia to come up with a proposal, but it was annoying just the same.

Then, of course, some states really were fearful because they were small. Little Delaware, for example, was afraid of being swallowed up, and definitely instructed her delegates to hold out for one state, one vote. New Jersey's finances were shaky and she was not on very good terms with its neighboring states, New York and Pennsylvania, because of interstate trade and money problems. She had come to the Convention determined to preserve the Articles of Confederation, unable to comprehend that governmental change might help solve her difficulties. While New York was not yet as populous as the "large" three states, she could see that her future was "large," with vast opportunities for trade, and was happy enough to keep herself prosperous and independent — as she thought she could be under the Articles of Confederation. Connecticut saw herself as self-sufficient, and preferred not to make great changes. Maryland wavered between the views of Virginia and New Jersey.

Yet we cannot explain the problem purely in terms of states, for the preferences of individuals come down to philosophical differences: those persons who see the rights of states as paramount, and those who look to a national, overall government as paramount. We can see how this approach to government has affected all our history — the states' rights convictions of the Civil War days, on down to recurrences in our own time when individuals or groups challenge the power of a national government in problems of religious freedom, civil rights and other social questions.

And so, as the first part of the Philadelphia drama ended and the delegates whiled away that Thursday, June 14, waiting for the new proposals which New Jersey would bring forward the following day, they surely knew that the divisions between them were now to come out into the open. They must have wondered — talking together, walking the streets — if the divisions would be so great that the Convention would collapse and all their work come to nothing.

VIII

INTERMISSION

As we become absorbed in the Convention debates, we sometimes assume all 55 delegates are participating. Actually, only about 11 states were represented at any one time with some 30 members present.

Behind the scenes, there was much coming and going among the players. Members drifted in all through May and June. New Hampshire did not name its delegates until June 27. Roger Sherman of Connecticut arrived May 30; Major William Pierce of Georgia came down May 31 from New York where he was a member of Congress under the Confederation government. William Blount of North Carolina, also a member of Congress, came from New York June 20. William Houstoun arrived from Georgia on June 1; John Lansing, Mayor of Albany, arrived the next day.

Luther Martin, the rough, gifted man from Maryland, took his seat June 9, siding with Paterson in the debates. He left in disgust August 4.

Others came and went for various reasons. George Wythe, one of the important Virginia delegates early in the Convention, resigned because of his wife's illness and his many duties as a judge and a professor at William and Mary College. Gouverneur Morris left June 7, for almost a month involved in personal business affairs. John Dickinson of Delaware, plagued by poor health, left for home September 15, asking George Read to sign the Constitution for him.

Captain Jonathan Dayton of New Jersey, at age 27 the youngest member of the Convention, arrived June 21 and lost no time in deciding the Virginia Plan was "an amphibious monster" which would never be accepted by the people.

The very last delegate to arrive was John Francis Mercer who came on August 6, opposed the direction the Convention was taking and left ten days later.

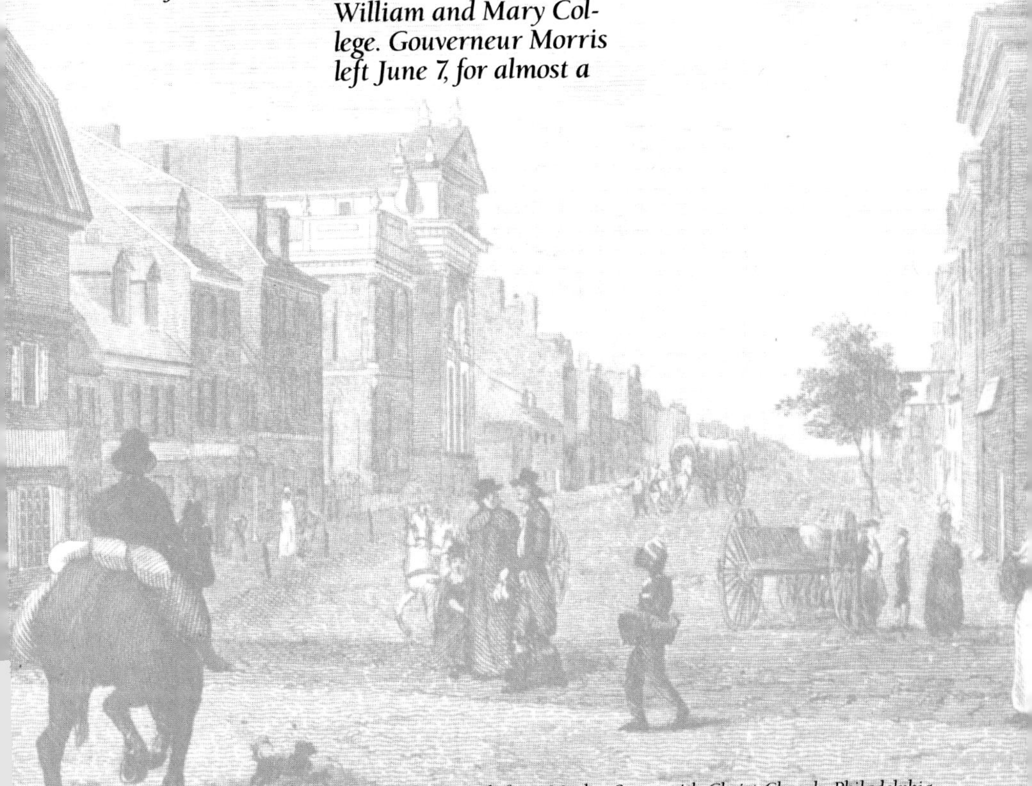

Second Street, North from Market Street with Christ Church, Philadelphia
by William Russell Birch, 1799.
Courtesy of the Library Company of Philadelphia.

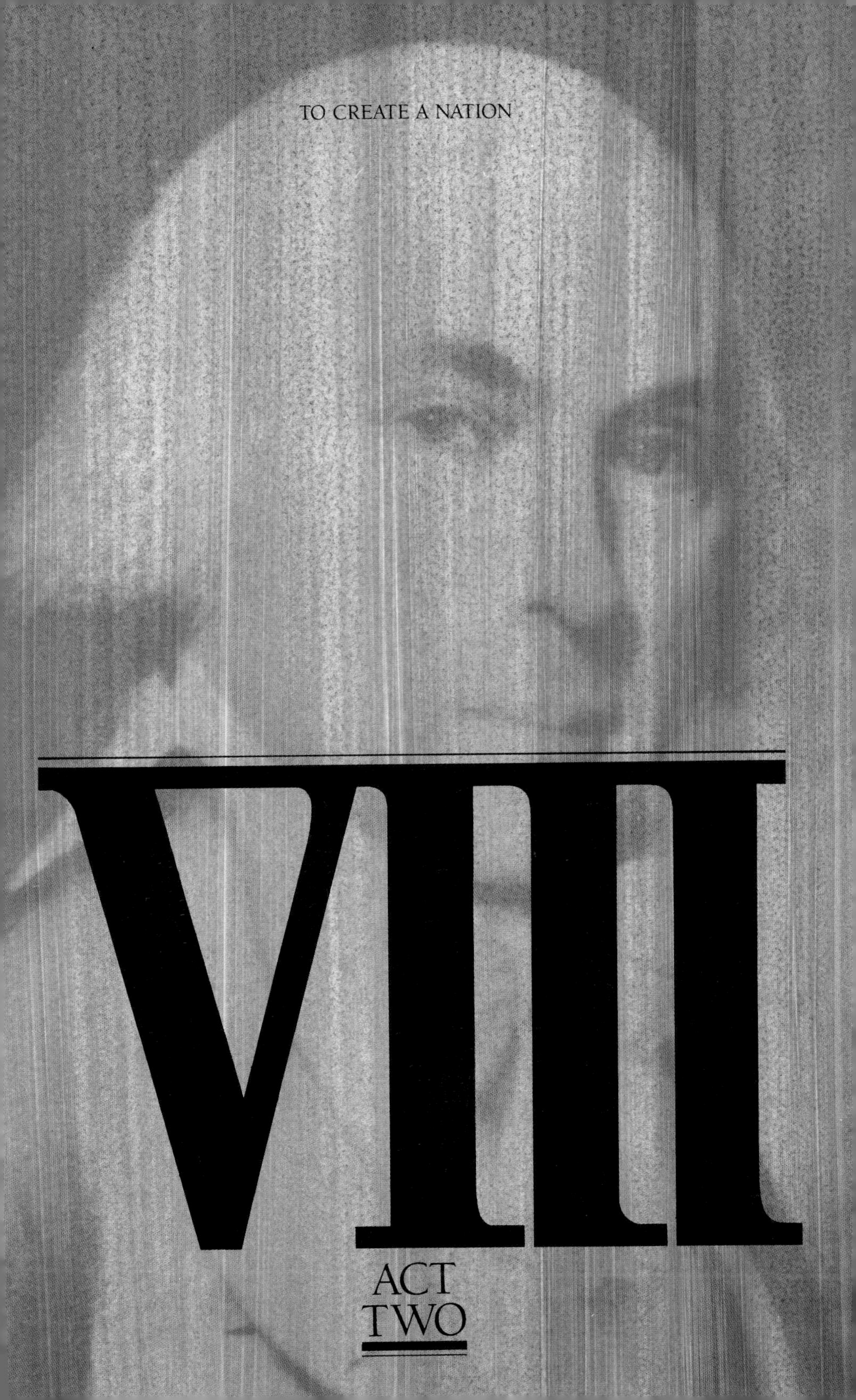

VIII

ACT TWO

VIII

ACT TWO

Friday June 15 W HEN PATERSON ROSE TO SPEAK, papers in hand, all attention was upon him. A new approach now must be considered. Paterson said that he wished to lay before the Convention a plan to be substituted "in place of that proposed by Mr. Randolph." It was agreed that it should be referred to the Committee of the Whole so that the two plans might be compared. But this was to take place the following day so that "friends of the plan proposed by Mr. Paterson would be better prepared to explain and support it, and all would have an opportunity of taking copies."

TO CREATE A NATION

James Madison by James Sharpes, Sr., ca. 1796-97. Courtesy of the Independence National Historic Park Collection.

Saturday June 16

On this morning, Lansing "called for the reading of the 1st Resolution of each plan, which he considered as involving principles directly in contrast; that of Mr. Paterson says he sustains the sovereignty of the respective States, that of Mr. Randolph distroys it: the latter requires a negative on all the laws of the particular States; the former, only certain general powers for the general good. The plan of Mr. R. in short absorbs all power except what may be exercised in the little local matters of the States which are not objects worthy of the supreme cognizance."

Lansing preferred the New Jersey plan, he said, mainly because the Convention did not have the power to discuss and propose a plan like the Virginia Resolves and because it was improbable that such a plan would be adopted anyway. He insisted that New York "would never have concurred in sending deputies to the convention, if she had supposed the deliberations were to turn on a consolidation of the States, and a National Government." As for his second objection,

"The States will never feel a sufficient confidence in a general Government to give it a negative on their laws. The Scheme is itself totally novel. There is no parallel to it to be found."

Paterson next took the floor in defense of his plan supporting the two points made by Lansing. "If the confederacy was radically wrong," he said, "let us return to our States, and obtain larger powers, not assume them of ourselves. I came here not to speak of my own sentiments, but the sentiments of those who sent me. Our object is not such a Government as may be best in itself, but such a one as our Constituents have authorized us to prepare, and as they will approve." In general, his other objections were to the ways the Virginia Plan deviated from the Articles of Confederation. He thought that the Convention should simply make minor corrections in its functions. He believed that with the additional powers for Congress proposed in the New Jersey Plan "Congress will act with more energy & wisdom than the proposed National Legislature." And finally, Paterson thought the Virginia Plan would be "enormously expensive" to put into operation because the government would be larger.

Wilson did his colleagues a great service when he rose and brilliantly made a direct comparison of the two plans. This was how he contrasted them:

Virginia: *two legislative branches*
New Jersey: *one legislative body*

Virginia: *legislative body represents the people at large*
New Jersey: *legislative body represents state legislatures*

Virginia: *one executive*
New Jersey: *more than one*

Virginia: *the majority of the people of the U.S. prevail*
New Jersey: *a minority can control*

Virginia: *the National Legislature can make laws on all national affairs*
New Jersey: *Congress to have additional power in a few cases*

Virginia: *veto power on state laws*
New Jersey: *coercion only*

Virginia: *Executive removable on impeachment & conviction*
New Jersey: *removable by the majority of the Executives of the states*

Virginia: *provision for inferior national tribunals*
New Jersey: *no provision*

Virginia: *revision of laws provided for*
New Jersey: *no check on laws*

Virginia: *jurisdiction of federal tribunals in certain cases*
New Jersey: *appellate jurisdiction only*

Virginia: *jurisdiction by national court in all cases affecting the National peace and harmony*
New Jersey: *small number of specific cases*

Virginia: *ratification of the Convention's document by the people*
New Jersey: *ratification by legislative authorities according to the 13th Article of Confederation*

Wilson went on to make his famous statement: "With regard to the *power of the Convention,* he conceived himself authorized to *conclude nothing,* but to be at liberty to *propose any thing* . . . . With *regard to the sentiments of the people,* he conceived it difficult to know precisely what they are. Those of the particular circle in which one moved, were commonly mistaken for the general voice. He could not persuade himself that the State Governments & Sovereignties were so much the idols of the people, nor a National Government so obnoxious to them, as some supposed. Why should a National Government be unpopular? Has it less dignity? will each Citizen enjoy under it less liberty or protection? Will a Citizen of *Delaware* be degraded by becoming a Citizen of the *United States?* Where do the people look at present for relief from the evils of which they complain? Is it from an internal reform of the Government? no, Sir. It is from the National Councils that relief is expected. For these reasons," he said, he "did not fear, that the people would not follow us into a national Government and it will be a further recommendation of Mr. R's plan that it is to be submitted to *them,* and not to the *Legislatures,* for ratification."

He continued on in his objections to a single legislature and a plural executive, obviously strongly opposed to the whole approach of the New Jersey plan.

Pinckney made a remark at this point which apparently was not heeded. It summed up one of the basic problems the delegates were as yet unable to face: "The whole comes to this," he said. "Give N. Jersey an equal vote, and she will dismiss her scruples, and concur in the National system."

But the debate moved on heatedly with Randolph on his feet. "When the salvation of the Republic was at stake, it would be treason to our trust, not to propose what we found necessary." Madison's notes indicate that "He painted in strong colours, the imbecility of the existing Confederacy, & the danger of delaying a substantial reform." We can imagine the strong language that was used to express these feelings.

Randolph went on to state that the New Jersey plan only proposed a limited right in Congress to employ force on uncomplying states, not even a full power of coercion. And coercion was *"impracticable, expensive, and cruel to individuals.* It tended also to habituate the instruments of it to shed the blood & riot in the spoils of their fellow Citizens, and consequently trained them up for the service of ambition. We must resort therefor to a National *Legislation over individuals,* for which Congress are unfit." He finished his impassioned remarks with "A National Government alone, properly constituted, will answer the purpose; and he begged it to be considered that the present is the last moment for establishing one. After this select experiment, the people will yield to despair."

With those somber remarks, the delegates adjourned for the day.

Monday June 18

The meeting started off with Dickinson moving that the delegates take up the issue "that the Articles of Confederation ought to be revised and amended, so as to render the Government of the U.S. adequate to the exigences, the preservation and the prosperity of the Union."

Immediately after the motion was passed, Hamilton who had not spoken before, stood up and talked almost six hours—the entire day that the Convention was in session. Up to now he had been silent, he said, "partly from respect to others whose superior abilities age & experience rendered him unwilling to bring forward ideas dissimilar to theirs, and

Convention at Philadelphia 1787 by Charles A. Goodrich from *History of the United States of America,* 1823.
Courtesy of the Library of Congress.

partly from his delicate situation with respect to his own State, to whose sentiments as expressed by his Colleagues, he could by no means accede."

Hamilton was "unfriendly" to both plans, and particularly opposed to the New Jersey plan, for he was convinced "that no amendment of the Confederation, leaving the States in possession of their Sovereignty could possibly answer the purpose." He spoke of his fears for a nation which broke up into small state interests and the only obstacle to a "truly national, a consolidated government was the size of the United States." He looked on the British government, he said, as "the best in the world" and "doubted much whether any thing short of it would do for America." It was the only government "which unites public strength with individual security." As for the Executive, "the English model was the only good one," a hereditary monarch with great wealth was above corruption from abroad, and was "both sufficiently independent and sufficiently controuled, to answer the purpose of the institution at home."

To achieve the stability represented by the British government, Hamilton recommended that the assembly aim for an organization with an executive and a Senate both of which served for life. Then he went on to suggest an 11-point plan saying that "he did not mean to offer the paper he had sketched as a proposition to the Committee. It was meant only to give a more correct view of his ideas, and to suggest the amendments which he should probably propose to the plan of Mr. R. in the proper stages of its future discussion."

His "paper" allowed the states only jurisdiction over local matters; they would elect the popular branch of the national legislature; the Senate's members were to be elected to serve during good behavior and hold major powers; the executive, also elected to serve during good behavior, would hold supreme powers including veto of laws "about to be passed"; the state governors would be appointed by the national government and could veto laws within their own states.

Judge Yates includes in his notes (not in the notes of Madison) the final remarks of Hamilton which have become famous. Hamilton noted that the New Jersey Plan was probably the nearest to the people's expectations. The plan he had just outlined and the Virginia Plan were "very remote from the idea of the people. But the people are gradually ripening in their opinions of government. They begin to be tired of an excess of democracy. And what even is the Virginia Plan but democracy checked by democracy, pork still with a little change of sauce?"

The exhausted delegation then adjourned for the day, and it can be imagined the anger stirring among the "small" state representatives hearing the extreme views of the brilliant, excitable member from New York.

Tuesday June 19

When the delegates met this morning, strangely there was no discussion of the thoughts put forward the day before by Hamilton, an oddity discussed by historians through the years. Perhaps it was so far from both plans being considered by the Convention, so far from acceptance that it seemed unnecessary to debate the views. One historian speculates that perhaps he deliberately outlined a system of government so radical that it would make the Virginia Plan look tame and the New Jersey Plan impossible. It could be that Hamilton's full day of talk had pulled the delegates away from their earlier wrangling and given them a chance to be somewhat cooler and more objective—at least for a short time. It was the very same thing that was so valuable in Franklin's long, gentle, humorous remarks which gave a calming influence to the Convention on so many occasions.

Returning to the earlier discussions of the Virginia and New Jersey Plans, Madison now rose to make in depth comparisons between the powers which a federal government would exercise and that of the states, and where such power came from. He asked, will the New Jersey Plan "prevent those violations of the law of nations & of Treaties which if not prevented must involve us in the calamities of foreign wars? . . . Will it prevent encroachments on the federal authority? . . . Will it prevent trespasses of the States on each other? . . . Will it secure the internal tranquility of the States themselves? . . . Will it secure a good internal legislation & administration to the particular States? . . . Will it secure the Union against the influence of foreign powers over its members?"

Madison "begged the smaller States which were most attached to Mr. Paterson's plan to consider the situation in which it would leave them." In this case, he was referring to the expense of maintaining delegates in Congress which would be harder financially for the small states than the larger ones. And finally he "begged them to consider the situation in which they would remain in case their pertinacious adherence to an inadmissible plan, should prevent the adoption of any plan. . . . Let the Union of the States be dissolved, and one of two consequences must happen. Either the States must remain individually independent & sovereign; or two or more Confederacies must be formed among them." He acknowledged that the stumbling block at this Convention was the problem of representation — fear by the small states that if they had only one vote and Virginia, say, had 16, they would be overwhelmed. Some members had suggested a repartitioning of the states so that they would be equal in size, but Madison referred to such impossible attempts in Europe.

At the end of Madison's carefully reasoned statement, the Committee of the Whole reported in favor of the Virginia Plan which then was resubmitted. The vote was seven to three for the Virginia Plan. The New Jersey Plan passed into history, a milestone in the Convention's difficult climb toward a viable form of government.

While yet in the Committee of the Whole, Wilson commented that "by a National Government he did not mean one that would swallow up the State Governments as seemed to be wished by some gentlemen." He wanted the states to live on "friendly terms" with the national government and believed "they were absolutely necessary for certain purposes which the [national government] could not reach."

King tried to clarify some of the terms which the delegates had been using interchangeably and inaccurately such as "sovereignty" and "national" and "federal." The states, for example, were not "Sovereigns" for they could not make war, peace, alliances or treaties; they could not of themselves raise troops or equip ships for war. "A Union of the States is a Union of the men composing them," he said, "from whence a *national* character results to the whole." He ended his clarifying remarks by saying that he very much doubted "the practicability of annihilating the States; but thought that much of their power ought to be taken from them."

To add further clarification to the views of the smaller states, Martin looked at the situation in a different way. When the 13 states separated from Great Britain, he thought they were "in a state of Nature towards each other; that they would have remained in that state till this time, but for the confederation; that they entered into the confederation on the footing of equality; that they met now to amend it on the same footing; and that he could never accede to a plan that would introduce an inequality and lay 10 States at the mercy of Virginia, Massachusetts and Pennsylvania."

Wilson replied that he could not believe the colonies, independent of Great Britain, then became independent also of each other. Referring to the Declaration of Independence, he said that the "*United Colonies* were declared to be free & independent States; and inferring that they were independent, not *individually* but *Unitedly* and that they were confederated as they were independent, States."

Hamilton spoke up supporting Wilson and disagreeing with Martin that the "States were thrown into a State of Nature." To allay the fears of the smaller states and make them feel more secure under a national government, he noted that the three largest states "were separated from each other by distance of place and equally so, by all the peculiarities which distinguish the interests of one State from those of another." He added that there was a gradation in size of the states from Virginia down to Delaware and that the states might combine their strengths in different ways. He concluded with "No combination has been seen among large Counties merely as such, against less Counties. The more close the Union of the States, and the more compleat the authority of the whole: the less opportunity will be allowed the stronger States to injure the weaker."

The meeting adjourned at this point. But, as we shall see, the smaller states were not convinced of their security in spite of all the arguments. The problem of representation was to be a major issue for weeks to come.

Wednesday June 20

On this day the delegates left the relaxed environment which the Committee of the Whole offered and met in full

Convention. Washington left his Virginia colleagues and took the chair, the first day since May 29 that he had sat through full debate. His presence on the podium gave the proceedings a heightened air of importance. Gorham, who had acted as chairman for the Committee of the Whole, rejoined the Massachusetts delegates.

The Convention now considered the Virginia Plan as it had been revised by the Committee of the Whole. The delegates were meticulous, going over each sentence with great care. The first momentous act this morning was to change "national government" to "government of the United States" in the First Virginia Resolve and therefore in all the rest of the document where "national government" appeared. Ellsworth, who moved for the alteration, felt that the states would not ratify the Convention's plan unless it appeared to be an amendment to the Articles of Confederation. And if the state legislatures were unwilling, "the people will be so too."

Lansing then rose to make a rambling complaint about how things were going in general. He said the true question was "whether the Convention would adhere to or depart from the foundation of the present Confederacy." He did not feel the delegates had the authority which they were exercising nor did he feel that the people would be in favor of it. He referred to Wilson's earlier remark that since the Convention was only to recommend, it could recommend what it pleased. He could not go along with this. "Any act whatever of so respectable a body must have a great effect, and if it does not succeed, will be a source of great dissentions."

Mason then spoke at some length about the tenor of public opinion, an area which was ever on the minds of the delegates. He was convinced that the public was for "Republican Government" and for "more than one branch in the Legislature." And while he was strongly in favor of a national government he could never "agree to abolish the State Governments or render them absolutely insignificant. They were as necessary as the General Government and he would be equally careful to preserve them." The Convention, he maintained, could not be expected to make "a faultless Government. And he would prefer trusting to posterity the amendment of its defects, rather than to push the experiment too far."

Martin then supported Mason's view on the importance of state governments, even at the expense of the national government.

Sherman was for two branches in the state legislatures but saw no need for two in the national government and argued at length in favor of this. As other delegates, he saw the disparity of size among the states as "the main difficulty." But unlike some of the others, he was ready to make compromises in order to overcome the unease of the smaller states.

Sherman's views, after many lengthy arguments, would be accepted. But it took time, countless hours of exposure to new ideas before the delegates could sort out what would be the best direction to take. Sherman's famous proposal was that "if the difficulty on the subject of representation can not be otherwise got over, he would agree to have two branches, and a proportional representation in one of them; provided each State had an equal voice in the other. This was necessary to secure the rights of the lesser States; otherwise three or four of the large States would rule the others as they please. Each State like each individual had its peculiar habits usages and manners, which constituted its happiness. It would not therefore give to others a power over this happiness, any more than an individual would do, when he could avoid it."

Wilson came forward urging that two branches were necessary, giving examples of governments through the ages, and then swung into further discussion of the problems of large and small states and the relationship of state and national governments, observing that "a private Citizen of a State is indifferent whether power be exercised by the General or State legislatures, provided it be exercised most for his happiness."

Sherman's idea was therefore buried — for the time being.

Thursday June 21

Johnson led off with a continuation of the discussion which was to go on for days. He suggested that if it could be shown that "the individuality of the States would not be endangered," many of those who were for the New Jersey Plan would no longer object to the Virginia Plan.

Wilson responded that one branch of the general government was to be appointed by the state legislatures and therefore would "have an opportunity of defending their rights. Ought not a reciprocal opportunity to be given to the General Government of defending itself by having an appointment of some one constituent branch of the State Governments? If a security be necessary on one side, it would seem reasonable to demand it on the other." Then he went on to say that he saw no danger to the states from the general government, and "in case of any proposition in the National Legislature to encroach on the State Legislatures, he conceived a general alarm would take place in the National Legislature itself, that it would communicate itself to the State Legislatures, and would finally spread among the people at large. The General Government will be as ready to preserve the rights of the States as the latter are to preserve the rights of individuals; all the members of the former, having a common interest, as representatives of all the people of the latter, to leave the State Governments in possession of what the people wish them to retain." He thought if there should be any potential danger, it would be encroachments from the state governments upon the general government.

Madison then amplified Wilson's remarks with the observation that if encroachments should occur, it would be "less fatal" if they were made by the general government upon the state governments than the reverse. The country's present Articles of Confederation were an example in point.

When he finished, the Convention agreed, in a divided vote, to have two branches in the legislature. Immediately, then, Pinckney moved "that the first branch, instead of being elected by the people, should be elected in such manner as the Legislature of each State should direct."

While Martin seconded the motion, a flood of divergent opinions followed. Hamilton spoke against it because it would increase state influence; Mason felt it should be elected by the people; Sherman preferred election by the legislatures but would accept election by the people; Rutledge also preferred election by the legislatures; Wilson "considered the election of the first branch by the people not only as the corner Stone, but as the foundation of the fabric" and he felt the legislatures were too removed from the people to be entrusted with choosing the House of Representatives. King agreed with him. After even more discussion, it was agreed

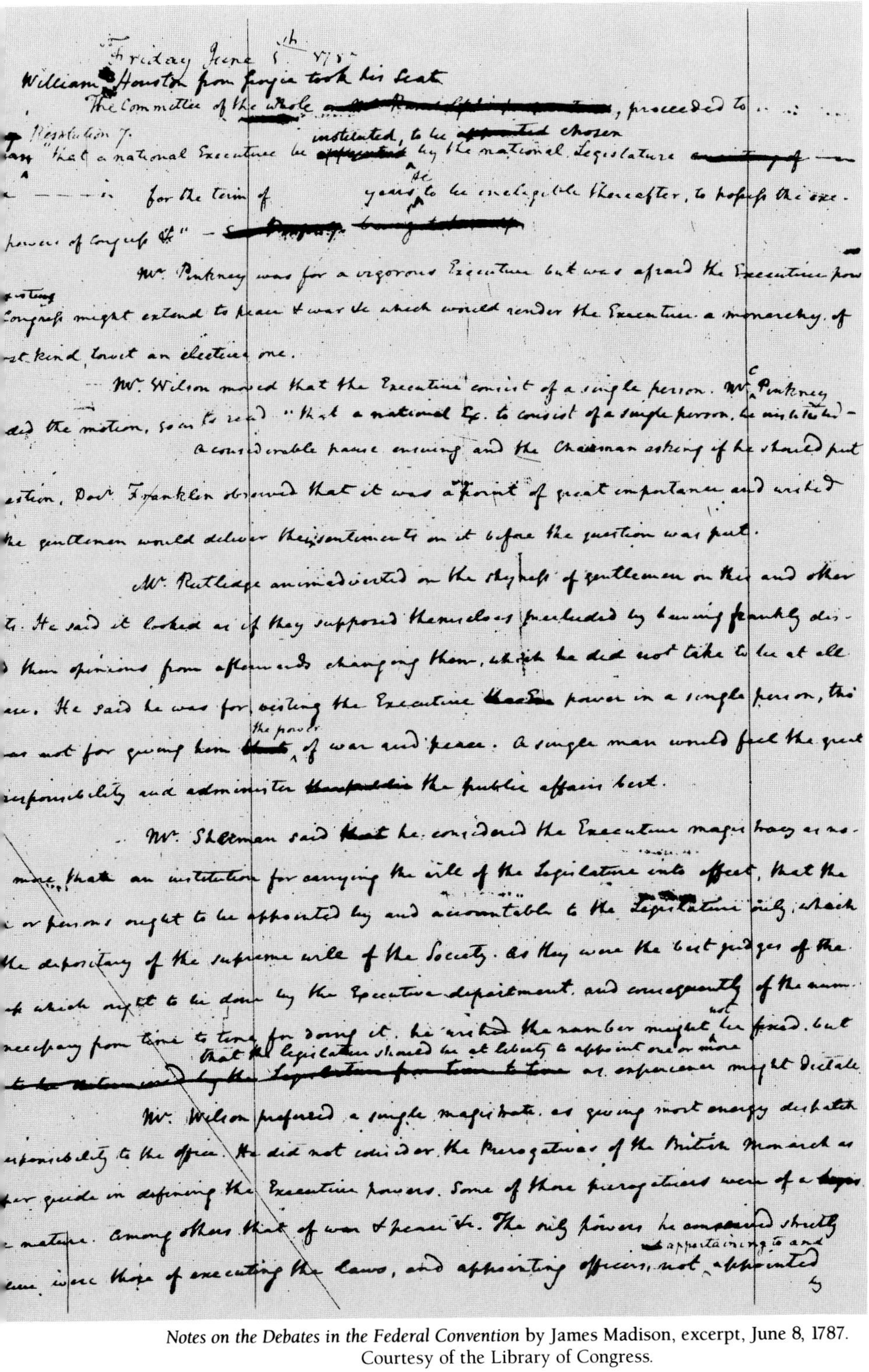

Friday June 1st 1787
William Houston from Georgia took his Seat
The Committee of the whole [redacted], proceeded to . . .
Resolution 7.
"that a national Executive be instituted, to be ~~appointed~~ chosen by the national Legislature [redacted]
— — — for the term of years &c to be ineligible thereafter, to possess the exe-
powers of Congress &c" — [redacted]
Mr. Pinkney was for a vigorous Executive but was afraid the Executive pow
existing Congress might extend to peace & war &c which would render the Executive a monarchy, of
st kind, towit an elective one.
Mr. Wilson moved that the Executive consist of a single person. Mr. C. Pinkney
ded the motion, so as to read "that a national Ex. to consist of a single person, be instituted."
A considerable pause ensuing and the Chairman asking if he should put
estion, Doct. Franklin observed that it was a point of great importance and wished
he gentlemen would deliver their sentiments on it before the question was put.
Mr. Rutledge animadverted on the shyness of gentlemen on this and other
ts. He said it looked as if they supposed themselves precluded by having frankly dis-
their opinions from afterwards changing them, which he did not take to be at all
se. He said he was for vesting the Executive [redacted] power in a single person, tho
as not for giving him ~~that~~ the power of war and peace. A single man would feel the great
responsibility and administer [redacted] the public affairs best.
Mr. Sherman said ~~that~~ he considered the Executive magistracy as no-
more than an institution for carrying the will of the Legislature into effect, that the
or persons ought to be appointed by and accountable to the Legislature only, which
the depositary of the supreme will of the Society. As they were the best judges of the
ss which ought to be done by the Executive department, and consequently of the num-
necessary from time to time for doing it, he wished the number might not be fixed, but
that the legislature should be at liberty to appoint one or more ~~to be determined by the Legislature from time to time~~ as experience might dictate.
Mr. Wilson preferred a single magistrate, as giving most energy dispatch
esponsibility to the office. He did not consider the Prerogatives of the British Monarch as
per guide in defining the Executive powers. Some of these prerogatives were of a [redacted]
nature. Among others that of war & peace &c. The only powers he conceived strictly
tive were those of executing the laws, and appointing officers, not appertaining to and appointed

Notes on the Debates in the Federal Convention by James Madison, excerpt, June 8, 1787.
Courtesy of the Library of Congress.

that the first branch of the national legislature would be elected by the people.

Next, the delegates considered whether or not this first branch would be elected for a term of three years. Randolph wanted the term changed to two years; Dickinson wanted a three-year term; Ellsworth preferred a one-year term; Wilson a one-year term; Mason was for two years; Hamilton for three years; and as usual, Sherman preferred annual elections but "would be content with biennial." When the delegates finally voted, it was for a two-year term for the first branch of the legislature.

Friday June 22, Saturday June 23

Now the Convention considered Virginia Resolve Number 3 in the version revised in the Committee of the Whole.

The delegates argued whether or not salaries would be paid from the state treasuries. They went on to consider age qualifications, re-election of House members, whether members could hold more than one position at once. Votes were close, indicating great division of thought in the Convention. They were clearly hard, tiring days of dealing with details of the document they were writing. The delegates' remarks often ranged far afield and there were heated arguments for and against each word and phrase. Votes often were inconclusive.

Monday June 25, Tuesday June 26

Resolve Number 4 was now taken up. This of course was a crucial time, for the delegates at last must wrestle with the concept of the second branch of the legislature—the Senate—how it was to be chosen, the number of members and the real nature of the body.

Pinckney led off the discussion with a long, thoughtful statement designed to remind the delegates of the extreme importance of this particular Resolve. "The efficacy of the System," he said, "will depend on this article. In order to form a right judgment in the case, it will be proper to examine the situation of this country more accurately than it has yet been done. The people of the U. States are perhaps the most singular of all we are acquainted with. Among them there are fewer distinctions of fortune & less of rank, than among the inhabitants of any other nation. Every freeman has a right to the same protection & security; and a very moderate share of property entitles them to the possession of all the honors and privileges the public can bestow: hence arises a greater equality, than is to be found among the people of any other country, and an equality which is more likely to continue — I say this equality is likely to continue, because in a new Country, possessing immense tracts of uncultivated lands, where every temptation is offered to emigration & where industry must be rewarded with competency, there will be few poor, and few dependent — Every member of the Society almost, will enjoy an equal power of arriving at the supreme offices & consequently of directing the strength & sentiments of the whole Community. None will be excluded by birth, & few by fortune, from voting for proper persons to fill the offices of Government — the whole community will enjoy in the fullest sense that kind of political liberty which consists in the power the members of the State reserve to themselves, of arriving at the public offices, or at least, of having votes in the nomination of those who fill them. . . . Much has been said of the Constitution of G. Britain. I will confess that I believe it to be the best Constitution in existence; but at the same time I am confident it is one that will not or can not be introduced into this Country, for many centuries."

Pinckney enlarged upon the equality of the American citizen in terms of wealth and hereditary background, a unique individual requiring an original form of government. "Our true situation appears to me to be this," he said, "a new extensive Country containing within itself the materials for forming a Government capable of extending to its citizens all the blessings of civil & religious liberty — capable of making them happy at home. . . . We mistake the object of our Government, if we hope or wish that it is to make us respectable abroad. Conquest or superiority among other powers is not or ought not ever to be the object of republican systems. If they are sufficiently active & energetic to rescue us from contempt & preserve our domestic happiness & security, it is all we can expect from them — it is more than almost any other Government ensures to its citizens." He divided Americans into three classes — professional, commercial and the landed interest — and urged that the government be suited to a population "among whom there are no distinctions of rank, and very few or none of fortune."

With this thoughtful introduction, the assembly settled down to considering what they wanted the second branch of the legislature to be. A back and forth argument soon began on the power of the states, whether the states should choose the members of the Senate and whether there should be proportional representation. In the play of ideas, Wilson reminded the delegates that "the General Government is not an assemblage of States, but of individuals for certain political purposes — it is not meant for the States, but for the individuals composing them; the *individuals* therefore not the *States,* ought to be represented in it."

The delegates nevertheless voted yes to the motion that the Senators be chosen by state legislatures and voted unanimously that the Senators must be at least 30 years of age. A decision on the ratio of representation was still postponed; the delegates had not yet taken firm positions on this all-important point or had not yet decided how best to compromise. It was as though they knew that the Convention itself might fall apart on this very issue and were waiting as long as possible before meeting it head-on.

A nine-year term for Senators was voted down in favor of a six-year term. Pay for the Senators should come from the national treasury rather than the states. As usual, Franklin was highly suspicious of the corrupting influence of wealth; he and Pinckney unsuccessfully tried to add the phrase "that no Salary should be allowed" to the Senators.

Wednesday June 27

This was the beginning day for dealing with the crucial problem facing the Convention. Rutledge moved to take up "the most fundamental points" — how members of the two houses of the legislature were to be chosen.

Madison writes in his journal that Martin taking the floor "contended at great length and with great eagerness that the General Government was meant merely to preserve the State Governments; not to govern individuals: that its powers ought to be kept within narrow limits; that if too little power was given to it, more might be added; but that if too much, it could never be resumed; that individuals as such have little to do but with their own States." Martin read passages from such authorities as Locke, Vattel, Lord Summers, Priestley and Samuel Rutherford to prove his points. His great fear was that the ten smaller states would become powerless, and as he continued, he repeated many of the earlier arguments, particularly that the delegates were exceeding their rights, they were downgrading the states and the kind of document they were forming would never be ratified.

Madison concludes the day's notes with "This was the substance of a speech which was continued more than three hours. He [Martin] was too much exhausted he said to finish his remarks, and reminded the House that he should tomorrow, resume them."

At that point, the assembly adjourned for the day. We can sense the weariness and gloom of the delegates as they filed away to their lodgings.

Thursday June 28

True to his word, Martin was on his feet again and "resumed his discourse," repeating much of what he had said the day before, but ending with the thought that he "had rather see partial confederacies take place, than the plan on the table." Madison's notes close with "This was the substance of the residue of his discourse which was delivered with much diffuseness & considerable vehemence."

At the close of Martin's long and emotional speech, Lansing and Dayton took advantage of the excitement aroused and moved that the Amended Virginia Resolution Number 7 should read "Resolved that the rights of suffrage in the first branch ought to be according to the rule established [by the Articles of] Confederation. . . ." This meant they wished to strike out the word "not" after the word "ought"—which would mean the Convention would reverse its earlier vote and return to equal votes for the states in the first branch of the legislature. The motion got nowhere.

Then the emotional debate continued, and to us today it may seem long-winded and purposeless. It undoubtedly was very necessary, however, in order to give the members a chance to express their deep convictions and to accept the fact that delegates of differing ideas held their own views with equal sincerity.

Williamson was concerned with the new states in the west which would be coming into the Union. "They would be small States," he said, "they would be poor States, they would be unable to pay in proportion to their numbers; their distance from market rendering the produce of their labour less valuable; they would consequently be tempted to combine for the purpose of laying burdens on commerce & consumption which would fall with greatest weight on the old States."

Madison tried to answer the fears of the smaller states in a calm, reasoned manner. Drawing from examples in ancient history and European countries of the 18th century, he cited cases where large governments were more likely to be hostile to each other than large against small. "Carthage & Rome tore one another to pieces instead of uniting their forces to devour the weaker nations of the Earth. The Houses of Austria & France were hostile as long as they remained the greatest powers of Europe. England & France have succeeded to the pre-eminence & to the enmity. To this principle we owe perhaps our liberty. A coalition between those powers would have been fatal to us."

As for Virginia, Massachusetts and Pennsylvania "the journals of Congress did not present any peculiar association of these States in the vote recorded." Their commerce was in tobacco, fish, flour — staple products "as dissimilar as any three other States in the Union."

But his words were falling on deaf ears; the smaller states would not be convinced.

It now was Franklin who spoke, addressing himself to Washington in the chair. "Mr. President, the small progress we have made after 4 or five weeks close attendance & continual reasonings with each other — our different sentiments on almost every question, several of the last producing as many noes as ayes, is methinks a melancholy proof of the imperfection of the Human Understanding. We indeed seem to feel our own want of political wisdom, since we have been running about in search of it. We have gone back to ancient history for models of Government, and examined the different forms of those Republics which having been formed with the seeds of their own dissolution now no longer exist. And we have viewed Modern States all round Europe, but find none of their Constitutions suitable to our circumstances.

"In this situation of this Assembly, groping as it were in the dark to find political truth, and scarce able to distinguish it when presented to us, how has it happened, Sir, that we have not hitherto once thought of humbly applying to the Father of lights to illuminate our understandings? In the beginning of the Contest with G. Britain, when we were sensible of danger we had daily prayer in this room for the divine protection.—Our prayers, Sir, were heard, & they were graciously answered. . . . I have lived, Sir, a long time, and the longer I live, the more convincing proofs I see of this truth—*that God Governs in the affairs of men*. . . . I therefore beg leave to move—that henceforth prayers imploring the assistance of Heaven, and its blessings on our deliberations, be held in this Assembly every morning before we proceed to business, and that one or more of the Clergy of this City be requested to officiate in that Service."

The delegates had great respect for their elder statesman, but probably thought it was a little late in the proceedings to start their days in this way. One pointed out that if the general public heard that the Convention at this stage was turning to prayerful guidance, they would believe things were going badly behind the closed doors. Another commented that the Convention had no funds to pay a cleric. Randolph, to smooth things over, proposed that on the Fourth of July a sermon be preached at the request of the Convention and prayers be used after that, but no vote was taken on the motion. Nevertheless, Franklin's words, as usual, had brought the Convention to a full stop—at least for the day. And as they adjourned and went home to their lodgings they must have thought about the solemnity of his speech.

Friday June 29

But the arguments continued, again with anger and frustration. Johnson brought up once more the proposal made much earlier by Sherman "that in *one* branch the *people*, ought to be represented; in the *other* the *States*."

But others were so filled with their own ideas that they apparently were not listening. Gorham asked that the small states "consider which are to give up most, they or the larger ones" by the plan the Convention was considering. He thought "a rupture of the Union would be an event unhappy for all, but surely the large States would be least unable to take care of themselves, and to make connections with one another. The weak therefore were most interested in establishing some general system for maintaining order. If among individuals, composed partly of weak, and partly of strong, the former most need the protection of law & Government, the case is exactly the same with weak & powerful States." He went on to assure his colleagues that he was willing to stay in the assembly just as long as any other State remained "in order to agree on some plan that could with propriety be recommended to the people."

An indication of how deep the divisions were can be seen by Ellsworth's remark at this point. He felt it necessary to say that he "did not despair," that he still trusted that some good plan of Government would be adopted.

Read went far afield, saying the states as such must be done away with, agreed with Hamilton's plan of government and wished that it be substituted for the one the assembly was now considering. No one seemed to be listening.

Madison was now pleading with the small states not to be adamant, "to renounce a principle which was confessedly unjust, which could never be admitted, & if admitted must infuse mortality into a Constitution which we wished to last forever. He prayed them to ponder well the consequences of suffering the Confederacy to go to pieces." He warned against the dangers to the freedom of the states should they stand separately and a foreign power bring military might against them.

Hamilton went even farther and speculated that the separate states or small combinations of states might form alliances with foreign powers. "Alliances will immediately be formed with different rival & hostile nations of Europes, who will foment disturbances among ourselves, and make us parties to all their own quarrels. Foreign Nations having American dominions are & must be jealous of us. Their representatives betray the utmost anxiety for our fate, & for the result of this meeting, which must have an essential influence on it.—It had been said that respectability in the eyes of foreign Nations was not the object at which we aimed; that the proper object of republican Government was domestic tranquility & happiness. This was an ideal distinction. No government could give us tranquility & happiness at home, which did not possess sufficient stability and strength to make us respectable abroad. This was the critical moment for forming such a Government. We should run every risk in trusting to future amendments. As yet we retain the habits of union. We are weak & sensible of our weakness. Henceforward the motives will become feebler, and the difficulties greater. It is a miracle that we were now here exercising our tranquil & free deliberations on the subject. It would be madness to trust to future miracles. A thousand causes must obstruct a reproduction of them."

But the arguments swung away from all the warnings. Gerry said that "we never were independent States, were not such now, & never could be even on the principles of the Confederation. The States & the advocates for them were intoxicated with the idea of their sovereignty. He was a member of Congress at the time the federal articles were formed. The injustice of allowing each State an equal vote was long insisted on. He voted for it, but it was against his Judgment, and under the pressure of public danger, and the obstinacy of the lesser States. The present confederation he considered as dissolving. The fate of the Union will be decided by the Convention. . . . He lamented that instead of coming here like a band of brothers, belonging to the same family, we seemed to have brought with us the spirit of political negociators."

While the assembly was voting in full Convention and not in the Committee of the Whole, it was possible to reverse a decision by calling for another vote the following day; this was done, slowing up the procedure and heightening the tension and frustration. On proportional representation, the four smaller states of Connecticut, New York, New Jersey and Delaware, and a divided Maryland, consistently opposed it in the first branch of the legislature. However, when put to a vote, the motion was passed against them.

Ellsworth moved that the rule of suffrage in the second branch of the legislature be the same as that established by the Articles of Confederation, hoping this "would become a ground of compromise. . . . We were partly national; partly federal. The proportional representation in the first branch was conformable to the national principle & would secure the large States against the small. An equality of voices was conformable to the federal principle and was necessary to secure the Small States against the large. He trusted that on this middle ground a compromise would take place." He went on to urge that they should find ground for compromise or America would divide in two. "Let a strong Executive, a Judiciary & Legislative power be created; but let not too much be attempted; by which all may be lost."

This was still another time the Connecticut delegates proposed giving all the states an equal voice in the Senate. The debate carried over to the next day.

Saturday June 30

But the convention began with Brearley moving that the President write to New Hampshire urging it to send its delegates; the business of the convention required their "immediate attendance." Madison drily adds parenthetically in his notes: "it was well understood that the object was to add N. Hampshire to the number of States opposed to the doctrine of proportional representation, which it was presumed from her relative size she must be adverse to."

Rutledge could not see "the necessity nor propriety of such a measure. They are not unapprized of the meeting, and can attend if they choose. Rho. Island might as well be urged to appoint & send deputies. Are we to suspend the business until the deputies arrive?" King said he had written more than once in private correspondence while Wilson wondered if such a step would be consistent with their rule of secrecy. The motion did not pass, and now the debate returned to Ellsworth's motion of the preceding day.

It was Wilson who responded at great length, denying the idea that the country would divide in two. "Can we forget for whom we are forming a Government?" he asked, passionately supporting the idea of proportional representation. "Is it for *men*, or for the imaginary beings called *States?* . . . The rule of suffrage ought on every principle to be the same in the second as in the first branch. If the Government be not laid on this foundation, it can be neither solid nor lasting." Once again he argued that the small states had nothing to fear from the larger ones. "Bad Governments are of two sorts. 1. that which does too little. 2. that which does too much: that which fails thro' weakness; and that which destroys thro' oppression. Under which of these evils do the U. States at present groan? Under the weakness and inefficiency of its Government. To remedy this weakness we have been sent to this Convention."

Ellsworth responded with "the capital objection of Mr. Wilson 'that the minority will rule the majority' is not true. The power is given to the few to save them from being destroyed by the many. If an equality of votes had been given to them in both branches, the objection might have had weight. Is it a novel thing that the few should have a check on the many? Is it not the case in the British Constitution the wisdom of which so many gentlemen have united in applauding? Have not the House of Lords, who form so small a proportion of the nation a negative on the laws, as a necessary defence of their peculiar rights against the encroachments of the Commons. . . . We are running from one extreme to another. We are razing the foundations of the building, when we need only repair the roof." He appealed to the delegates to remember their plighted faith "under which each State small as well as great, held an equal right of suffrage in the general Councils" and reminded his listeners that he represented a state of "middle rank" and therefore his arguments were not "the result of partial or local views."

But Madison was very strong in disagreement. Almost rude. He said that on one occasion Ellsworth described the large states as "Aristocratic" and now the small states were compared to the House of Lords which needed to have a defense against the more numerous House of Commons. As for his appeal "to the faith plighted in the existing federal compact" he felt that "of all the States however Connecticut was perhaps least able to urge this plea. Besides the various omissions to perform the stipulated acts from which no State was free, the Legislature of that State had by a pretty recent vote, *positively, refused* to pass a law for complying with the Requisitions of Congress and had transmitted a copy of the vote to Congress."

Madison then went on to a subject which had not yet been discussed fully: "the States were divided into different interests not by their difference of size, but by other circumstances; the most material of which resulted partly from climate, but principally from the effects of their having or not having slaves. These two causes concurred in forming the great division of interests in the U. States. It did not lie between the large & small States: It lay between the Northern & Southern, and if any defensive power were necessary, it ought to be mutually given to these two interests. He was so strongly impressed with this important truth that he had been casting about in his mind for some expedient that would answer the purpose. The one which had occurred was that instead of proportioning the votes of the States in both branches, to their respective numbers of inhabitants computing the slaves in the ratio of 5 to 3, they should be represented in one branch according to the number of free inhabitants only; and in the other according to the whole not counting the slaves as if free." This would give the Southern States the advantage in one House, and the Northern in the other.

But Ellsworth, smarting from Madison's remarks about Connecticut, turned the attention away from Madison's new proposal. "Whatever might be thought of the Representatives of Connecticut," Ellsworth said, "the State was entirely federal in her disposition." He referred "to her great exertions during the war, in supplying both men & money. The muster rolls would show she had more troops in the field than Virginia. If she had been Delinquent, it had been from inability, and not more so than other States."

Ellsworth's remarks undoubtedly struck home for more than one delegate; Davie of North Carolina spoke up in support of Ellsworth's motion for equal representation in the Senate. The number of Senators, he thought, was a problem.

Wilson agreed, "If the smallest States be allowed one, and the others in proportion, the Senate will certainly be too numerous. He looked forward to the time when the smallest States will contain 100,000 souls at least. Let there be then one Senator in each for every 100,000 souls and let the States not having that number of inhabitants be allowed one. He was willing himself to submit to this temporary concession to the small States; and threw out the idea as a ground of compromise."

It looked as though the delegates were beginning to realize that compromise of some kind was necessary.

Franklin seized upon the mood: "The diversity of opinions turns on two points. If a proportional representation takes place, the small States contend that their liberties will be in danger. If an equality of votes is to be put in its place, the large States say their money will be in danger. When a broad table is to be made, and the edges of planks do not fit, the artist takes a little from both, and makes a good joint. In like manner here both sides must part with some of their demands, in order that they may join in some accommodating proposition. He had prepared one which he would read, that it might lie on the table for consideration."

He suggested that there be an equal number of Senators from each state; vote equally in all matters involving state sovereignty, but in money matters "have suffrage in proportion to the Sums which their respective States do actually contribute to the Treasury." He went on, "Where a Ship had many owners this was the rule of deciding on her expedition. He had been one of the Ministers from this Country to France during the joint war and would have been very glad if allowed a vote in distributing the money to carry it on."

Tempers were high by this time, however, and not even the respect of the delegates for their senior member could hold them down. King went right on with the observation "that the simple question was whether each State should have an equal vote in the 2nd branch; that it must be apparent to those gentlemen who liked neither the motion for this equality, nor the report as it stood, that the report was as susceptible of melioration as the motion. . . ." He warned that "we were in fact cut in sunder already, and it was in vain to shut our eyes against it; that he was however filled with astonishment that if we were convinced that every *man* in America was secured in all his rights, we should be ready to sacrifice this substantial good to the phantom of *State* sovereignty; that his feelings were more harrowed & his fears more agitated for his Country than he could express, that he conceived this to be the last opportunity of providing for its liberty & happiness; that he could not therefore but repeat his amazement that when a just Govenrment founded on a fair representation of the *people* of America was within our reach, we should renounce the blessing, from an attachment to the ideal freedom & importance of States. . . ."

Dayton added that "he considered the system on the table as a novelty, an amphibious monster; and was persuaded that it never would be received by the people." And Martin went on to say that he "would never confederate if it could not be done on just principles."

But Madison stuck by his earlier views: "The plan in its present shape makes the Senate absolutely dependent on the States. The Senate therefore is only another edition of Congress. He knew the faults of that Body & had used a bold language against it. Still he would preserve the State rights, as carefully as the trials by jury."

Bedford now rose, obviously very angry, and argued with heat and recklessness. He contended that self-interest was motivating the delegates rather than the common good. "If any gentleman doubts it let him look at the votes. Have they not been dictated by interest, by ambition? Are not the large States evidently seeking to aggrandize themselves at the expense of the small? They think no doubt that they have right on their side, but interest had blinded their eyes. Look at Georgia. Though a small State at present, she is actuated by the prospect of soon being a great one. S. Carolina is actuated both by present interest & future prospects. She hopes too to see the other States cut down to her own dimensions. N. Carolina has the same motives of present & future interest. Virginia follows. Maryland is not on that side of the Question. Pennsylvania has a direct and future interest. Massachusetts has a decided and palpable interest in the part she takes. Can it be expected that the small States will act from pure disinterestedness. . . . The three large States have a common interest to bind them together in commerce. But whether a combination as we suppose, or a competition as others suppose, shall take place among them, in either case, the smaller States must be ruined. We must like Solon make such a Government as the people will approve. Will the smaller States ever agree to the proposed degradation of them. . . . We have been told with a dictatorial air that this is the last moment for a fair trial in favor of a good Government. It will be the last indeed if the propositions reported from the Committee go forth to the people. He was under no apprehensions. The Large States dare not dissolve the Confederation. If they do the small ones will find some foreign ally of more honor and good faith, who will take them by the hand and do them justice. He did not mean by this to intimidate or alarm. It was a natural consequence; which ought to be avoided by enlarging the federal powers not annihilating the federal system."

Bedford had gone farther than any member of the Convention by threatening an alliance with a foreign power. His words had a sobering effect upon all present. King had to take "some notice of the language of the honorable gentleman from Delaware [Mr. Bedford]. It was not he that had uttered a dictatorial language. This intemperance had marked the honorable gentleman himself. It was not he who with a vehemence unprecedented in that House, had declared himself ready to turn his hopes from our common Country, and court the protection of some foreign land. This too was the language of the Honorable member himself. He was grieved that such a thought had entered into his heart. He was more grieved that such an expression dropped from his lips. The gentleman could only excuse it to himself on the score of passion. For himself whatever might be his distress, he would never court relief from a foreign power."

With this rebuke to Bedford's outburst, the angry, uneasy members adjourned for the weekend.

Monday July 2

The delegates must have assembled this morning with trepidation, fearful that the Convention was nearing a complete breakup, yet unwilling to seek out a compromise acceptable to everyone. Warily they took up Ellsworth's motion for allowing each State to have one vote in the Senate. A tie was the result. Pinckney in searching for some way out, said he was "extremely anxious that something should be done, considering this as the last appeal to a regular experiment. Congress have failed in almost every effort for an amendment of the federal System. Nothing has prevented a dissolution of it, but the appointment of this Convention; and he could not express his alarms for the consequences of such an event."

General Pinckney thought some kind of compromise had to be found "the States being exactly divided on the question for an equality of votes in the 2nd branch." He suggested that "a Committee consisting of a member from each State should be appointed to devise & report some compromise."

Martin did not object but reiterated firmly that "no modifications whatever could reconcile the Smaller States to the least diminution of their equal Sovereignty."

There must have been a silence, an uneasy stirring among the delegates, finding themselves in such a dilemma.

Sherman spoke up with "we are now at a full stop" but he supposed the delegates did not wish to break up the Convention without trying to find a solution. He was in favor of appointing a committee.

Gouverneur Morris agreed, while adding in a long speech his own wish that the members of the Senate be appointed for life by the executive. No one commented on that suggestion which did little to influence opinions.

When Morris at last finished, Randolph went back to Bedford's "rash language" of the Saturday before and concluded that the large states could not survive alone any more than could the smaller ones and said that he was "determined to pursue such a scheme of Government as would secure us against such a calamity" as a divided country. Strong also spoke up for a committee and Williamson said "If we do not concede on both sides, our business must soon be at an end." As a smaller body, he felt the committee could work toward a compromise "with more coolness."

Both Wilson and Madison opposed the committee idea, perhaps fearing that it would propose a compromise unfavorable to the larger states. Before the vote, Gerry spoke in favor of forming a committee saying "Something must be done, or we shall disappoint not only America, but the whole world. . . . We must make concessions on both sides."

The delegates then voted for a committee; with its members elected by ballot. They were Gerry of Massachusetts, Ellsworth of Connecticut, Yates of New York, Paterson of New Jersey, Franklin of Pennsylvania, Bedford of Delaware, Martin of Maryland, Mason of Virginia, Davie of North Carolina, Rutledge of South Carolina, and Baldwin of Georgia — a member from each state.

At this crucial time, Independence Day had come. The delegates adjourned for the holiday and to give the committee time to work out a compromise. It was a somber time, the realization of how narrowly they had escaped a breakup of the Convention, with only the uncertain possibility that the committee could find a way out of the impasse.

And now the uneasy delegates must face Philadelphia's happy celebration of Independence Day—with special honors for them.

IX

INTERMISSION

It was a time of mingling — Convention delegates uneasy with their secrets, and the people of Philadelphia glowing with their Independence Day pride and confidence that the Convention would be a new beginning for the country.

Philadelphia's bells rang out. In the taverns there was singing and drinking to the Glorious Fourth. It was customary to down 13 toasts with appropriately high-flown oratory to honor the 13 original states. On the Commons behind the State House a rousing gun salute was fired after which the throng marched to the Lutheran Church on Race Street where many of the delegates heard an oration addressed to them: "To you, your country looks with anxious expectations. . . . How fallen would be the character we have acquired in the establishment of our liberties, if we discover inability to form a suitable Government to preserve them! Is the science

South East Corner of Third and Market Streets, Philadelphia by William Russell Birch, 1799.
Courtesy of the Library Company of Philadelphia.

of Government so difficult that we have not men among us capable of unfolding its mysteries and binding our States together by mutual interests and obligations?"

And as if this were not enough prodding, newspapers and speakers around the country addressed the delegates with their hopes for a successful outcome from the Convention. The Pennsylvania Herald *was among them: "With zeal and confidence we expect from the Federal Convention a system of government adequate to the security and preservation of those rights which were promulgated by the ever memorable Declaration of Independence."*

The whole country was awaiting results. After the brief Independence Day holiday, the delegates were aware more than ever of their awesome responsibility. It could not have been a lighthearted group which filed once again into the sealed-off room of the State House.

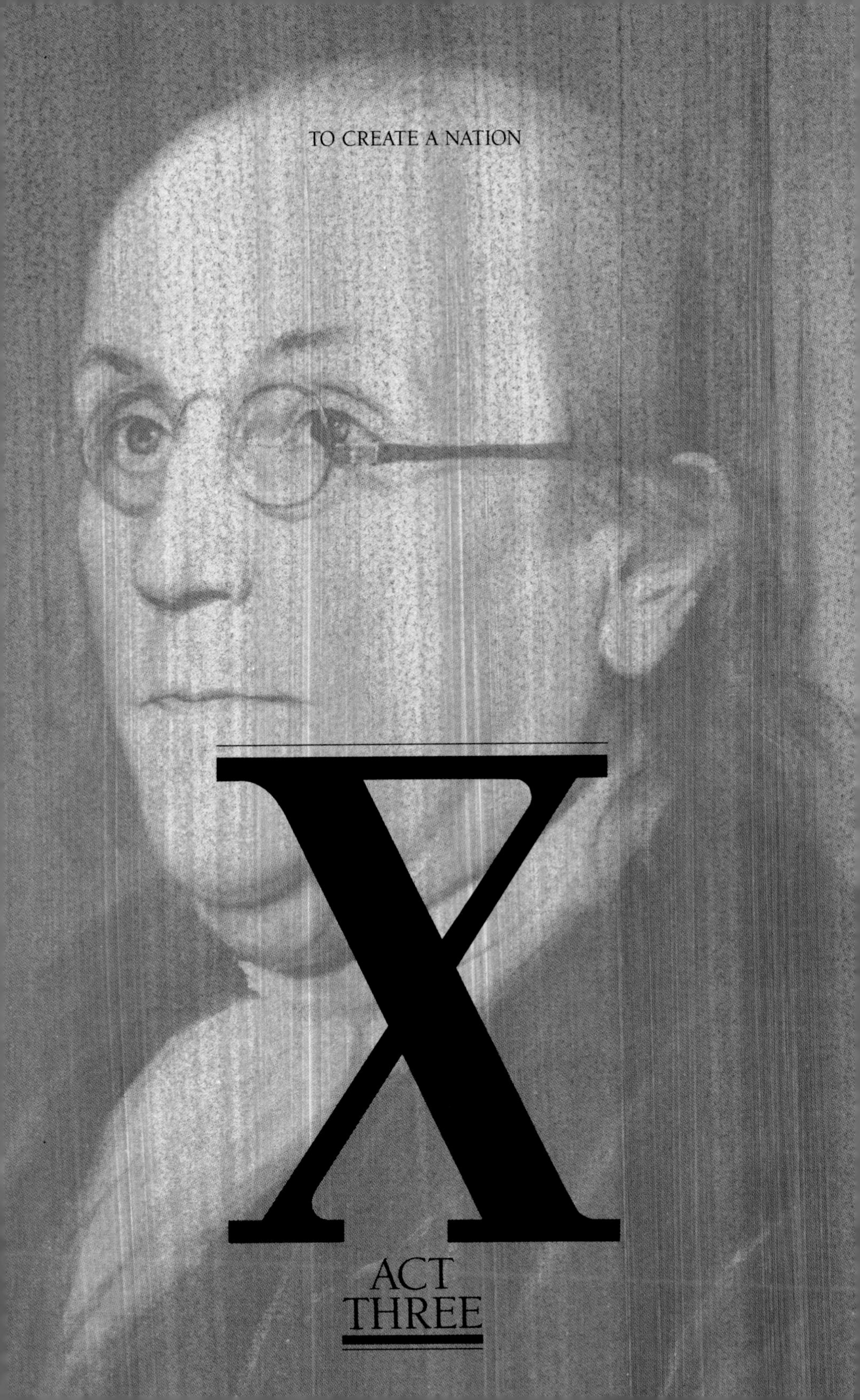

TO CREATE A NATION

X

ACT THREE

TO CREATE A NATION

Benjamin Franklin by Charles Willson Peale, 1785. Courtesy of the Pennsylvania Academy of Fine Arts.

Thursday July 5

IT WAS GERRY, THE CHAIRMAN, who delivered the report from the Committee of the States. It read: "That the subsequent propositions be recommended to the Convention on the condition that both shall be generally adopted. I. That in the first branch of the Legislature each of the States now in the Union shall be allowed 1 member for every 40,000 inhabitants of the description reported in the 7th Resolution of the Committee of the whole House: that each State not containing that number shall be allowed 1 member; that all bills for raising or appropriating money, and for fixing the Salaries of the officers of the Government of the U. States shall originate in the 1st branch of the Legislature, and shall not be altered or amended by the 2nd branch; and that no money shall be drawn from the public Treasury, but in pursuance of appropriations to be originated in the 1st branch. II. That in the 2nd branch each State shall have an equal vote."

The committee had had a hot potato to handle, that of finding an acceptable compromise for the opposing sides which the delegates had taken in Convention: proportional representation versus equal representation in the national legislature. Early in the Convention debates, as we have seen, Sherman had proposed that there be proportional representation in the lower branch and equal representation in the upper branch. Franklin had agreed with this idea for the upper branch, but felt that in money matters, the Senate votes should be according to the amount of contributions coming from the various states.

When the Committee of the States had met to work out the disagreement, both Sherman and Franklin were able to offer solutions. Ellsworth, indisposed, had been replaced by

Sherman on the Committee. Sherman suggested equal representation for the states in the upper house "provided that no decision therein should prevail unless the majority of States concurring should also comprize a majority of the inhabitants of the U. States." This suggestion did not satisfy the Committee members. It was Franklin who introduced wording which, when somewhat modified, the Committee would accept.

After Gerry presented the Committee's report, Gorham asked for an explanation of why the Committee had made the "propositions mutually conditional."

Gerry replied that because of the differing opinions both in the Committee and in the Convention, this had been a way to find "some ground of accommodation" for the opposing viewpoints.

Clearly, the larger states were unhappy. Madison argued strongly against concessions made to the smaller states, and "could not regard the exclusive privilege of originating money bills as any concession on the side of the small States. Experience proved that it had no effect. If seven States in the upper branch wished a bill to be originated, they might surely find some member from some of the same States in the lower branch who would originate it. The restriction as to amendments was of as little consequence. Amendments could be handed privately by the Senate to members in the other house. . . . It could not therefore be deemed any concession on the present, and left in force all the objections which had prevailed against allowing each State an equal voice. He conceived that the Convention was reduced to the alternative of either departing from justice in order to conciliate the smaller States, and the minority of the people of the U.S. or of displeasing these by justly gratifying the larger States and the majority of the people. He could not himself hesitate as to the option he ought to make. The Convention with justice & the majority of the people on their side, had nothing to fear. With injustice and the minority on their side they had every thing to fear. It was in vain to purchase concord in the Convention on terms which would perpetuate discord among their Constituents. The Convention ought to pursue a

John Dickinson's
7 august 1787

WE the People of the States of New-Hampſhire, Maſſachuſetts, Rhode-Iſland and Providence Plantations, Connecticut, New-York, New-Jerſey, Pennſylvania, Delaware, Maryland, Virginia, North-Carolina, South-Carolina, and Georgia, do ordain, declare and eſtabliſh the following Conſtitution for the Government of Ourſelves and our Poſterity.

ARTICLE I.

The ſtile of this Government ſhall be, "The United States of America."

II.

The Government ſhall conſiſt of ſupreme legiſlative, executive and judicial powers.

III.

The legiſlative power ſhall be veſted in a Congreſs, to conſiſt of two ſeparate and diſtinct bodies of men, a Houſe of Repreſentatives, and a Senate; each of which ſhall, in all caſes, have a negative on the other. The Legiſlature ſhall meet on the firſt Monday in December in every year.

IV.

Sect. 1. The Members of the Houſe of Repreſentatives ſhall be choſen every ſecond year, by the people of the ſeveral States comprehended within this Union. The qualifications of the electors ſhall be the ſame, from time to time, as thoſe of the electors in the ſeveral States, of the moſt numerous branch of their own legiſlatures.

Sect. 2. Every Member of the Houſe of Repreſentatives ſhall be of the age of twenty-five years at leaſt; ſhall have been a citizen in the United States for at leaſt three years before his election; and ſhall be, at the time of his election, a reſident of the State in which he ſhall be choſen.

Sect. 3. The Houſe of Repreſentatives ſhall, at its firſt formation, and until the number of citizens and inhabitants ſhall be taken in the manner herein after deſcribed, conſiſt of ſixty-five Members, of whom three ſhall be choſen in New-Hampſhire, eight in Maſſachuſetts, one in Rhode-Iſland and Providence Plantations, five in Connecticut, ſix in New-York, four in New-Jerſey, eight in Pennſylvania, one in Delaware, ſix in Maryland, ten in Virginia, five in North-Carolina, five in South-Carolina, and three in Georgia.

Sect. 4. As the proportions of numbers in the different States will alter from time to time; as ſome of the States may hereafter be divided; as others may be enlarged by addition of territory; as two or more States may be united; as new States will be erected within the limits of the United States, the Legiſlature ſhall, in each of theſe caſes, regulate the number of repreſentatives by the number of inhabitants, according to the proviſions herein after made, at the rate of one for every forty thouſand.

Sect. 5. All bills for raiſing or appropriating money, and for fixing the ſalaries of the officers of government, ſhall originate in the Houſe of Repreſentatives, and ſhall not be altered or amended by the Senate. No money ſhall be drawn from the public Treaſury, but in purſuance of appropriations that ſhall originate in the Houſe of Repreſentatives.

Sect. 6. The Houſe of Repreſentatives ſhall have the ſole power of impeachment. It ſhall chooſe its Speaker and other officers.

Sect. 7. Vacancies in the Houſe of Repreſentatives ſhall be ſupplied by writs of election from the executive authority of the State, in the repreſentation from which they ſhall happen.

V.

The First Preliminary Draft of the Constitution with Changes in the Hand of John Dickinson.
Courtesy of the Library Company of Philadelphia.

plan which would bear the test of examination, which would be espoused & supported by the enlightened and impartial part of America, & which they could themselves vindicate and urge. . . . He could not suspect that Delaware would brave the consequences of seeking her fortunes apart from the other States, rather than submit to such a Government much less could he suspect that she would pursue the rash policy of courting foreign support, which the warmth of one of her representatives [Mr. Bedford] had suggested, or if she should that any foreign nation would be so rash as to hearken to the overture. As little could he suspect that the people of N. Jersey notwithstanding the decided tone of the gentlemen from that State, would choose rather to stand on their own legs, and bid defiance to events, than to acquiesce under an establishment founded on principles the justice of which they could not dispute, and absolutely necessary to redeem them from the exactions levied on them by the commerce of the neighbouring States. A review of other States would prove that there was as little reason to apprehend an inflexible opposition elsewhere. Harmony in the Convention was no doubt much to be desired. Satisfaction to all the States, in the first instance still more so. But if the principal States comprehending a majority of the people of the U.S. should concur in a just & judicious plan, he had the firmest hopes, that all the other States would by degress accede to it."

Madison's warm expression of his objections was followed and supported by Gouverneur Morris in an equally strong fashion. "He came here as a Representative of America; he flattered himself he came here in some degree as a Representative of the whole human race; for the whole human race will be affected by the proceedings of this Convention. He wished gentlemen to extend their views beyond the present moment of time; beyond the narrow limits of place from which they derive their political origin. If he were to believe some things which he had heard, he should suppose that we were assembled to truck and bargain for our particular States. . . . Much has been said of the sentiments of the people. They were unknown. They could not be known. All that we can infer is that if the plan we recommend be reasonable & right; all who have reasonable minds and sound intentions will embrace it, notwithstanding what had been said by some gentlemen. Let us suppose that the larger States shall agree; and that the smaller refuse: and let us trace the consequences. The opponents of the system in the smaller States will no doubt make a party, and a noise for a time, but the ties of interest, of kindred & of common habits which connect them with the other States will be too strong to be easily broken. In N. Jersey particularly he was sure a great many would follow the sentiments of Pennsylvania & N. York. This Country must be united. If persuasion does not unite it, the sword will." Morris went on to warn of civil war, the dangers of foreign intervention. As for the Committee report, he felt no good would come of following its suggestions. "State attachments, and State importance have been the bane of this Country. We can not annihilate; but we may perhaps take out the teeth of the serpents. . . ."

Bedford, who had been chided a number of times for his heated threat some days earlier of reaching out to a foreign power, took this chance to protest that he had been misunderstood. "He did not mean that the small States would court the aid & interposition of foreign powers. He meant that they would not consider the federal compact as dissolved untill it should be so by the Acts of the large States. In this case the consequence of the breach of faith on their part, and the readiness of the small States to fulfill their engagements, would be that foreign Nations having demands on this country would find it their interest to take the small States by the hand, in order to do themselves justice. This is what he meant. But no man can foresee to what extremities the small States may be driven by oppression. He observed also in apology that some allowance ought to be made for the habits of his profession in which warmth was natural & sometimes necessary. But is there not an apology in what was said by Mr. Gouverneur Morris that the sword is to unite: by Mr. Gorham that Delaware must be annexed to Pennsylvania and N. Jersey divided between Pennsylvania and N. York. To hear such language without emotion, would be to renounce the feelings of a man and the duty of a Citizen. . . ." He ended his support of the Committee's findings with "It will be better that a defective plan should be adopted, than that none should be recommended. He saw no reason why defects might not be supplied by meetings 10, 15 or 20 years hence."

Now Williamson could "not conceive that Mr. Gouverneur Morris meant that the sword ought to be drawn against the smaller states. He only pointed out the probable consequences of anarchy in the U.S." And Paterson "complained of the manner in which Mr. Madison and Mr. Gouverneur Morris had treated the small States." The delegates were on the edge of casting doubt upon each other's motives as they angrily wrestled with their differences.

Gerry warned of dangers should they not compromise. Although he had assented to the report in Committee he did have objections to it. "We were however in a peculiar situation. We were neither the same Nation nor different Nations. We ought not therefore to pursue the one or the other of these ideas too closely. If no compromise should take place what will be the consequence. A secession he foresaw would take place; for some gentlemen seem decided on it; two different plans will be proposed; and the result no man could foresee. If we do not come to some agreement among ourselves some foreign sword will probably do the work for us."

Mason followed him with the assurance that the report was not meant as specific propositions to be adopted "but merely as a general ground of accommodation. There must be some accommodation on this point, or we shall make little further progress in the work. Accommodation was the object of the House in the appointment of the Committee; and of the Committee in the Report they had made. And however liable the Report might be to objections, he thought it preferable to an appeal to the world by the different sides, as had been talked of by some Gentlemen. It could not be more inconvenient to any gentleman to remain absent from his private affairs, than it was for him: but he would bury his bones in this City rather than expose his Country to the Consequences of a dissolution of the Convention without any thing being done."

The Convention was lucky to have a number of delegates who would speak up as Gerry and Mason just had for the importance of compromise and putting aside personal concerns and differences for the good of the country. The extremists seemed determined to have their way and only those willing to hold middle ground could hold the Convention together.

Returning to the report, both Gouverneur Morris and Rutledge spoke against the proposal that there be one member in the lower house for every 40,000 inhabitants, both of them believing that property should be included in the estimate along with the number of inhabitants. Rutledge commented that "property was certainly the principal object of Society," and asked whether the delegates had considered how the new states in the west were to be apportioned. He favored "suffrages of the several States be regulated and proportioned according to the sums to be paid towards the general revenue by the inhabitants of each State respectively. . . ."

The Convention adjourned without having come to any conclusions.

Friday July 6

After some discussion, the delegates agreed to postpone a decision on that part of the report which related to one member in the lower house for every 40,000 inhabitants, with a small committee appointed to give the matter more detailed study. These committee members, chosen by ballot, were Gouverneur Morris, Gorham, Randolph, Rutledge and King.

The clause which related to the originating of money bills was then taken up, with Gouverneur Morris objecting to restricting this right to either branch of the legislature. Wilson refused to see this proposal as a concession made by the smaller states. "If both branches were to say yes or no, it was of little consequence which should say yes or no first, which last." And he felt the "least numerous body" would more appropriately originate money bills if it were to be done in a single body.

Mason explained that the Committee had felt that the lower house would be "the immediate representatives of the people," while the upper house would not. Therefore, if the upper house should "have the power of giving away the people's money, they might soon forget the source from whence they received it. We might soon have an aristocracy."

Gouverneur Morris came back with "there never was, nor ever will be a civilized Society without an aristocracy. His endeavor was to keep it as much as possible from doing mischief."

Franklin further clarified the thinking of the committee: "as it had been asked what would be the use of restraining the 2nd branch from meddling with money bills, he could not but remark that it was always of importance that the people should know who had disposed of their money, & how it had been disposed of. It was a maxim that those who feel, can best judge. . . . This was his inducement to concur in the report. As to the danger or difficulty that might arise from a negative in the 2nd branch where the people would not be proportionally represented, it might easily be got over by declaring that there should be no such Negative: or if that will not do, by declaring that there shall be no such branch at all."

The Convention then agreed in a split vote to let the clause on money bills stand as part of the report.

Saturday July 7

The clause allowing each state one representative in the Senate was debated this day. But because the delegates knew that later a vote would be taken on the whole of the committee report, debate was not acrimonious and the Convention agreed that the states should have an equal vote. However, Paterson warned that if proportional representation was to be the rule in the lower house the small states then must surely have equality of votes in the upper house. "There was no other ground of accommodation. His resolution was fixt. He would meet the large States on that Ground and no other."

And Gouverneur Morris chided him with "he had no resolution unalterably fixed except to do what should finally appear to him right," and lamented that "it had been one of our greatest misfortunes that the great objects of the nation had been sacrificed constantly to local views; in like manner as the general interests of States had been sacrificed to those of the Counties. . . . Particular States ought to be injured for the sake of a majority of the people, in case their conduct should deserve it. Suppose they should insist on claims evidently unjust, and pursue them in a manner detrimental to the whole body. Suppose they should give themselves up to foreign influence. Ought they to be protected in such cases. They were originally nothing more than colonial corporations. On the declaration of Independence, a Government was to be formed. The small States aware of the necessity of preventing anarchy, and taking advantage of the moment, extorted from the large ones an equality of votes. Standing now on that ground, they demand under the new system greater rights as men, than their fellow Citizens of the large States. The proper answer to them is that the same necessity of which they formerly took advantage, does not now exist, and that the large States are at liberty now to consider what is right, rather than what may be expedient."

Monday July 9

Gouverneur Morris gave the report from the small committee considering the proper ratio of representatives in the lower house with one to every 40,000 inhabitants. Basing their conclusions on the population estimates of 1774, the committee came up with the figure of 56 members for the lower house — New Hampshire 2, Massachusetts 7, Rhode Island 1, Connecticut 4, New York 5, New Jersey 3, Pennsylvania 8, Delaware 1, Maryland 4, Virginia 9, North Carolina 5, South Carolina 5, Georgia 2. But as the situation would change "in point of wealth as in the number of their inhabitants, that the Legislature be authorized from time to time to augment the number of Representatives."

Again the "point of wealth" had been brought up and it engendered more debate. Gorham explained "the views of the Committee" which were that the representation would become too numerous if there were one member for every 40,000 inhabitants; also, there was a fear that the Western states eventually might out-vote the Atlantic states. With a combination of wealth and population as the rule, "the Atlantic States having the Government in their own hands, may take care of their own interest, by dealing out the right of Representation in safe proportions to the Western States."

Other delegates also believed both wealth and population should count in representation and the Convention voted to have the legislature regulate the state's representation "upon the principles of their wealth and number of inhabitants." A committee was appointed with a member from each state to determine the number of representatives there should be at the present time. These members were King, Sherman, Yates, Brearley, Gouverneur Morris, Read, Carroll, Madison, Williamson, Rutledge and Houstoun.

Tuesday July 10

The committee formed the day before reported in with the proposal that the lower house begin with 65 members—New Hampshire 3, Massachusetts 8, Rhode Island 1, Connecticut 5, New York 6, New Jersey 4, Pennsylvania 8, Delaware 1, Maryland 6, Virginia 10, North Carolina 5, South Carolina 5, Georgia 3.

Then of course debate began over the apportionment. Some of the delegates wanted New Hampshire reduced to 2; some felt this committee's report was less favorable to the Southern states while others said the dividing state was Pennsylvania with six states to the north, six to the south. When the question of New Hampshire's representation was put to a vote, the delegates left the number at 3 and turned down motions by Southerners to have their numbers increased.

Madison then moved that the number allowed to each state be doubled. "A *majority* of a *Quorum* of 65 members, was too small a number to represent the whole inhabitants of the U. States; they would not possess enough of the confidence of the people, and would be too sparsely taken from the people, to bring with them all the local information which would be frequently wanted." But after further discussion, the Convention voted to leave the figure at 65.

Wednesday July 11

The debates continued over relative representation, south versus north and west versus east. Randolph urged that a census be taken "under the direction of the General Legislature. The States will be too much interested to take an impartial one for themselves."

Butler and Pinckney felt "that blacks be included in the rule of Representation, *equally* with the Whites; and for that purpose moved that the words 'three fifths' be struck out." Such a change in Resolution 7 would greatly enlarge representation for the Southern states. But Gorham replied that "this ratio was fixed by Congress as a rule of taxation. Then it was urged by the Delegates representing the States having slaves that the blacks were still more inferior to freemen. At present when the ratio of representation is to be established, we are assured that they are equal to freemen."

Scene at the Signing of the Constitution by Howard Chandler Christie, 1940.
Courtesy of the Architect of the Capitol.

Butler insisted "that the labour of a slave in S. Carolina was as productive & valuable as that of a freeman in Massachusetts, that as wealth was the great means of defence and utility to the Nation they were equally valuable to it with freemen; and that consequently an equal representation ought to be allowed for them in a Government which was instituted principally for the protection of property, and was itself to be supported by property."

However, the Convention voted Butler's motion down and the ratio remained at counting three fifths of the slaves to all of the white inhabitants. Again, the whole problem of reckoning wealth came up for debate. Sherman "thought the number of people alone the best rule for measuring wealth as well as representation. . . ."

Madison now made a case for not discriminating against the Western states. He pointed out that when the Mississippi was opened up to them, their trade would increase, bringing the Westerners wealth, and as their products passed through the Atlantic states the Easterners would benefit.

As the delegates returned to the problem of counting blacks in deciding the number of representatives a state should have, various views came to light. Wilson "did not well see on what principle the admission of blacks in the proportion of three fifths could be explained. Are they admitted as Citizens? then why are they not admitted on an equality with White Citizens? are they admitted as property? then why is not other property admitted into the computation?" Gouverneur Morris "could never agree to give such encouragement to the slave trade as would be given by allowing them a representation for their negroes, and he did not believe those States would ever confederate on terms that would deprive them of that trade."

Thursday July 12

This morning, Gouverneur Morris came forward with the idea of "empowering the Legislature to vary the Representation according to the principles of wealth & number of inhabitants a 'proviso that taxation shall be in proportion to Representation.'"

This shed a different light upon how the blacks should

be counted. While South Carolina and Georgia agreed to pay taxes on all their slaves if all of them were counted, other Southern states with large numbers of blacks could not agree. Davie said "he was sure that North Carolina would never confederate on any terms that did not rate them at least as three fifths." Randolph supported him. Pinckney wanted blacks equal to the whites in the ratio of representation. This he said "was nothing more than justice. The blacks are the labourers, the peasants of the Southern States; they are as productive of pecuniary resources as those of the Northern States. They add equally to the wealth, and considering money as the sinew of war, to the strengh of the nation." The delegates passed the motion "as proportioning representation to direct taxation & both to the white & three fifths of black inhabitants, & requiring a Census within six years—& within every ten years afterwards."

Friday July 13

This was not, after all, an unlucky day for the Convention because they came to a decision about property and its relationship to the government document they were trying to form. Randolph asked that the word "wealth" be struck out of the motion made July 9 which authorized the Legislature "to adjust from time to time, the representation upon the principles of *wealth* & numbers of inhabitants. . . ." There was disagreement, but Wilson was the delegate who was able to remind his colleagues of the larger goals of their work. "Conceiving that all men wherever placed have equal rights and are equally entitled to confidence, he viewed without apprehension the period when a few States should contain the superior number of people. The majority of people wherever found ought in all questions to govern the minority. If the interior Country should acquire this majority, it will not only have the right, but will avail itself of it whether we will or no. This jealousy misled the policy of G. Britain with regard to America. The fatal maxims espoused by her were that the Colonies were growing too fast, and that their growth must be stinted in time. What were the consequences? first, enmity on our part, then actual separation. Like consequences will result on the part of the interior settlements, if like jealousy & policy be pursued on ours. Further, if numbers be not a proper rule, why is not some better rule pointed out. No one has yet ventured to attempt it. Congress have never been able to discover a better. No State as far as he had heard, has suggested any other. In 1783, after elaborate discussion of a measure of wealth all were satisfied that the rule of numbers, does not differ much from the combined rule of numbers & wealth. Again he could not agree that property was the sole or the primary object of Government & society. The cultivation & improvement of the human mind was the most noble object. With respect to this object, as well as to other *personal* rights, numbers were surely the natural & precise measure of Representation. And with respect to property, they could not vary much from the precise measure."

The day ended with the word "wealth" stricken from the clause. By coincidence, on this same day, the Congress of the Confederation passed the Ordinance of 1787 for the government of the Northwest Territory. This important document provided that the territory be ruled at first by a governor, a secretary and three judges who would be named by Congress. When any region had 5000 free male inhabitants, a legislature was to be elected and a non-voting delegate could be sent to Congress. When the population reached 60,000, it would be admitted to the Union and write its own constitution. The Ordinance provided for five states which became Ohio, Indiana, Illinois, Wisconsin and Michigan. Slavery was prohibited and a bill of rights guaranteed freedom of worship, *habeas corpus*, trial by jury and security of contracts. Thus, the new states would enter the Union on an equal footing with the original 13.

Saturday July 14

Even so, the fears of the eastern state representatives remained and on this Saturday Gerry asked that "the attention of the House might be turned to the dangers apprehended from Western States. He was for admitting them on liberal terms, but not for putting ourselves into their hands. They will if they acquire power like all men, abuse it. They will oppress commerce, and drain our wealth into the Western Country. To guard against these consequences, he thought it necessary to limit the number of new States to be admitted into the Union, in such a manner, that they should never be able to outnumber the Atlantic States."

The delegates looked uneasily to the west. They were aware that western areas of Pennsylvania already were in conflict with the eastern part of the state as was true in South Carolina. And in these mushrooming western "states" the people were generally restless, adventurous and had little wealth. How, the delegates wondered, would they be able to pay their share in the Union.

Sherman replied to Gerry that he thought "there was no probability that the number of future States would exceed that of the Existing States. If the event should ever happen, it was too remote to be taken into consideration at this time. Besides We are providing for our posterity, for our children & our grand Children, who would be as likely to be citizens of new Western States, as of the old States. On this consideration we ought to make no such discrimination. . . ."

Gerry was not soothed: "If some of our children should remove, others will stay behind, and he thought it incumbent on us to provide for their interests. There was a rage for emigration from the Eastern States to the Western Country, and he did not wish those remaining behind to be at the mercy of the Emigrants. Besides foreigners are resorting to that country, and it is uncertain what turn things may take there." His motion was that "in order to secure the liberties of the States already confederated, the number of Representatives in the 1st branch, of the States which shall hereafter be established, shall never exceed in number, the Representatives from such of the States as shall accede to this confederation." The motion was defeated.

Delegates Martin and Sherman were asking that the Convention vote on the whole report of the Committee of the States which had been given July 5. But it was as though the delegates were fearful of bringing the report to a vote, dreading the outcome if the Convention were deadlocked. The arguments began again, sharper than ever. Strong reminded the delegates that "the Convention had been much divided in opinion. In order to avoid the consequences of it, an accommodation had been proposed. A committee had been appointed; and though some of the members of it were averse to an equality of votes, a Report has been made in favor of it. It is agreed on all hands that Congress are nearly at an end. If no Accommodation takes place, the Union itself must soon be dissolved."

But this did not stop the debate. Both Madison and Wilson vehemently spoke against the finding of the Committee, both knowing that time was running out and the vote inevitably would be taken.

Monday July 16

On this day, probably the most important one of the Convention, the delegates voted on the whole report as amended and including the proviso for equality of votes in the lower house. It was passed, with Connecticut, New Jersey, Delaware, North Carolina, Maryland approving; Pennsylvania, Virginia, South Carolina and Georgia voting against it. Massachusetts was divided.

It was Randolph who broke the tension by saying that the morning's vote "had embarrassed the business extremely. All the powers given in the Report from the Committee of the whole, were founded on the supposition that a Proportional representation was to prevail in both branches of the Legislature. When he came here this morning his purpose was to have offered some propositions that might if possible have united a great majority of votes, and particularly might provide against the danger suspected on the part of the smaller States, by enumerating the cases in which it might lie, and allowing an equality of votes in such cases. But finding from the preceding vote that they persist in demanding an equal vote in all cases, that they have succeeded in obtaining it, and that N. York if present would probably be on the same side, he could not but think we were unprepared to discuss this subject further. It will probably be in vain to come to any final decision with a bare majority on either side. For these reasons he wished the Convention might adjourn, that the large States might consider the steps proper to be taken in the present solemn crisis of the business, and that the small States might also deliberate on the means of conciliation."

Paterson retorted that he "thought with Mr. Randolph that it was high time for the Convention to adjourn that the rule of secrecy ought to be rescinded, and that our Constituents should be consulted. No conciliation could be admissible on the part of the smaller States on any other ground than that of an equality of votes in the 2nd branch. If Mr. Randolph would reduce to form his motion for an adjournment *sine die,* he would second it with all his heart."

General Pinckney hastily asked if Randolph had meant an end to the Convention or merely for the day. Poor Randolph quickly said he "had never entertained an idea of an adjournment *sine die;* & was sorry that his meaning had been so readily & strangely misinterpreted. He had in view merely an adjournment till tomorrow, in order that some conciliatory experiment might if possible be devised, and that in case the smaller States should continue to hold back, the larger might then take such measures, he would not say what, as might be necessary."

Paterson was willing to adjourn until the next day, but even on this motion the states were divided. Rutledge said "he could see no need of an adjournment because he could see no chance of a compromise. The little States were fixt. They had repeatedly & solemnly declared themselves to be so. All that the large States then had to do, was to decide whether they would yield or not. For his part he conceived that altho' we could not do what we thought best, in itself, we ought to do something. Had we not better keep the Government up a little longer, hoping that another Convention will supply our omissions, than abandon every thing to hazard. Our Constituents will be very little satisfied with us if we take the latter course."

When the Convention adjourned that evening, the future of the country hung precariously in the balance. Our own lives would be utterly different had the delegates decided to give up and go home. Given the depth of the convictions of these men, it was an excruciating process to forge a compromise. Had their personal pride prevailed, the United States would be not at all as we know it.

On the morning of July 17, according to Madison's journal, "before the hour of the convention a number of the members from the larger States, by common agreement met for the purpose of consulting on the proper steps to be taken in consequence of the vote in favor of an equal Representation in the 2nd branch, and the apparent inflexibility of the smaller States on that point. Several members from the latter States also attended. The time was wasted in vague conversation on the subject, without any specific proposition or agreement."

While some were willing to end the Convention, others felt they had opposed the smaller states to no avail long enough. Some thought the larger states should form a constitution of their own, offer it to Congress and those states that were willing to join could do so. But no firm direction to which all could agree was arrived at. Madison closes this portion of his diary with "It is probable that the result of this consultation satisfied the smaller States that they had nothing to apprehend from a union of the larger, in any plan whatever against the equality of votes in the 2nd branch."

The acceptance of the Committee Report has come to be known as the Great Compromise, the Sherman Compromise and the Connecticut Compromise. The smaller states had agreed to proportional representation in the lower house and the larger states had agreed to equal representation in the upper house. The idea of a confederation was ended while a federal system was born: A unique combination of states with their own rights and privileges agreeing to follow federal laws which applied to the whole. No other country had ever attempted such a government.

Generally, in a compromise, no one side feels completely satisfied, and the wounds from the weeks of argument undoubtedly went deep. Other convictions expressed at this time have recurred in the country's history. The slavery issue already showed itself to be a divisive force in the nation. Argument has recurred through the years over the rights of the states versus the powers of the national government. For a long time there was a sense of guarded acceptance between the Eastern and Western states. And Presidents have swung sometimes between a determinedly "just folks" attitude and a faintly regal regime. It is remarkable that such a unique combination of power at state and national level has worked, aside from the conflicting special interests of the various regions.

Tuesday July 17

After one more feeble attempt, the large states accepted the fact that they had been beaten, and the compromise agreement became history.

Now the Convention needed to re-examine the Virginia Plan which had been discussed in the Committee of the

Whole. It was agreed that the legislature of the United States should have the power "to legislate in all cases for the general interests of the Union, and also in those to which the States are separately incompetent, or in which the harmony of the U. States may be interrupted by the exercise of individual Legislation."

And then in a reversal of an earlier vote, the delegates now voted against the national government having "the power of negativing laws of States." Gouverneur Morris thought such a negative would "disgust the States." And in addition, "a law that ought to be negatived will be set aside in the Judiciary department and if that security should fail; may be repealed by a National Law."

Legislative acts of the new government, it was agreed, must harmonize with the Constitution they were now constructing and "all Treaties made & ratified under the authority of the U.S. shall be the supreme law of the respective States, as far as those acts or treaties shall relate to the said States, or their Citizens and inhabitants—& that the Judiciaries of the several States shall be bound thereby in their decisions, any thing in the respective laws of the individual States to the contrary notwithstanding."

This decided, the Convention turned once more to consideration of the national executive, agreeing again that it be represented in a single person. He was to be chosen by the national legislature, but Gouverneur Morris objected, saying "he will be the mere creature of the Legislature: if appointed & impeachable by that body. He ought to be elected by the people at large, by the freeholders of the Country." Mason, the liberal from Virginia, surprisingly thought "it would be as unnatural to refer the choice of a proper character for chief Magistrate to the people, as it would, to refer a trial of colours to a blind man. The extent of the Country renders it impossible that the people can have the requisite capacity to judge of the respective pretensions of the Candidates."

Term of office for the chief executive was once more set at seven years, but he was to be allowed a second term. Madison, however, sounded a warning that the legislature and executive and judicial branches must be kept separate as "essential to the preservation of liberty." Yet "the Executive could not be independent of the Legislature, if dependent on the pleasure of that branch for a reappointment." It was a problem that was to be taken up again at a later day.

Wednesday July 18

It was time to look again at the national judiciary. While it had been agreed that there should be one supreme tribunal, how those judges would be chosen now came up for discussion. Gorham suggested "that the Judges be appointed by the Executive with the advice & consent of the 2nd branch [of the legislature], in the mode prescribed by the constitution of Massachusetts. This mode had been long practised in that country, & was found to answer perfectly well." Madison "suggested that the Judges might be appointed by the Executive with the concurrence of one-third at least, of the 2nd branch." But a vote was not taken at that time. The delegates did agree "that National Legislature be empowered to appoint inferior tribunals," and that "the jurisdiction shall extend to all cases arising under the National laws: And to such other questions as may involve the National peace & harmony."

According to author Carl Van Doren in his book *The Great Rehearsal*, "Nothing then or later was explicitly said about giving the Supreme Court the power to pass on the constitutionality of acts of Congress. It was an implied power which did not come into existence until the power of Congress had been limited, with the implication that there must be some power to enforce the limitations." The Court under Chief Justice John Marshall, to a great extent, defined its powers in relation to the other branches of government.

As a final order of business on this Wednesday, the Convention moved "that a Republican form of Government shall be guarantied to each State & that each State shall be protected against foreign & domestic violence."

Thursday July 19

The whole day's debates were on the subject of the executive—how he should be chosen, the length of his term, whether or not he could serve a second time. The term was changed to six years and if he were to serve again, the delegates decided that he must be chosen once more by electors appointed by the state legislators.

Friday July 20

Again the day was taken up with considering the executive—how many electors from the states would appoint the executive and whether or not he should "be removeable on impeachment and conviction for mal practice or neglect of duty." Mason held that "no point is of more importance than that the right of impeachment should be continued. Shall any man be above Justice?"

Madison agreed, feeling "it indispensable that some provision should be made for defending the Community against the incapacity, negligence or perfidy of the chief Magistrate." After considerable discussion, the Convention voted that the executive could be impeached.

Saturday July 21

This morning, Wilson reverted to his earlier argument that "the supreme National Judiciary should be associated with the Executive in the Revisionary power." He argued that "laws may be unjust, may be unwise, may be dangerous, may be destructive; and yet may not be so unconstitutional as to justify the Judges in refusing to give them effect. Let them have a share in the Revisionary power, and they will have an opportunity of taking notice of these characters of a law, and of counteracting, by the weight of their opinions the improper views of the Legislature."

Madison gave the idea his support. "It would be useful to the Judiciary department by giving it an additional opportunity of defending itself against Legislative encroachments; It would be useful to the Executive, by inspiring additional confidence & firmness in exerting the revisionary power; It would be useful to the Legislature by the valuable assistance it would give in preserving a consistency, conciseness, perspicuity & technical propriety in the laws, qualities peculiarly necessary; & yet shamefully wanting in our republican Codes. It would moreover be useful to the Community at large as an additional check against a pursuit of those unwise & unjust measures which constituted so great a portion of our calamities."

While some supported the motion, others worried that the separation of powers would not be maintained between the three branches of government, and the motion lost. Many students of the Constitution regret that some form of Wilson's idea had not become a part of the document; that much more precision in the lawmaking process could have been attained.

The Convention voted for executive veto power, Virginia Resolve 10, as reported out by the Committee of the Whole.

Monday July 23

Delegates this Monday had come to consideration of how the Constitution was to be ratified. While Ellsworth and Paterson were for referring it to the state legislatures for approval, others argued that the general public must be involved in the decision. It was again the importance of the rights of the states in some of the delegates' minds as opposed to power vested directly in the people. Gouverneur Morris noted that "the amendment moved by Mr. Ellsworth erroneously supposes that we are proceeding on the basis of the Confederation. This Convention is unknown to the Confederation." After debate, the Convention voted "to refer the Constitution after the approbation of Congress to assemblies chosen by the people."

Then Gouverneur Morris and King "moved that the representation in the second branch consist of BLANK members from each State, who shall vote per capita." The delegates went on to vote for two Senators from each state who were empowered to cast their votes not in a state bloc but individually.

Tuesday July 24, Wednesday July 25

The delegates went back to considering the appointment of the executive by electors. The discussion ranged over the length of the executive's term, whether the electors should be appointed by the state or the national legislature, whether the executive should be eligible for a second term. They obviously were turning arguments over in their minds, feeling the weight of the decisions they were making. No doubt many of them wondered if they were building in enough ways to keep their executive from eventually becoming a king. Rulers in their times did not conform to the kind of executive they were creating.

Delegates discussed at length and voted for the election of the executive by national legislature.

Thursday July 26

After the long debates of the two days before, the delegates voted for a term of seven years for the executive, without reelection. All kinds of proposals had been made as to how he would be chosen—the people at large, the legislatures of the states, the executives of the states, electors chosen by the people. Mason said "that an election by the National Legislature as originally proposed, was the best," but at this time the Convention committed itself only to the length of service. The qualifications of the electors were discussed, but the Convention was not yet ready to decide how they would be appointed and how they would carry out the electing of the executive.

It was now time to turn over the Convention's materials to a Committee of Detail which would put them into a clearer form for the delegates to reconsider. The deliberations given to the Committee were in a large folio of seven pages containing 23 Resolutions which had been passed. This important Committee was made up of five members: Randolph of Virginia, Wilson of Pennsylvania, Gorham of Massachusetts, Ellsworth of Connecticut and Rutledge of South Carolina. The Committee was given 11 days to bring in a "report," and the Convention adjourned until August 6.

While the outside world speculated in newspapers and correspondence upon what was going on, the delegates were faithful to their code of secrecy. General Washington set off with Gouverneur Morris to the nearby Valley Forge area for some trout fishing. While Morris was fishing, Washington rode over to where the Revolutionary Army had spent the terrible winter of 1777. The old cantonment was now in ruins, a fading scene from the past. Some of the delegates went home, others went sightseeing to neighboring areas while most of them found diversions in the city of Philadelphia.

Monday August 6

Rutledge gave the report from the Committee of Detail—the amended Virginia Plan which the Convention had labored over since a quorum arrived at the State House on May 25. The Committee had organized the delegates' decisions, making it possible once more to go over the work., In this report, the preamble read: "We the people of the States of New Hampshire, Massachusetts, Rhode-Island and Providence Plantations, Connecticut, New-York, New-Jersey, Pennsylvania, Delaware, Maryland, Virginia, North-Carolina, South-Carolina, and Georgia, do ordain, declare, and establish the following Constitution for the Government of Ourselves and our Posterity." Twenty-three Articles followed and the Convention adjourned until the next day while the delegates pondered and annotated their printed copies.

Tuesday August 7

According to the Convention rules, any portion of the report which the Committee had presented to the delegates could still be argued and voted on again. This fact undoubtedly took some of the uneasiness out of seeing their work taking shape as a powerful document which would affect the lives of everyone living under its influence.

Cautiously, the Convention accepted the preamble and the first two articles which merely stated that the government would be The United States Of America and would consist of "supreme legislative, executive, and judicial powers."

Picking their way slowly, considering every phrase and every word with care, the delegates moved on. The legislative body was now called "a Congress" while the lower house was "a House of Representatives" and the upper house "a Senate." As it had earlier, the problem of who should elect the members of the House of Representatives showed the differing opinions. According to Article IV in the Committee's Report, qualifications for voters for House members should be the same as that for choosing members "of the most numerous branch of their own [state] legislatures."

Wilson explained that "It was difficult to form any uniform rule of qualifications for all the States." (In these years, citizens could not vote unless they owned property or paid taxes, but the qualifications differed from state to state, sometimes were not even the same for the two branches of the several legislatures.) Gouverneur Morris noted that Article IV made "the qualifications of the National Legislature depend on the will of the States, which he thought not proper."

Ellsworth replied that "The right of suffrage was a tender point, and strongly guarded by most of the State Constitutions. The people will not readily subscribe to the National

Constitution if it should subject them to be disfranchised. The States are the best Judges of the circumstances & temper of their own people."

Dickinson wanted voting rights to be restricted to "the freeholders of the Country," considering them as "the best guardians of liberty."

Ellsworth wanted to know "How shall the freehold be defined? Ought not every man who pays a tax, to vote for the representative who is to levy & dispose of his money? Shall the wealthy merchants & manufacturers, who will bear a full share of the public burdens be not allowed a voice in the imposition of them — taxation & representation ought to go together." This, a reminder of one of the reasons why the American Revolution had been fought.

But Gouverneur Morris countered with "Give the votes to people who have no property, and they will sell them to the rich who will be able to buy them. We should not confine our attention to the present moment. The time is not distant when this Country will abound with mechanics & manufacturers who will receive their bread from their employers. Will such men be the secure & faithful Guardians of liberty?"

Mason, however, opposed the whole freehold idea. "A Freehold is the qualification in England, & hence it is imagined to be the only proper one. The true idea in his opinion was that every man having evidence of attachment to & permanent common interest with the Society ought to share in all its rights & privileges. . . . Ought the merchant, the monied man, the parent of a number of children whose fortunes are to be pursued in his own Country, to be viewed as suspicious characters, and unworthy to be trusted with the common rights of their fellow citizens."

Madison said that "Whether the Constitutional qualifications ought to be a freehold, would with him depend much on the probable reception such a change would meet with in States where the right was now exercised by every description of people. In several of the States a freehold was now the qualification. Viewing the subject in its merits alone, the freeholders of the Country would be the safest depositories of Republican liberty. In future times a great majority of the people will not only be without land, but any other sort of, property. These will either combine under the influence of their common situation: In which case, the rights of property & the public liberty, will not be secure in their hands: or which is more probable, they will become the tools of opulence & ambition. . . ."

Franklin made a noble case for trusting and giving power to the common people. He said, "It is of great consequence that we should not depress the virtue & public spirit of our common people; of which they displayed a great deal during the war, and which contributed principally to the favorable issue of it" and gave examples of heroic acts of American seamen during the Revolution as contrasted to the spirit of the British seamen. "This proceeded," he said, "from the different manner in which the common people were treated in America and G. Britain. He did not think that the elected had any right in any case to narrow the privileges of the electors."

Wednesday August 8

When the vote came, the Convention upheld Article IV as the Committee had reported it; that is, property qualifications were not to be required for voters choosing members of the House of Representatives.

As for the qualifications of the members of the House of Representatives, the delegates decided that the Congressmen should be citizens of the United States for seven instead of the three years in the report. Mason said that he "was for opening a wide door for emigrants; but did not chuse to let foreigners and adventurers make laws for us & govern us. Citizenship for three years was not enough for ensuring that local knowledge which ought to be possessed by the Representative. This was the principal ground of his objection to so short a term. It might also happen that a rich foreign Nation, for example Great Britain, might send over her tools who might bribe their way into the Legislature for insidious purposes."

As the discussion moved to the provision of allocating one representative for every 40,000 inhabitants, several of the delegates spoke up against the slave trade and the method of counting slaves in determining the number of a state's representatives. King, Sherman and Gouverneur Morris were among those voicing objections. King asked "If slaves are to be imported shall not the exports produced by their labor, supply a revenue the better to enable the General Government to defend their masters?. . . He had hoped that some accommodation would have taken place on this subject; that at least a time would have been limited for the importation of slaves." Sherman "regarded the slave trade as iniquitous" but did not quarrel with the method of representation. Gouverneur Morris "never would concur in upholding domestic slavery. It was a nefarious institution. It was the curse of heaven on the States where it prevailed. . . . Upon what principle is it that the slaves shall be computed in the representation? Are they men? Then make them Citizens and let them vote. Are they property? Why then is no other property included?"

But the "federal ratio" was finally agreed upon; that is, any navigation act must have a two-thirds vote in both houses of Congress, the import tax on slaves would not go higher than ten dollars a person, and slaves would be counted, for representation and taxes, five slaves to three free white inhabitants. Importation of slaves was to cease — a decision reached on August 25 — in 1808.

The problem was argued again and again during the summer months without the delegates ever finding a real solution, only an uneasy compromise.

Thursday August 9

At this stage of proceedings, the Convention considered the choosing of Senators and what their qualifications should be. Once more some of the members voiced concern that "foreigners" might meddle in the governing of the country. Butler said that they would "bring with them, not only attachments to other Countries; but ideas of Government so distinct from ours that in every point of view they are dangerous."

Again Franklin brought his rationality to the discussion. He "was not against a reasonable time [for newcomers to have lived in the United States before being qualified to hold office], but should be very sorry to see any thing like illiberality inserted in the Constitution. The people in Europe are friendly to this Country. Even in the Country with which we have been lately at war, we have now & had during the war, a great many friends not only among the people at large but in both houses of Parliament. . . . When foreigners after looking about for some other Country in which they can obtain more happiness, give a preference to ours it is a proof of attachment which ought to excite our confidence & affection."

Wilson, the native Scotsman, noted that "if the ideas of some gentlemen should be pursued," he would be "incapacitated from holding a place under the very Constitution, which he had shared in the trust of making."

The delegates finally agreed that Senators must have been United States citizens for at least nine years before election.

Friday August 10, Saturday August 11

Section 2 of Article VI read—as reported by the Committee of Detail: "The Legislature of the United States shall have authority to establish such uniform qualifications of the members of each House, with regard to property, as to the said Legislature shall seem expedient."

Pinckney felt "that the members of the Legislature, the Executive, and the Judges, should be possessed of competent property to make them independent & respectable. It was prudent when such great powers were to be trusted to connect the tie of property with that of reputation in securing a faithful administration. . . . Were he to fix the quantum of property which should be required, he should not think of less than one hundred thousand dollars for the President, half of that sum for each of the Judges, and in like proportion for the members of the National Legislature. He moved that all these officials 'should be required to swear that they were respectively possessed of a cleared unencumbered Estate' of amounts to be determined."

Once again, Franklin came to the rescue. He "expressed his dislike of every thing that tended to debase the spirit of the common people. If honesty was often the companion of wealth, and if poverty was exposed to peculiar temptation, it was not less true that the possession of property increased the desire of more property. Some of the greatest rogues he was ever acquainted with, were the richest rogues. We should remember the character which the Scripture requires in Rulers, that they should be men hating covetousness. This Constitution will be much read and attended to in Europe, and if it should betray a great partiality to the rich, will not only hurt us in the esteem of the most liberal and enlightened men there, but discourage the common people from removing into this Country."

Madison's notes read: "The Motion of Mr. Pinckney was rejected by so general a *no,* that the States were not called." And this section relating to property was deleted from the document. Through those hot summer days, the delegates were examining every Article with incredible persistence and awareness of the importance of their work.

Monday August 13

This morning the Convention went back to the qualifications for members of the House of Representatives and changed the requirement for citizenship from three to "at least seven years before his election." The fear of foreign powers meddling in their government's affairs was deep.

A long discussion went on during the day on where bills for raising money should originate and whether or not the Senate could alter or amend them. Mason held that "the Senate did not represent the *people,* but the *States* in their political character. It was improper therefore that it should tax the people." He, of course, was right, for at this stage in its creation the Constitution read that the Senate was to be chosen by the legislatures of the states, a method which did not change until the 17th amendment. The money issue was not finally resolved until September 8 when the Section read: "All Bills for raising revenue shall originate in the House of Representatives: but the Senate may propose or concur with amendments as on other bills."

Tuesday August 14, Wednesday August 15

On Wednesday, Rutledge "complained much of the tediousness of the proceedings." The delegates struggled on with details of the document they were writing, often voicing at great length their special convictions with which by now their colleagues were very familiar. Congressional members were declared ineligible during their terms to hold other government offices, the right to originate bills was again debated, as was the question of whether or not the Judiciary should interpret the Constitution. Mercer "disapproved of the

Doctrine that the Judges as expositors of the Constitution should have authority to declare a law void." Dickinson agreed with him "as to the power of the Judges to set aside the law. He thought no such power ought to exist. He was at the same time at a loss what expedient to substitute." As for overriding the Presidential veto, the Convention at this stage believed that three-fourths of each House must dissent with the President.

Thursday August 16, Friday August 17

Commerce and trade, money and insurrection were the subjects on these hot August days. At one point, when the delegates were debating the question of a national force, Gouverneur Morris observed that "we are acting a very strange part. We first form a strong man [the national legislature] to protect us, and at the same time wish to tie his hands behind him. The legislature may surely be trusted with such a power to preserve the public tranquility."

Saturday August 18

Rutledge moved this Saturday that a "Grand Committee" be appointed to "consider the necessity and expediency of the U. States assuming all the State debts — a regular settlement between the Union & the several States would never take place. The assumption would be just as the State debts were contracted in the common defence. It was necessary, as the taxes on imports the only sure source of revenue were to be given up to the Union. It was politic, as by disburdening the people of the State debts it would conciliate them to the plan." His motion passed and the committee members were Langdon, King, Sherman, Livingston, Clymer, Dickinson, McHenry, Williamson, Pinckney and Baldwin.

Ellsworth "observed that a Council had not yet been provided for the President. He conceived there ought to be one. His proposition was that it should be composed of the President of the Senate—the Chief-Justice, and the ministers as they might be established for the departments of foreign & domestic affairs, war, finance and marine, who should advise but not conclude the President."

As the Convention picked its way through the tedious detail work, delegates must have chafed at the endless task.

Rutledge "remarked on the length of the Session, the probable impatience of the public and the extreme anxiety of many members of the Convention to bring the business to an end; concluding with a motion that the Convention meet henceforward precisely at 10 OC. A.M. and that precisely at 4 OC. P.M. the President adjourn the House without motion for the purpose, and that no motion to adjourn sooner be allowed." His motion carried.

Monday August 20

Following Ellsworth's remarks the Saturday before concerning a Council for the President, Pinckney submitted a "Council of State" which included the Chief Justice, a Secretary of Domestic Affairs, a Secretary of Commerce and Finance, Secretary of Foreign Affairs, Secretary of War, Secretary of the Marine, Secretary of State "who shall be Secretary to the Council of State, and also public Secretary to the President. . . . The President may from time to time submit any matter to the discussion of the Council of State, and he may require the written opinions of any one or more of the members: But he shall in all cases exercise his own judgment, and either Conform to such opinions or not as he may think proper; and every officer above-mentioned shall be responsible for his opinion on the affairs relating to his particular Department." These officers were to be "liable to impeachment & removal from office for neglect of duty malversation [evil conduct], or corruption." It is interesting that such a council did not find its way into the final Constitution, but a Presidential Cabinet did come into being, at the pleasure of the President.

The nature of treason and how to deal with it was among the subjects debated on this Monday. Gouverneur Morris "was for giving to the Union an exclusive right to declare what should be treason," while Mason believed "The United States will have qualified sovereignty only. The individual States will retain a part of the Sovereignty. An Act may be treason against a particular State which is not so against the U. States." Franklin noted that "prosecutions for treason were generally virulent: and perjury too easily made use of against innocence." Wilson said that "treason may sometimes be practised in such a manner, as to render proof extremely difficult—as in a traitorous correspondence with an Enemy." Randolph did not think the President should have the power to pardon traitors, but King thought the power should not be granted to Congress.

And so it went. The delegates were still very close to the war and well aware of the many different opinions and loyalties in the young Republic. They also knew, from the history of not-so-distant times, rulers had often used the excuse of treason to extend their power. The Convention this day debated and voted seven different times to change the wording of Article VII, Section 2, a section consisting of four sentences.

In the end, the Constitution omits any mention of treason against a state and the power of punishment is lodged in the Congress to be used in very specific situations listed in Article III, Section 2.

Tuesday August 21

The Convention now listened to the report from the Committee of Eleven which had been set up on August 18 to deal with the questions of the nature of the militia and the debts of the states. Livingston gave the report, but the delegates moved that it "should lie on the table," and the Convention went on to the thorny problem of taxation. The Southern delegates feared the right of the Federal Government to tax their exports of agricultural products because the Northern states, in the majority, might levy ruinous duties on them. Williamson warned that if Congress were given this power "it would distroy the last hope of an adoption of the plan [the Constitution]." Gerry, too, "was strenuously opposed to the power over exports." He envisioned a kind of sinister blackmail: "It might be made use of to compel the States to comply with the will of the General Government, and to grant it any new powers which might be demanded. We have given it more power already than we know how will be exercised. It will enable the General Government to oppress the States as much as Ireland is oppressed by Great Britain." Even Mason agreed, going "on a principle often advanced & in which he concurred, that 'a majority when interested will oppress the minority.' This maxim had been verified by our own Legislature [of Virginia]. If we compare the States in this point of view the 8 Northern States have an interest different from the five Southern States; and have in one branch of the legislature 36 votes against 29, and in the other, in the proportion of 8 against 5. The Southern States had therefore good ground for their suspicions. The case of Exports was not the same with that of imports. The latter were the same throughout the States: The former very different."

Madison, who as usual argued for a strong central government, said that "we aught to be governed by national and permanent views, it is a sufficient argument for giving the power over exports that a tax, tho' it may not be expedient at present, may be so hereafter. A proper regulation of exports may & probably will be necessary hereafter, and for the same purposes as the regulation of imports; viz, for revenue — domestic manufactures — and procuring equitable regulations from other nations. An Embargo may be of absolute necessity, and can alone be effectuated by the General authority."

Wilson supported him. To take away from the Federal Government its power to tax exports "is to take from the Common Government half the regulation of trade. It was his opinion that a power over exports might be more effectual than that over imports in obtaining beneficial treaties of commerce."

But the Southern states, with Massachusetts and Connecticut voting with them, sustained the Committee of Detail's Section 4, Article VII: "No tax or duty shall be laid by the Legislature on articles exported from any State. . . ."

The second part of this same section dealt with the problem of a tax on slaves: that there be no tax or duty "on the migration or importation of such persons as the several States shall think proper to admit; nor shall such migration or importation be prohibited."

When this part of Section 4 was taken up, Martin made a proposal for "a prohibition or tax on the importation of slaves. 1. as five slaves are to be counted as 3 free men in the apportionment of Representatives; such a clause would leave an encouragement to this trafic. 2. slaves weakened one part of the Union which the other parts were bound to protect: the privilege of importing was therefore unreasonable. 3. it was inconsistent with the principles of the revolution and dishonorable to the American character to have such a feature in the Constitution."

Rutledge replied that he "did not see how the importation of slaves could be encouraged by this Section. He was not apprehensive of insurrections and would readily exempt the other States from the obligation to protect the Southern [States] against them. — Religion & humanity had nothing to do with this question. Interest alone is the governing principle with nations. The true question at present is whether the Southern States shall or shall not be parties to the Union. If the Northern States consult their interest, they will not oppose the increase of Slaves which will increase the commodities of which they will become the carriers."

Ellsworth was for letting "every State import what it pleases. The morality or wisdom of slavery are considerations belonging to the States themselves. What enriches a part enriches the whole, and the States are the best judges of their particular interest. The old confederation had not meddled with this point, and he did not see any greater necessity for bringing it within the policy of the new one."

And Pinckney warned that "South Carolina can never receive the plan if it prohibits the slave trade. In every proposed extension of the powers of the Congress, that State has expressly & watchfully excepted that of meddling with the importation of negroes. If the States be all left at liberty on this subject, S. Carolina may perhaps by degrees do of herself what is wished, as Virginia & Maryland have already done." He was speaking of the laws passed by Virginia and Maryland against slave importation. New Hampshire, Massachusetts, Rhode Island, Connecticut, New York and Pennsylvania had similar laws.

Wednesday August 22

The delegates continued the debates they had left the day before with Sherman leading off with the suggestion that Section 4 not be changed. "He disapproved of the slave trade; yet as the States were now possessed of the right to import slaves, as the public good did not require it to be taken from them, & as it was expedient to have as few objections as possible to the proposed scheme of Government, he thought it best to leave the matter as we find it. He observed that the abolition of Slavery seemed to be going on in the U.S. & that the good sense of the several States would probably by degrees compleat it."

Mason of Virginia gave the strongest condemnation of the slave trade to be heard at the Convention. "This infernal trafic originated in the avarice of British Merchants. The British Government constantly checked the attempts of Virginia to put a stop to it. The present question concerns not the importing States alone but the whole Union. The evil of having slaves was experienced during the late war. Had slaves been treated as they might have been by the Enemy, they would have proved dangerous instruments in their hands." He called to mind slave insurrections during the past in other countries. "Maryland & Virginia he said had already prohibited the importation of slaves expressly. N. Carolina had done the same in substance. All this would be in vain if S. Carolina & Georgia be at liberty to import. The Western people are already calling out for slaves for their new lands, and will fill that Country with slaves if they can be got thro' S. Carolina & Georgia. Slavery discourages arts & manufactures. The poor despise labor when performed by slaves. They prevent the immigration of Whites, who really enrich & strenghten a Country. They produce the most pernicious effect on manners. Every master of slaves is born a petty tyrant. They bring the judgment of heaven on a Country. As nations can not be rewarded or punished in the next world they must be in this. By an inevitable chain of causes & effects providence punishes national sins, by national calamities. He lamented that some of our Eastern brethren had from a lust of gain embarked in this nefarious traffic. As to the States being in possession of the Right to import, this was the case with many other rights, now to be properly given up. He held it essential in every point of view that the General Government should have power to prevent the increase of slavery."

Ellsworth observed "that if it was to be considered in a moral light we ought to go farther and free those already in the Country. . . . Let us not intermeddle. As population increases poor laborers will be so plenty as to render slaves useless. Slavery in time will not be a speck in our Country. Provision is already made in Connecticut for abolishing it. And the abolition has already taken place in Massachusetts. As to the danger of insurrections from foreign influence, that will become a motive to kind treatment of the slaves."

But Pinckney justified the owning of slaves with examples through history and "the sanction given by France, England, Holland & other modern States. In all ages one half of mankind have been slaves. If the S. States were let alone they will probably of themselves stop importations. He would himself as a Citizen of S. Carolina vote for it. An attempt to take away the right . . . will produce serious objections to the Constitution which he wished to see adopted."

His Cousin, General Pinckney, agreed with him saying that it was "his firm opinion that if himself & all his colleagues were to sign the Constitution & use their personal influence, it would be of no avail towards obtaining the assent of their Constituents."

Wilson noted "that if S.C. and Georgia were themselves disposed to get rid of the importation of slaves in a short time as had been suggested, they would never refuse to Unite because the importation might be prohibited. As the Section now stands all articles imported are to be taxed. Slaves alone are exempt. This is in fact a bounty on that article."

And Dickinson "considered it as inadmissible on every principle of honor & safety that the importation of slaves should be authorised to the States by the Constitution. The true question was whether the national happiness would be promoted or impeded by the importation, and this question ought to be left to the National Government not to the States particularly interested."

Langdon agreed. He wanted to give "the power to the General Government. He could not with a good conscience leave it with the States who could then go on with the traffic, without being restrained by the opinions here given that they will themselves cease to import slaves."

General Pinckney was honest. He declared "candidly that he did not think S. Carolina would stop her importations of slaves in any short time, but only stop them occasionally as she now does."

Rutledge was vehement. "If the Convention thinks that N.C., S.C. & Georgia will ever agree to the plan, unless their right to import slaves be untouched, the expectation is vain.

The people of those States will never be such fools as to give up so important an interest."

Sherman thought it better to let the Southern states import slaves than to lose them to the Union, something that was becoming more and more clearly evident. "He acknowledged that if the power of prohibiting the importation should be given to the General Government that it would be exercised. He thought it would be its duty to exercise the power."

The Convention was in a deadlock. The only possibility of finding a way out was to refer the problem to a committee. General Pinckney moved that this be done. Randolph spoke up for it "in order that some middle ground might, if possible, be found. He could never agree to the clause as it stands. He would sooner risk the constitution. He dwelt on the dilemma to which the Convention was exposed. By agreeing to the clause, it would revolt the Quakers, the Methodists, and many others in the States having no slaves. On the other hand, two States might be lost to the Union."

Seven states were for forming a committee, three opposed. And so a committee was appointed, the members being Langdon, King, Johnson, Livingston, Clymer, Dickinson, Luther Martin, Madison, Williamson, Charles Cotesworth Pinckney, and Baldwin.

Thursday August 23, Friday August 24

The report of the Committee of Eleven which had been set up on August 18 to define the nature of the militia and state debts was studied in great detail these two days. The national legislature was given the power "To provide for calling forth the militia to execute the laws of the Union, suppress insurrections, and repel invasions;

"To make laws for organizing, arming, and disciplining the militia, and for governing such part of them as may be employed in the service of the U.S. reserving to the States, respectively, the appointment of Officers, and the authority of training the militia according to the discipline prescribed."

This, after arguments by those delegates urging the rights of states. Martin said he "was confident that the States would never give up the power over the Militia" and Gerry stormed "Let us at once destroy the State Governments have an Executive for life or hereditary, and a proper Senate, and then there would be some consistency in giving full powers to the General Government but as the States are not to be abolished, he wondered at the attempts that were made to give powers inconsistent with their existence. He warned the Convention against pushing the experiment too far. Some people will support a plan of vigorous Government at every risk. Others of a more democratic cast will oppose it with equal determination, and a Civil war may be produced by the conflict."

Legislative powers continued to be defined and strengthened. Usually such movement was resisted by the delegates who were ever alert to any diminishing of state power. But all agreed with the concept that the President should be a "single person."

On August 24, Livingston, who was chairman of the committee formed on the 22nd to resolve the thorny problem of a tax on slaves, gave as a compromise solution that importation of slaves be allowed until 1800, but a duty be laid on them "at a rate not exceeding the average of the duties laid on imports." No poll (capitation) tax was to be required "unless in proportion to the census hereinbefore directed to be taken." The section requiring that any navigation act should be passed by two thirds of both houses of the Legislature was to be stricken out.

The reality behind this compromise was that the Southern states could continue to import slaves, pay duty on them, until 1800. Congress had to levy poll taxes according to census reports and not arbitrarily levy a heavy poll tax on slaves. With these gains, the Southern states must then give up the two-thirds requirements for passage of navigation acts in favor of a simple majority in Congress.

Saturday August 25

Today, the cutoff date for importation of slaves was increased to 1808, even though Madison warned that "twenty years will produce all the mischief that can be apprehended from liberty to import slaves. So long a term will be more dishonorable to the National character than to say nothing about it in the Constitution." General Pinckney, who had slaves, brought up the motion while Gorham, whose state had no slaves but had ships to transport them, seconded the motion which was passed. The delegates were uneasy about using the term "slaves" in the Constitution, and agreed to refer to them as "such persons." Another Convention crisis was averted at a high cost to be paid almost a century later with the Civil War. But in 1787, the delegates found no other way to keep the Southern states in the Union.

Monday August 27, Tuesday August 28, Wednesday August 29

A wide variety of miscellaneous problems were taken up during these days, from the wording of the Presidential oath of office to the salaries for judges; from coinage of money to raising revenue. Because of the yielding of the Northern states to the demands of the Southern states on the slavery issue, there was an atmosphere at this time of co-operation and civility. It was in this mood of compromise that it was agreed that navigation acts would be passed with a simple majority rather than a two-thirds vote in Congress. Agreement immediately followed that "If any person bound to service or labor in any of the U. States shall escape into another State, he or she shall not be discharged from such service or labor, in consequence of any regulations subsisting in the State to which they escape, but shall be delivered up to the person justly claiming their service or labor."

It is interesting that no delegate raised his voice against this Article XV dealing with runaway slaves because undoubtedly they were fearful of bringing to the surface again the distrust the Southerners had of the motives of the Middle and Northern states. They surely were remembering the long road they had followed, trying to build enough confidence to make unity possible, but must have secretly wondered if the compromises they were required to make were too great. Indicative was Randolph's comment "that there were features so odious in the constitution as it now stands, that he doubted whether he should be able to agree to it."

Thursday August 30

Among points of detail discussed this day, the members considered the admission of new States into the Union. It was agreed that "New States may be admitted by the Legislature into this Union; but no new State shall be hereafter formed or erected within the jurisdiction of any of the present States, without the consent of the Legislature of such State as well as of the general Legislature." This laid to rest lingering fears which might have resulted from earlier discussions of abolishing states or state mergers.

The delegates also passed Article XVIII which guaranteed each state a Republican form of government and provided protection for individual States "against foreign invasions, and, on the application of its Legislature [or Executive], against domestic violence."

Friday August 31

A discussion which had begun the day before was continued on how many states would need to approve the Constitution in order for it to become law. Carroll had said that 13 states should certainly be required for dissolving the Confederacy which had been established unanimously. Others suggested seven, eight and nine states. There also was the question of whether ratification be done by a state convention or the state legislatures. Madison was for conventions because "the powers given to the General Government being taken from the State Governments the Legislatures would be more disinclined than conventions composed in part at least of other men; and if disinclined, they could devise modes apparently promoting, but really, thwarting the ratification." On the other hand, Martin "insisted on a reference to the State Legislatures."

Finally, the assembly agreed that the approval of nine states would be sufficient for ratification and that the Constitution should first be laid before the Congress with the opinion of the delegates that it "should be afterwards submitted to a Convention chosen in each State, under the recommendation of its Legislature, in order to receive the ratification of such Convention."

This was done with the despairing remarks from Mason "that he would sooner chop off his right hand than put it to the Constitution as it now stands;" and Gouverneur Morris saying "he had long wished for another Convention, that will have the firmness to provide a vigorous Government, which we are afraid to do;" and Randolph suggesting that "in case the final form of the Constitution should not permit him to accede to it, that the State Conventions should be at liberty to propose amendments to be submitted to another General Convention which may reject or incorporate them, as shall be judged proper."

The long debates, the hot, stuffy days, the compromises with deeply held beliefs were taking their toll.

Saturday September 1, Monday September 3, Tuesday September 4

As part of the final approval of the Legislature's powers, the Convention authorized it "to exercise exclusive legislation in all cases whatsoever over such district (not exceeding ten miles square) as may by cession of particular States and the acceptance of the Legislature become the seat of the Government of the United States. . . ." From this sentence came the creation of the District of Columbia and its long battle for self-government which extends even to today.

The Convention also discussed the mode of electing the President and the plan of the Electoral College in which each state appoints a number of Electors equal to its members in Congress. The Electors meet in their respective states and vote by ballot for two persons, at least one of whom is not a citizen of that same state, and send their votes to the President of the Senate. The person with the greatest number of votes is President; if more than one has a majority, the House of Representatives by ballot chooses the President.

Gouverneur Morris gave as an explanation for this method of selection that "as the Electors would vote at the same time throughout the U.S. and at so great a distance from each other, the great evil of cabal was avoided. It would be impossible also to corrupt them."

Through this method of election, the delegates were attempting to avoid "the danger of intrigue & faction if the appointment should be made by the Legislature" and thus make the executive and legislative branches separate.

Wednesday September 5, Thursday September 6, Friday September 7, Saturday September 8

At the beginning of the Convention the members had expected to be finished by September; they now were impatient to end the tedious examination of the Constitution's details. Citizens barred from their activities were equally impatient to learn what was going on and this gave the delegates an additional feeling of urgency. There was more discussion of the mode of electing the President and a sense of dissatisfaction with the method they had worked out, yet no better solution appeared.

The Convention also considered a number of duties of the President including his power to make treaties "with the advice and consent of the Senate." Some of the members urged that two thirds of the Senate must approve treaties, for there was concern among Southern states and Western areas that navigation rights on the Mississippi be maintained and not given away to Spain or some other foreign power. As finally passed, the Constitution read that "no Treaty shall be made without consent of two thirds of the Members present."

Once again, the question of a council (cabinet) for the President was brought up with Mason warning "that in rejecting a Council to the President we were about to try an experiment on which the most despotic Governments had never ventured." Franklin agreed with him, saying "a Council would not only be a check on a bad President but a relief to a good one."

Gouverneur Morris demurred; he said the Committee of Eleven had considered the question of a Council but "judged that the President by persuading his Council, to concur in his wrong measures, would acquire their protection for them." The Convention went along with the Committee decision.

Finally, a Committee was appointed by Ballot "to revise the stile of and arrange the articles which had been agreed to by the House." The members of this important Committee were Johnson of Connecticut, Hamilton of New York, Gouverneur Morris of Pennsylvania, Madison of Virginia and King of Massachusetts. Johnson was named chairman.

Monday September 10

The Convention met this day to gather up final loose ends before the Committee of Style went to work in earnest. A few pet ideas were repeated, a few small skirmishes as though they were loathe — now that the final days were approaching — to let go of the document.

Tuesday September 11

"The report of the Committee of Stile & arrangement not being made & being waited for, The House Adjourned."

Wednesday September 12

"Doctor Johnson from the Committee of stile etc. reported a digest of the plan, of which printed copies were ordered to be furnished to the members. He also reported a letter to accompany the plan, to Congress."

These are Madison's words in his journal for the day. Once more, let us read the original preamble and compare it with the inspiring one which the Committee wrote:

"We the people of the States of New Hampshire, Massachusetts, Rhode-Island and Providence Plantations, Connecticut, New-York, New-Jersey, Pennsylvania, Delaware, Maryland, Virginia, North-Carolina, South-Carolina, and Georgia, do ordain, declare and establish the following Constitution for the Government of Ourselves and our Posterity."

And the rewritten preamble: "WE, THE PEOPLE OF THE UNITED STATES, IN ORDER TO FORM a more perfect union, to establish justice, insure domestic tranquility, provide for the common defence, promote the general welfare, and secure the blessings of liberty to ourselves and our posterity, do ordain and establish this Constitution for the United States of America." (Minor changes were made later.)

Gouverneur Morris, a particularly strong advocate of centralized government, is credited with giving this document its clear and inspiring language, with the concurrence of the rest of the Committee of Style. This beautifully-expressed preamble shows an important difference from the earlier version: the all-encompassing phrase "people of the United States" is used rather than naming the states to emphasize the national character of the government and its direct connection with the people.

By agreement the Constitution's ratification would be accomplished by any nine of the states. The much debated requirements for approval were expressed in the final Article VII: "The ratification of the conventions of nine States, shall be sufficient for the establishment of this constitution between the States so ratifying the same."

A cumbersome document of 23 articles had been turned over to the members of the Committee of Style; in only four days they had simplified and shortened it to the document of seven articles which — with slight changes made in September — we have today.

Along with the document, the Committee had drafted a letter to accompany it to be signed by George Washington. In final form it began: "Sir, We have now the honor to submit to the consideration of the United States in Congress assembled, that Constitution which has appeared to us the most adviseable." The letter went on to explain what they had done and why. "Individuals entering into society must give up a share of liberty to preserve the rest. The magnitude of the sacrifice must depend as well on situation and circumstance, as on the object to be obtained. It is at all times difficult to draw with precision the line between those rights which must be surrendered, and those which may be reserved; and on the present occasion this difficulty was encreased by a difference among the several States as to their situation, extent, habits, and particular interest.

"In all our deliberations on this subject we kept steadily in our view, that which appears to us the greatest interest of every true American, the consolidation of our union, in which is involved our prosperity, felicity, safety, perhaps our national existence. This important consideration, seriously and deeply impressed on our minds, led each State in the Convention to be less rigid on points of inferior magnitude, than might have been otherwise expected; and thus the Constitution, which we now present, is the result of a spirit of amity, and of that mutual deference and concession which the peculiarity of our political situation rendered indispensible."

Evidently the letter did not cause debate. It was not printed with the Constitution, but was read and agreed to paragraph by paragraph. But the delegates began immediately going through the new version of the Constitution, making final changes. Williamson asked that the delegates reconsider the clause requiring three fourths of each House to overrule a Presidential veto. He was for a two thirds vote as were Sherman and others. Mason agreed, with a view "to guard against too great an impediment to the repeal of laws." The clause was changed to two-thirds.

Mason "wished the plan [Constitution] had been prefaced with a Bill of Rights, & would second a Motion if made for the purpose. It would give great quiet to the people; and with the aid of the State declarations, a bill might be prepared in a few hours." Gerry agreed and the idea was put in the form of a motion.

Sherman "was for securing the rights of the people where requisite. The State Declarations of Rights are not repealed by this Constitution; and being in force are sufficient."

The delegates were tired, eager to be done. They had spent much longer away from home than they had intended. More days of work on the document could not be tolerated. They all voted against the motion which, had it been brought up earlier in the summer, might have passed, or at least would have been considered more carefully, even by those who thought the enumeration of rights unnecessary. It was one of the few errors in judgment the Convention made — and one which caused considerable difficulty during the ratification process.

Thursday September 13

Johnson made another report from the Committee of Style which used Articles 22 and 23 from the Constitution as the basis for a separate Resolution of the Convention to be signed by George Washington. The resolution stated that the preceding Constitution "laid before the U. States in Congress assembled," and then submitted to state conventions. It also stated "that it is the opinion of this Convention, that as soon as the Conventions of nine States shall have ratified this Constitution," it would go into effect with the choosing of the various members of government.

Friday September 14

Among the many small changes and additions brought up by the delegates, Madison and Pinckney moved "to insert in the list of powers vested in Congress a power— 'to establish an University in which no preferences or distinctions should be allowed on account of Religion.'" Gouverneur Morris thought it was "not necessary" and the motion was voted down.

Pinckney and Gerry moved to insert a declaration "that the liberty of the Press should be inviolably observed." This time, Sherman said "It is unnecessary. The power of Congress does not extend to the Press" and this, too, was voted down.

Saturday September 15

On this final working day of the Convention, Carroll "reminded the House that no address to the people had yet been prepared. He considered it of great importance that such an one should accompany the Constitution. The people had been accustomed to such on great occasions, and would expect it on this." But Rutledge objected to the delay it would cause and besides he felt it would be improper to address the people "before it was known whether Congress would approve and support the plan." The delegates went along with him.

In these final hours, Randolph, Mason and Gerry showed increasing dissatisfaction with the document. When Article V, relating to the amending of the Constitution, was being discussed, Mason said he "thought the plan of amending the Constitution exceptional & dangerous" fearing that "no amendments of the proper kind would ever be obtained by the people, if the Government should become oppressive, as he verily believed would be the case."

A short while later, he expressed "his discontent at the power given to Congress by a bare majority to pass navigation acts, which he said would not only enhance the freight, a consequence he did not so much regard—but would enable a few rich merchants in Philadelphia, N. York & Boston, to monopolize the Staples of the Southern States. . . ."

Randolph now also expressed his dissatisfaction with "the indefinite and dangerous power given by the Constitution to Congress, expressing the pain he felt at differing from the body of the Convention, on the close of the great & awful subject of their labours, and anxiously wishing for some accommodating expedient which would relieve him from his embarrassments." He moved that amendments to the Constitution be offered by the state conventions, which would then be submitted to and finally decided on by another general convention. "Should this proposition be disregarded," he said, "it would be impossible for him to put his name to the instrument. Whether he should oppose it afterwards he would not then decide but he would not deprive himself of the freedom to do so in his own State, if that course should be prescribed by his final judgment."

This must have been dismaying, coming from the person who had read to the Convention in May the Virginia Plan, the very basis for the Constitution. During the many weeks of debate, Randolph gradually had come to the conclusion that another convention was needed to rework the document. Without doubt the views of his esteemed colleague George Mason had a strong effect upon his decision.

Mason seconded Randolph's motion and "followed Mr. Randolph in animadversions of the dangerous power and structure of the Government, concluding that it would end either in monarchy, or a tyrannical aristocracy; which, he was in doubt, but one or other, he was sure. This Constitution had been formed without the knowledge or idea of the people. A second Convention will know more of the sense of the people, and be able to provide a system more consonant to it. It was improper to say to the people, take this or nothing. As the Constitution now stands, he could neither give it his support or vote in Virginia; and he could not sign here what he could not support there. With the expedient of another Convention as proposed, he could sign."

The delegates, exhausted, eager for it all to be over, anxious that their weeks of work not be for nought, must have been appalled at this reaction from two of their most respected colleagues. How much effect would these two dissenters have upon some of the other delegates who might still be sitting on the fence? They may have regretted their haste and lack of deliberation when considering Mason's numerous motions during the last few weeks. There was no doubt that Mason had been annoyed by the obvious hurry of the delegates to bring the meeting to an end. In our own times, we have only to recall the deliberations of Congress during the final days of a long, tiring session to understand the weariness and pressures on these men.

But there was, of course, much more to Mason's objections to the Constitution and the Convention than mere pique at having his ideas overriden. He thought the

Constitution should have a Bill of Rights, he was against the compromises made on the slavery issue, he feared the Southern states would lack the power to control their commerce, and he felt deeply that the people should somehow be brought into the government-making process.

It was Pinckney, another Southerner, who spoke to the objections of the two men. He began with "these declarations from members so respectable at the close of this important scene, give a peculiar solemnity to the present moment. He descanted on the consequences of calling forth the deliberations & amendments of the different States on the subject of Government at large. Nothing but confusion & contrariety could spring from the experiment. The States will never agree in their plans, and the Deputies to a second Convention coming together under the discordant impressions of their Constituents, will never agree. Conventions are serious things, and ought not to be repeated. He was not without objections as well as others to the plan. He objected to the contemptible weakness & dependence of the Executive. He objected to the power of a majority only of Congress over Commerce. But apprehending the danger of a general confusion, and an ultimate decision by the sword, he should give the plan his support."

The final speaker this day was Gerry who also stated he would not sign the document. He listed his objections: "1. the duration and reeligibility of the Senate. 2. the power of the House of Representatives to conceal their journals. 3. the power of Congress over the places of election. 4. the unlimited power of Congress over their own compensations. 5. Massachusetts has not a due share of Representatives allotted to her. 6. three-fifths of the Blacks are to be represented as if they were freemen. 7. Under the power over commerce, monopolies may be established. 8. The vice president being made head of the Senate. He could however he said get over all these, if the rights of the Citizens were not rendered insecure 1. by the general power of the Legislature to make what laws they may please to call necessary and proper. 2. raise armies and money without limit. 3. to establish a tribunal without juries, which will be a Star-chamber as to Civil cases. Under such a view of the Constitution, the best that could be done he conceived was to provide for a second general Convention."

No one replied. Randolph's motion for a second Convention was put to a vote: "All the States answered — no."

Then, "On the question to agree to the Constitution, as amended. All the States ay.

"The Constitution was then ordered to be engrossed.

"And the House adjourned."

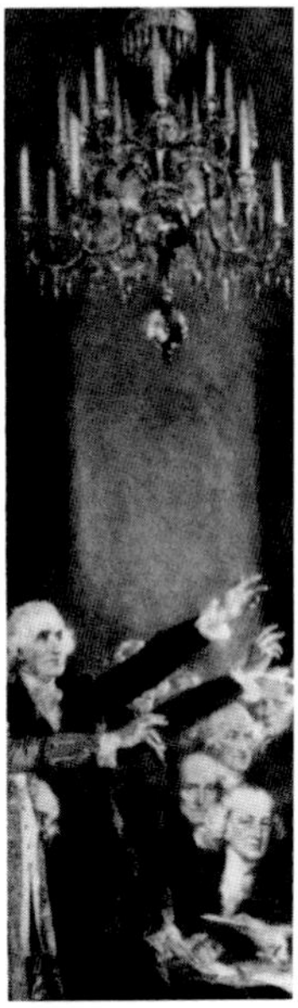

Monday September 17

Over the weekend, the Constitution had been engrossed (copied on parchment in fine script) and this morning it was read aloud to the Convention. There had been 55 delegates who had been present at one time or another; this morning there were 40.

After the document was read, their oldest, most diplomatic member — Benjamin Franklin — "rose with a speech in his hand, which he had reduced to writing for his own conveniency, and which Mr. Wilson read in the words following.

"Mr. President

"I confess that there are several parts of this constitution which I do not at present approve, but I am not sure I shall never approve them: For having lived long, I have experienced many instances of being obliged by better information, or fuller consideration, to change opinions even on important subjects, which I once thought right, but found to be otherwise. It is therefore that the older I grow, the more apt I am to doubt my own judgment, and to pay more respect to the judgment of others. Most men indeed as well as most sects in Religion, think themselves in possession of all truth, and that wherever others differ from them it is so far error. . . . But though many private persons think almost as highly of their own infallibility as of that of their sect, few express it so naturally as a certain french lady, who in a dispute with her sister, said 'I don't know how it happens, Sister but I meet with no body but myself, that's always in the right — *Il n'y a que moi qui a toujours raison.*

"In these sentiments, Sir, I agree to this Constitution with all its faults, if they are such; because I think a general Government necessary for us, and there is no form of Government but what may be a blessing to the people if well administered, and believe farther that this is likely to be well administered for a course of years, and can only end in Despotism, as other forms have done before it, when the people shall become corrupted as to need despotic Government, being incapable of any other. I doubt too whether any other Convention we can obtain, may be able to make a better Constitution. For when you assemble a number of men to have the advantage of their joint wisdom, you inevitably assemble with those men, all their prejudices, their passions, their errors of opinion, their local interests, and their selfish views. From such an assembly can a perfect production be expected? It therefore astonishes me, Sir, to find this system approaching so near to perfection as it does; and I think it will astonish our enemies, who are waiting with confidence to hear that our councils are confounded like those of the Builders of Babel; and that our States are on the point of separation, only to meet hereafter for the purpose of cutting one another's throats. Thus I consent, Sir, to the Constitution because I expect no better, and because I am not sure, that it is not the best."

Franklin then went on to emphasize that what objections he might have to it, he would keep to himself rather than giving encouragement to those who would oppose the Convention's work, He ended with "On the whole, Sir, I can not help expressing a wish that every member of the convention who may still have objections to it, would with me, on this occasion doubt a little of his own infallibility, and to make manifest our unanimity, put his name to this instrument.—"

Franklin then "moved that the Constitution be signed by the members and offered the following as a convenient form viz. 'Done in Convention by the unanimous consent of the States present the 17th of September & c — In Witness whereof we have hereunto subscribed our names.'"

Madison noted at this point that "the ambiguous form" had been drawn up by Gouverneur Morris and given to Franklin to present, for in this way it "might have the better chance for success." By wording the sentence "the unanimous consent of the States" it would appear to the public that all the delegates had agreed to the document.

Before the motion came to a vote, Gorham said "if it was not too late" he would like to see a Representative for every

30,000 persons, rather than for every 40,000 in order to lessen objections to the Constitution.

And for the first time the whole summer, George Washington rose to offer an opinion. He said "that although his situation had hitherto restrained him from offering his sentiments on questions depending in the House, and it might be thought, ought now to impose silence on him, yet he could not forbear expressing his wish that the alteration proposed might take place. It was much to be desired that the objections to the plan recommended might be made as few as possible. The smallness of the proportion of Representatives had been considered by many members of the Convention an insufficient security for the rights & interests of the people. He acknowledged that it had always appeared to himself among the exceptionable parts of the plan, and late as the present moment was for admitting amendments, he thought this of so much consequence that it would give much satisfaction to see it adopted."

The Convention, undoubtedly startled and somewhat awed to hear an opinion from Washington after all these weeks, agreed unanimously.

But still they could not let the curtain fall. Randolph had shown earlier that his loyalties were divided and that he had difficulty making up his mind. The moral power of both Franklin and Washington must have made him feel it was necessary to further explain his motives. He rose "and with an allusion to the observations of Doctor Franklin apologized for his refusing to sign the Constitution notwithstanding the vast majority & venerable names that would give sanction to its wisdom and its worth. He said however that he did not mean by this refusal to decide that he should oppose the Constitution without doors. He meant only to keep himself free to be governed by his duty as it should be prescribed by his future judgment. He refused to sign, because he thought the object of the Convention would be frustrated by the alternative which it presented to the people. Nine States will fail to ratify the plan and confusion must ensue. With such a view of the subject he ought not, he could not, by pledging himself to support the plan, restrain himself from taking such steps as might appear to him most consistent with the public good."

It is doubtful that his face-saving statement fooled his canny colleagues that his position was more than fence-sitting, waiting to see how the new document would fare in coming months.

Gouverneur Morris followed him by noting that "he too had objections, but considering the present plan as the best that was to be attained, he should take it with all its faults. The majority had determined in its favor and by that determination he should abide." Williamson, trying to find a way to bring everyone into the signing process, "suggested that the signing should be confined to the letter accompanying the Constitution to Congress, which might perhaps do nearly as well, and would he found be satisfactory to some members who disliked the Constitution. For himself he did not think a better plan was to be expected and had no scruples against putting his name to it."

Hamilton, who had not spoken up for weeks, now "expressed his anxiety that every member should sign. A few characters of consequence, by opposing or even refusing to sign the Constitution, might do infinite mischief by kindling the latest sparks which lurk under an enthusiasm in favor of the Convention which may soon subside. No man's ideas were more remote from the plan than his were known to be; but is it possible to deliberate between anarchy and Convulsion on one side, and the chance of good to be expected from the plan on the other." His colleagues, remembering his long, impassioned speech weeks before favoring a government tantamount to a monarchy, could not but be impressed by his support.

Blount, a North Carolina delegate who had not spoken before at the Convention, announced that although he had indicated earlier he would not sign, "was relieved by the form proposed and would without committing himself attest the fact that the plan was the unanimous act of the States in Convention." Gouverneur Morris' clever wording therefore added Blount to the signers.

Once more, Franklin made a bid to persuade Randolph. He "expressed his fears from what Mr. Randolph had said, that he thought himself alluded to in the remarks offered this morning to the House. He declared that when drawing up that paper he did not know that any particular member would refuse to sign his name to the instrument, and hoped to be so understood. He professed a high sense of obligation to Mr. Randolph for having brought forward the plan in the first instance, and for the assistance he had given in its progress, and hoped that he would yet lay aside his objections, and by concurring with his brethren, prevent the great mischief which the refusal of his name might produce."

But Randolph would not be persuaded, even by a master persuader like Franklin. He "could not but regard the signing in the proposed form, as the same with signing the Constitution. The change of form therefore could make no difference with him. He repeated that in refusing to sign the Constitution, he took a step which might be the most awful of his life, but it was dictated by his conscience, and it was not possible for him to hesitate, much less, to change. He repeated also his persuasion that the holding out this plan with a final alternative to the people of accepting or rejecting it in toto, would really produce the anarchy & civil convulsions which were apprehended from the refusals of individuals to sign it."

Gerry, another of the dissidents, "described the painful feelings of his situation, and the embarrassment under which he rose to offer any further observations on the subject which had been finally decided." He feared civil war, he said, in Massachusetts particularly where "there are two parties, one devoted to Democracy, the worst he thought of all political evils, the other as violent in the opposite extreme. From the collision of these in opposing and resisting the Constitution, confusion was greatly to be feared. He had thought it necessary, for this & other reasons that the plan should have been proposed in a more mediating shape. . . . He could not therefore by signing the Constitution pledge himself to abide by it at all events."

General Pinckney did not care for "the ambiguity of the proposed form of signing. He thought it best to be candid and let the form speak the substance. . . . He should sign the Constitution with a view to support it with all his influence, and wished to pledge himself accordingly."

Franklin, recognizing the hard road ahead, remarked that "it is too soon to pledge ourselves before Congress and our Constituents shall have approved the plan."

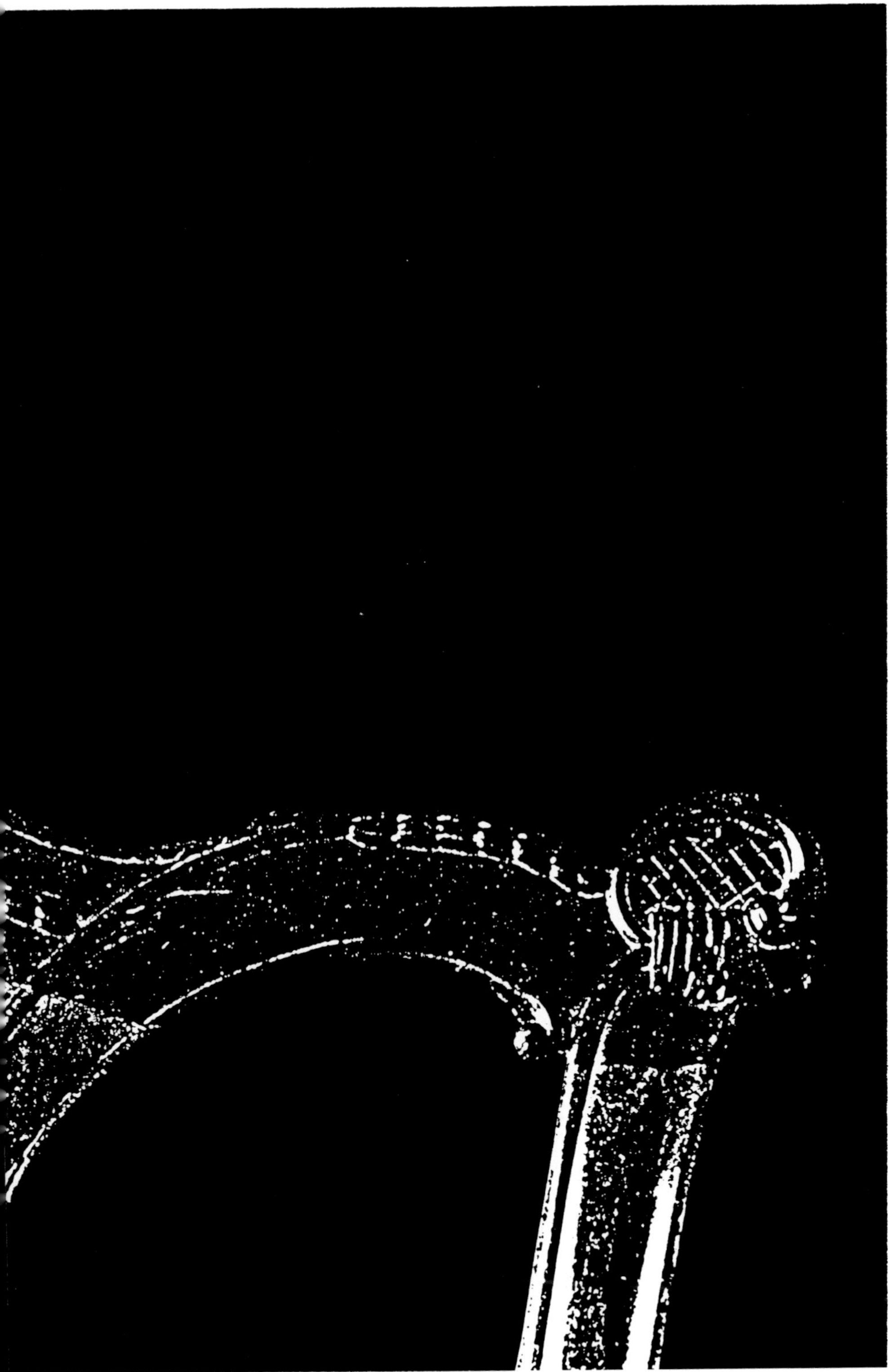

President's chair.

Ingersoll, who had not spoken before at the Convention, saw the signing not as a pledge of support "But as a recommendation of what, all things considered, was the most eligible."

It was finally time to vote on Franklin's motion on the form of signing the document. It passed.

King then suggested that the Journals of the Convention either be destroyed or deposited in the custody of the President for, if made public, "a bad use would be made of them by those who would wish to prevent the adoption of the Constitution." Wilson thought they should be held by the President so that there would be documents of proof should "false suggestions" be made later. This latter motion also passed.

Washington asked what the Convention wanted him to do with the records and whether copies were to be given to members on request. It was resolved unanimously "that he retain the Journal and other papers, subject to the order of the Congress, if ever formed under the Constituion."

It now was the moment to sign, the last act of the historic summer in this hallowed room. Members stepped forward according to their geographical order beginning with New Hampshire and down through Georgia. As they inscribed their names, one by one, they claimed for themselves the highest place in their nation's history, alongside those who had signed the Declaration of Independence here just 11 years earlier. One man, Roger Sherman, had actually signed the Continental Association of 1774, the Declaration of Independence and the Articles of Confederation before adding his name to the Constitution. With our knowledge today of the long, heated debates, the reluctant compromises, the lost individual goals that took place in this room during the summer, we can be sure that many of the delegates signed the document with misgivings and often with disappointment. With our present vantage point, Franklin's words earlier in the meeting take on a special wisdom: "I consent to this Constitution because I expect no better, and because I am not sure, that it is not the best."

And it was his words which were last recorded in Madison's precious journal: "Whilst the last members were signing it Doctor Franklin looking towards the President's

Chair, at the back of which a rising sun happened to be painted, observed to a few members near him, that Painters had found it difficult to distinguish in their art a rising from a setting sun. I have, said he, often and often in the course of the Session, and the vicissitudes of my hopes and fears as to its issue, looked at that behind the President without being able to tell whether it was rising or setting: But now at length I have the happiness to know that it is a rising and not a setting Sun."

Madison finished his awesome work with the simple sentence: "The Constitution being signed by all members except Mr. Randolph, Mr. Mason, and Mr. Gerry who declined giving it the sanction of their names, the Convention dissolved itself by an Adjournment *sine die* — "

William Jackson, the Convention's secretary, burned miscellaneous papers that afternoon. Washington later received from him the formal Journal of the Convention and the journal of the Committee of the Whole.

We have one final glimpse of that historic day from the words of George Washington's diary: "The business being closed, the Members adjourned to the City Tavern, dined together and took a cordial leave of each other; after which I returned to my lodgings, did some business with, and received the papers from the Secretary of the Convention, and retired to meditate on the momentous work which had been executed, after not less than five, and for a large part of the time, Six, and sometimes 7 hours sitting every day, except Sundays and the ten days adjournment to give a committee opportunity and time to arrange the business, for more than four months."

XI

EPILOGUE

TO CREATE A NATION

Federal Hall, the Seat of Congress, Washington's Inauguration, by A. Doolittle after Peter Lacour, 1790. Courtesy of the New York Public Library.

THE CURTAIN FALLS ON THE GREAT AMERICAN DRAMA of summer 1787. The weary players, unsure of the work upon which they toiled for many hot weeks, packed their bags and one by one quit Philadelphia. Carriages were engaged; horses and boats sought to take the travelers home or to New York. Ten of the delegates to the Philadelphia Convention, including Madison, were also members of Congress and it was crucial that they be in New York to further the cause of the Constitution as it was brought before that body.

The very next day after the Convention wound up its business, its secretary, Major William Jackson, left Philadelphia with a copy of the new document. He laid it before Congress two days later and that assembly set September 26 as the date it would consider the Constitution and decide whether or not to refer it to the States for ratification. It took them three days of debate to reach that decision.

And then the struggle to win the country's approval began. Secrecy was gone. The delegates were again out among their relatives and friends who were avid to know what had transpired those long weeks behind closed doors. Faint intimations had seeped out from evasive letters and conversations. Newspapers had helped keep interest alive by reporting rumors and commentary. Now the delegates were ready to speak—for and against—about what they had done, and their work was ready for all to read. On September 19, just two days after the Convention ended, the *Pennsylvania Packet* was the first newspaper to publish the Constitution. It devoted its entire issue to the document. As soon as they could get their hands on it, other newspapers followed suit.

Besides the newspapers, one of the most important ways the Constitution and its philosophy became known was by correspondence. Delegates sent copies and their own views to friends and political acquaintances who in turn passed on the information. Franklin gave out copies of his final remarks at the Convention, hoping to bolster support for ratification. One of the most prolific letter writers was Washington who sent messages of support far and wide. Documents from that period show that Mount Vernon was a focal point for spreading ideas about government-making, as guests and letters came and went. When he sent copies of the Constitution to three important Virginia leaders who would be involved in the ratification process—Patrick Henry, Benjamin Harrison and Thomas Nelson—Washington included a very carefully-worded note: "I wish the Constitution which is offered had been made more perfect, but I sincerely believe it is the best that could be obtained at this time; and, as a constitutional door is opened for amendment hereafter, the adoption of it under the present circumstances of the Union is, in my opinion, desirable." Patrick Henry's opposition, he knew, would be formidable.

The Federal Constitution was the prime creation of this period [colonial to federal union]: a work of genius, since it set up what every earlier political scientist had thought impossible, a sovereign union of sovereign states.
—SAMUEL ELIOT MORISON & HENRY STEELE COMMAGER

The approach Washington used seems to have been the common view of most of the delegates. In the autobiography of Charles Biddle of Philadelphia, published in 1802, this prominent man commented that he had been told by members of the Convention that "they did not believe a single member was *perfectly* satisfied with the Constitution, but they believed it was the best they could ever agree upon, and that it was infinitely better to have such a one than break up without fixing on some form of government. . . ."

By far the most long-lasting effort in this contest of ideas was that carried out by three men—Alexander Hamilton, James Madison and John Jay. Hamilton, the principal figure, began the series of essays signed "Publius" and called *The Federalist*. They were started initially to help win the fight for ratification in the State of New York where there was strong opposition. The foes of the Constitution were so powerful there that the state did not enter the Union until after the first nine states had ratified.

The essays, written largely by Hamilton and Madison, appeared in New York newspapers during the crucial months of public debate and were the most thought-provoking writing to appear at the time. Later brought together in a collection of 85 essays as *The Federalist Papers,* they take up various aspects of the constitutional process as was currently being argued among the general public. They have come down to us as masterpieces of understanding of the Constitution as intended by the framers.

It is interesting that Hamilton's brilliant support for the Constitution came from one who, on the last day of the Convention in Philadelphia, had said that "no man's ideas were more remote from the plan than his were known to be," yet who saw the new governmental concept as a "chance of good" away from anarchy and general disorder.

After the Convention, it did not take long for the people to begin taking sides. Those in favor of the centralized government as proposed by the Constitution became known as the Federalists; those who were opposed were called the Antifederalists. Most state ratification conventions were even more emotional than the Constitutional Convention in Philadelphia.

Feelings ran high among the general public as well, and often violent outbreaks occurred. Catherine Drinker Bowen in her book, *Miracle in Philadelphia,* recounts one such eruption when Pennsylvania ratified the document after particularly heated debates. James Wilson, the very effective delegate at Philadelphia, had played a leading part in guiding the Constitution through passage in his home state. "On December twenty-seventh, an outdoor rally was held at Carlisle, to celebrate the Constitution. There was a bonfire, and speeches. A mob of Antifeds (now so called), armed with clubs, rushed toward the fire and attacked James Wilson. When Wilson fought back they knocked him down and began to beat him as he lay. He would have been killed, it was said, had not an old soldier thrown himself on Wilson's body and taken the blows."

Bitter fights occurred in the state conventions themselves, particularly in Virginia, New York and North Carolina. In Virginia, Randolph—the man who had proposed the

Virginia Resolves back in May at the Convention and one of the three men who refused to sign the Constitution—surprised George Mason and other Antifederalists by reversing himself and supporting the document back home. The reason he gave was that after eight states had ratified, it was too late to demand amendments before adoption. Thereafter he supported Madison and the other Federalists, risking a potential duel with Patrick Henry, the stubborn Antifederalist leader who questioned the motives behind Randolph's changed position.

The Constitution is an experiment, as all life is an experiment.
—OLIVER WENDELL HOLMES.

In New York, the Antifederalists were well organized under the former Governor, George Clinton. Hamilton led the Federalists. He was greatly helped by the timely ratification by New Hampshire, the ninth state, followed by Virginia. New York's close passing vote of 30 to 27 was won with the belief that another Federal Convention would be called.

Delaware was the first to ratify, although its delegates at the Convention had been strictly forbidden in their instructions to support any change of the Articles of Confederation which affected their one-state one-vote rule. The final compromise on legislative representation certainly had done this with proportional representation in the House of Representatives. The other eight ratifying states which made the Constitution the law of the land were Pennsylvania, New Jersey, Georgia, Connecticut, Massachusetts, Maryland, South Carolina and New Hampshire. On June 21, 1788, just 13 months after the Constitutional Convention first began its deliberations, the approval of the country had been won.

It took two state conventions before North Carolina came into the Union on November, 1789, well after the new national government was organized. Rhode Island, which had not sent delegates to Philadelphia, did not enter the Union until 1790. After all the other states had made the Constitution the law of the land, the Senate of the new government passed a bill breaking commercial relations with the little hold-out state. Only then, did Rhode Island vote to enter the Union with a narrow margin of 34 to 32. Soon after ratification, Washington wrote to the state's Governor, Arthur Fenner: "Since the bond of union is now complete, and we once more consider ourselves as one family, it is much to be hoped that reproaches will cease and prejudice be done away;

for we should all remember that we are members of that community upon whose general success depends our particular and individual welfare; and, therefore, if we mean to support the Liberty and Independence which it has cost us so much blood and treasure to establish, we must drive far away the daemon of party spirit and local reproach."

After New Hampshire and Virginia ratified the Constitution, Congress put in motion the forming of the new government. On August 6, 1788, Congress agreed electors were to be chosen and on April 30, 1789, George Washington was inaugurated the first President of the United States. At the very first session of the new Congress the first ten amendments, the nation's Bill of Rights, were proposed to the states. They became effective December 15, 1791, a vital addition to the Constitution. While the Philadelphia Convention had failed to recognize the need for these guarantees, the clamor from individuals and state ratifying conventions for the protection of basic rights made such amendments one of the first orders of business. The Bill of Rights made the Constitution one in which people as a whole had had a part in shaping.

Considering the widely divergent opinions held among the population, the difficulty of bringing news and ideas from one place to another, the passionate hold certain convictions had upon some leaders, it seems almost impossible that the Constitution could have been accepted so quickly. But the country had a singularly precious element: A public deeply interested in government, a distrust of unlimited power and an eagerness to discuss politics at every possible occasion. The average person who cared nothing for politics, who was uninterested in the functioning of his government, was looked down upon by his compatriots. Visitors from Europe were amazed at how caught up in politics the general public was and how well-informed the average person was about political theories of the day. It was an age of ferment both in America and in Europe and the young country had been closely involved in the nature of government and power.

There is no doubt, however, that the making of the Constitution broke new ground. As we look back through the pages of this book which follow Madison's notes on the Convention, we cannot help but see that the drama the delegates enacted in Philadelphia was an education in itself.

Many of the delegates began the Convention with somewhat hazy ideas of how the Articles of Confederation were defective. Even delegates so astute as Madison and Wilson were to learn something about the importance of proportional versus one-state one-vote representation in a national legislature. As the drama unfolded through the weeks, we can see how in the interchange of ideas the delegates came to grips with the fundamentals of self-government. They left Philadelphia changed men, far wiser in the art of government than when they first arrived.

One more time let us glance around that small room and single out a few of those remarkable figures, perspiring in their formal attire—bored, angry, earnest, through that amazing summer:

Washington, sitting silently in the President's chair or moving down to vote with the Virginia delegation, giving little indication of his views. A presence needed to hold the meeting in order, a moral influence. A faithful, quiet presence, breaking silence only to demand that the rule of secrecy be kept and on the last day to offer an amendment to the article on proportional representation. Yet we know from his letters how worried he was about the outcome of the event.

Franklin, the 81-year-old sage, who deliberately used the veneration of his fellow delegates to calm them in times of anger during the debates, to project his own spirit of compromise—and particularly on the last day to remind them that one's judgment is not infallible.

Madison, sitting day after day, scribbling his precious notes, using every debater's strategy to win support for his stand on congressional representation. Yet when he had to accept the Grand Compromise, he went on to fight for other goals with unabated purpose and energy.

Wilson, ally of Madison, Washington and Franklin, who expressed issues with great clarity and brought home to his fellow delegates the fundamentals they should be addressing in a particular debate.

Gouverneur Morris, the flamboyant figure in the room, given to florid speeches, yet, as a member of the Committee of Style, turning a pedantic document into the clear, ringing words of the Constitution which the general public can read and understand.

It will be considered, I believe, as a most extraordinary epoch in the history of mankind that in a few years there should be so essential a change in the minds of men. 'Tis really astonishing that the same people, who have just emerged from a long and cruel war in defence of liberty, should now agree to fix an elective despotism upon themselves and their posterity.
—RICHARD HENRY LEE

Hamilton, not quite accepted by the other delegates, whose early speech advocating a kingly government helped members make up their minds to form a very different system than he proposed. An individual able to take a wider view and accept a document contrary to his desires yet one which might save the country from ruin.

The good sense of Sherman, suggesting early on a solution which eventually became the Great Compromise; Charles Pinckney who at a crucial moment deflected the strong arguments of Randolph and Mason for a second Federal Convention; Mason who repeatedly reminded the delegates of their responsibility to the people. Paterson, Dickinson, Gerry and other "small" state dissenters performing a great service in helping the Convention to produce a document which preserved the rights of the states and was more responsive to the average citizen. The yeasty mix of personalities and ideas produced many examples of individual delegates expressing the right idea at the right moment.

These men of the Convention, once the battle for ratification was over, were to take places of prominence in the new government. Washington and Madison became Presidents; Madison also a Secretary of State; Hamilton, Secretary of the Treasury; McHenry, Secretary of War; Rutledge, Chief Justice of the United States; Paterson, Wilson and Blair, Associate Justices of the Supreme Court; Langdon, Gilman, King, Johnson, Sherman, Dayton, Gouverneur Morris, Robert Morris, Read, Bassett, Carroll, Blount, Butler, Few and Baldwin, Senators; Clymer, FitzSimons, Spaight, Williamson, Representatives; Dayton, Speaker of the House; King, Minister to Great Britain; Gouverneur Morris and Charles Cotesworth Pinckney, Ministers to France; Charles Pinckney, Minister to Spain; Brearley, Ingersoll, Bedford, federal judges; Gerry, Representative in the First Congress and Vice-President under Madison; Randolph, Attorney General and Secretary of State under Washington.

The new government, therefore, was strengthened in its first years by having in its ranks a large number of the delegates involved — men who could remember the compromises and debates and knew why the government was formed in the manner it had been, and how the Convention had meant it to function. This early involvement cannot be ignored as a vital force in helping to set the new nation upon its course. Strong advocates of the Constitution and violent dissenters joined to make it work successfully.

Their fellow citizens had not had the advantage of the educational process of the Convention. They had not gone through the long days, sometimes inspiring but often tedious, of working out compromises, listening to opinions quite different from their own, learning the social and economic concerns of those from another part of the country. For that reason, the delegates as they came forth from Philadelphia were essential to the general process of country-wide understanding. It was a new perspective for the average person to see himself not just as the citizen of a state but as the citizen of a union of states. A man from Connecticut now must think of the important economics of export shipments of rice and indigo for the State of Georgia. And the Virginia gentleman must be aware of the importance of foreign trade to the Port of New York.

It was a revolution of ideas, an expansion of horizons. In our own time, we can consider how our own views have expanded. While deepening our attachment to the United States, we see ourselves much more as members of the human community living together on this planet. Like our 18th-century ancestors who began to consider the fate of their brothers in other states, so we realize we must be concerned about the welfare of people living in China or Australia.

In its time, the Constitution was a new kind of governing instrument, coming from a new breed of people different from those of any other continent. A system of checks and balances among three branches of government, designed to control the use of power and make government the tool not the tyrant of its citizens. A system preserving the rights of statehood, yet also a central body elected by the people, which ruled the whole nation. Such a remarkable balancing act had never been tried before. And as the Constitution continued to work effectively through the decades, other countries, particularly emerging nations after World War II, used it as a guide in drafting their own constitutions. Other countries which have shed old forms not responsive to the people, have revised their governments

> ***In all governments, whatever is their form, however they may be constituted, there must be a power established from which there is no appeal, and which is therefore called absolute, supreme, and uncontrollable. The only question is where that power is lodged? . . . for in truth, it remains and flourishes with the people.***
> — JAMES WILSON, *delegate from Pennsylvania*

with ideas taken from the Philadelphia document. Fundamental in creating the kind of individuals we are in the United States, it also is one of the major contributions our nation has made to the world.

While recognizing the formidable achievement of the Philadelphia delegates, we can join them in wishing that the document could have been more perfect than it apparently was possible at that time. Besides failing to recognize the importance of having a Bill of Rights, the Convention almost forgot to spell out the nature of the federal court system. According to Max Farrand in *The Fathers of the Constitution*, "Nowhere in the document itself is there any word as to that great power which has been exercised by the Federal courts of declaring null and void laws or parts of laws that are regarded as in contravention to the Constitution." There is a paragraph, however, toward the end of the document which says that the Constitution "shall be the supreme Law of the Land" and that "judges in every State shall be bound thereby" (Article VI), which does define the national power over the states. It was, of course, John Marshall, Chief Justice of the United States, who set the direction the Supreme Court has followed down to this day. According to Justice Felix Frankfurter, "When Marshall came to the Supreme Court, the Constitution was still essentially a virgin document. By a few opinions—a mere handful—he gave institutional direction to the inert ideas of a paper scheme of government." Again, the country is fortunate that it had such a Chief Justice at that crucial time.

Students of government also wonder if some way could have been found at the Convention to determine the constitutionality of a law as soon as it is passed by Congress. The delegates saw no method of determination without violating the separation of powers between the executive and judiciary. Yet if a way could be found to accomplish this, unconstitutional laws would no longer stay in force, as they do today, until they have been finally challenged in federal court—a process which often takes years.

There are other flaws from which we were not saved. In our time, we look in vain for any recognition of the rights of women, a situation which was not changed until August 1920 after much pain and struggle by suffragettes to pass an amendment guaranteeing voting rights to women. Far more devastating to the country was the Convention's inability or failure to come to grips with the slavery issue. Particularly, we would wish that some of the leading delegates had joined with Mason in trying to find a better way of confronting the slavery problem, pushing for a shorter time limit on the importation of slaves and indentured servants, searching for extra inducements which would have secured Georgia and South Carolina for the Union, yet would have brought the custom to a foreseeable end. As we read George Mason's remarks in the notes of the Convention, it appears he somehow lacked the tenacity of a Madison or a Wilson to insist upon his admirable ideas and to gather support for them.

We are now really another people.
— THOMAS PAINE

But by the time the Convention took place, the whole life and economy of the Southern states were embedded in a slave-holding culture. And finally, to wonder why such gross errors were made is to rip the Philadelphia Convention out of the context of the 18th century. It was an accepted thing that women had no legal status then, just as slavery was practiced in many parts of the world and had been for centuries. The delegates reflected their qualms about the practice, but came to the view that the Union would not hold and the Constitution would be unacceptable to the South if they tampered with this basic tenent of their society.

The delegates, feeling the document they had created was imperfect, left room for change, and 26 amendments have been added to address new needs. We, in the years of the Bicentennial of our government's creation, re-examine the document for possible amendments to make it more compatible with our own times—as the delegates would certainly have wished us to do.

It is remarkable in this re-examination that we find so few ways to improve the 200-year-old plan. An august Committee on the Constitutional System looks for ways to make our government function more effectively; historians and students of government have suggestions on their own. One of these asks for controls on campaign expenditures. Campaign costs in recent years has made it almost prohibitive for a person of modest means—however highly qualified—to run for office unless he or she accepts funds from individuals or groups who have special agenda in mind.

According to the Committee's statistics, in the 1986 election, $350 million was spent by national legislative candidates, and most of it was contributed by single-interest groups. This was 50 percent above the amount spent four years earlier. "Nothing does more to weaken party cohesion," the Committee members say, "and to produce a hodgepodge of inconsistent government actions." Historian Henry Steele Commager suggests that Congress refuse to seat anyone who has exceeded a certain fixed amount of money to get elected.

An amendment to the Constitution advocated by the Committee is a change in the length of term for Congress members. They recommend that members of the House of Representatives be elected for four instead of two years, and Senators for eight-year terms. The House terms would run simultaneously with the Presidential term along with half the Senators. The electorate would be besieged with fewer campaign periods and legislators could make more effective use of in-office time.

Other students of government feel that through law or amendment, powers of the executive branch should be more sharply defined. They point out specifically a clarification of the power to declare war, the nature of "national security," executive secrecy in relationship to the legislative branch. Some express concern that the governmental process conceivably could slide into a more "kingly" form of government than was originally intended—except, of course, by Alexander Hamilton.

Other suggested reforms come from biographer Ronald Steel, for Parliament-style monthly visits of the President to Capitol Hill for questioning; and from Jimmy Carter for treaty ratification by a majority of the Senate rather than the two-thirds vote.

We today must join hands with those Philadelphia leaders in trying to find ways to make government responsive to problems in our rapidly changing world. It is our debt to the political fathers of the Convention who made possible our bountiful life; it is our duty to ourselves today; and especially it is our responsibility toward the next generations who must find their way in the new century. This precious gift of choice, of freedom to change, which has been bequeathed to us, is forever beyond price.

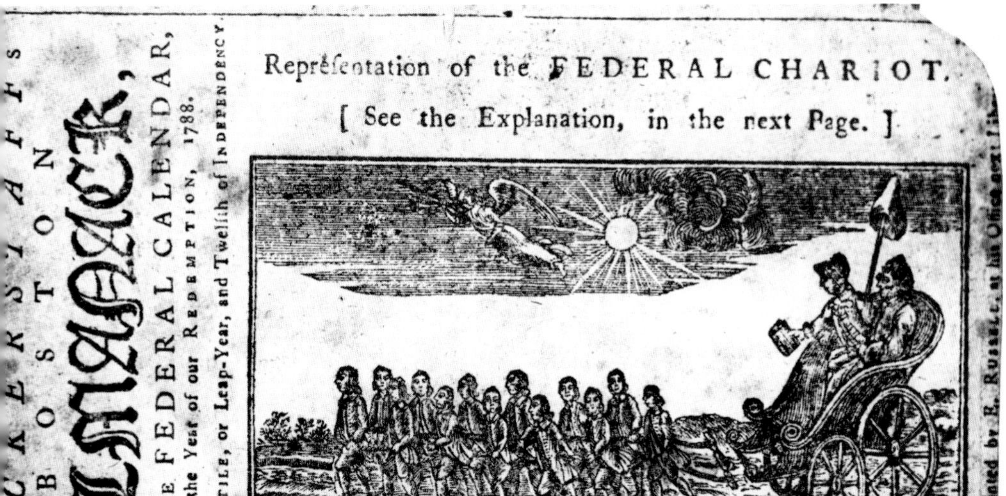

Bickerstaff's Boston Almanack,
or The Federal Calendar (detail),
Washington and Franklin
driving the "Federal Chariot,"
pulled by the 13 states, toward ratification, 1788.
Courtesy of the American Antiquarian Society.

THE CONSTITUTION AND AMENDMENTS

We the People

of the United States, in order to form a more perfect union, establish justice, insure domestic tranquility, provide for the common defense, promote the general welfare, and secure the blessings of liberty to ourselves and our posterity, do ordain and establish this Constitution for the United States of America.

ARTICLE I.

SECTION 1. All legislative powers herein granted shall be vested in a Congress of the United States, which shall consist of a Senate and House of Representatives.

SECTION 2. The House of Representatives shall be composed of members chosen every second year by the people of the several states, and the electors in each state shall have the qualifications requisite for electors of the most numerous branch of the state legislature.

No person shall be a representative who shall not have attained to the age of 25 years, and been seven years a citizen of the United States, and who shall not, when elected, be an inhabitant of that state in which he shall be chosen.

Representatives and direct taxes shall be apportioned among the several states which may be included within this union, according to their respective numbers, which shall be determined by adding to the whole number of free persons, including those bound to service for a term of years, and excluding Indians not taxed, three-fifths of all other persons. The actual enumeration shall be made within three years after the first meeting of the Congress of the United States, and within every subsequent term of ten years, in such manner as they shall by law direct. The number of representatives shall not exceed one for every 30,000, but each state shall have at least one representative; and until such enumeration shall be made, the state of New Hampshire shall be entitled to choose three, Massachusetts eight, Rhode Island and Providence Plantations one, Connecticut five, New York six, New Jersey four, Pennsylvania eight, Delaware one, Maryland six, Virginia ten, North Carolina five, South Carolina five, and Georgia three.

When vacancies happen in the representation from any state, the executive authority thereof shall issue writs of election to fill such vacancies.

The House of Representatives shall choose their speaker and other officers; and shall have the sole power of impeachment.

SECTION 3. The Senate of the United States shall be composed of two Senators from each State, [chosen by the Legislature thereof,] for six Years; and each Senator shall have one Vote.

Immediately after they shall be assembled in Consequence of the first Election, they shall be divided as equally as may be into three Classes. The Seats of the Senators of the first Class shall be vacated at the Expiration of the second Year, of the second Class at the Expiration of the fourth Year, and of the third Class at the Expiration of the sixth Year, so that one-third may be chosen every second Year; [and if Vacancies happen by Resignation, or otherwise, during the Recess of the Legislature of any State, the Executive thereof may make temporary Appointments until the next Meeting of the Legislature, which shall then fill such Vacancies.]

No Person shall be a Senator who shall not have attained to the Age of thirty Years, and been nine Years a Citizen of the United States, and who shall not, when elected, be an Inhabitant of that State for which he shall be chosen.

The Vice President of the United States shall be President of the Senate, but shall have no Vote, unless they be equally divided.

The Senate shall chuse their other Officers, and also a President pro tempore, in the absence of the Vice President, or when he shall exercise the Office of President of the United States.

The Senate shall have the sole Power to try all Impeachments. When sitting for that Purpose, they shall be on Oath or Affirmation. When the President of the United States is tried, the Chief Justice shall preside: And no Person shall be convicted without the Concurrence of two thirds of the Members present.

Judgment in Cases of Impeachment shall not extend further than to removal from Office, and disqualification to hold and enjoy any Office of honor, Trust or Profit under the United States: but the Party convicted shall nevertheless be liable and subject to Indictment, Trial, Judgment and Punishment, according to Law.

SECTION 4. The Times, Places and Manner of holding Elections for Senators and Representatives, shall be prescribed in each State by the Legislature thereof; but the Congress may at any time by Law make or alter such Regulations, except as to the Place of Chusing Senators.

The Congress shall assemble at least once in every Year, and such Meeting shall [be on the first Monday in December,] unless they shall by Law appoint a different Day.

SECTION 5. Each House shall be the Judge of the Elections, Returns and Qualifications of its own Members, and a Majority of each shall constitute a Quorum to do Business; but a smaller number may adjourn from day to day, and may be authorized to compel the Attendance of absent Members, in such Manner, and under such Penalties as each House may provide.

Each House may determine the Rules of its Proceedings, punish its Members for disorderly Behavior, and, with the Concurrence of two thirds, expel a Member.

Each House shall keep a Journal of its Proceedings, and from time to time publish the same, excepting such Parts as may in their Judgment require Secrecy; and the Yeas and Nays of the Members of either House on any question shall, at the Desire of one fifth of those Present, be entered on the Journal.

Neither House, during the Session of Congress, shall, without the Consent of the other, adjourn for more than three days, nor to any other Place than that in which the two Houses shall be sitting.

SECTION 6. The Senators and Representatives shall receive a Compensation for their Services, to be ascertained by Law, and paid out of the Treasury of the United States. They shall in all Cases, except Treason, Felony and Breach of the Peace, be privileged from Arrest during their Attendance at the Session of their respective Houses, and in going to and returning from the same; and for any Speech or Debate in either House, they shall not be questioned in any other Place.

No Senator or Representative shall, during the Time for which he was elected, be appointed to any civil Office under the Authority of the United States, which shall have been created, or the Emoluments whereof shall have been encreased during such time; and no Person holding any Office under the United States, shall be a Member of either House during his Continuance in Office.

SECTION 7. All Bills for raising Revenue shall originate in the House of Representatives; but the Senate may propose or concur with Amendments as on other Bills.

Every Bill which shall have passed the House of Representatives and the Senate, shall, before it become a Law, be presented to the President of the United States; If he approve he shall sign it, but if not he shall return it, with his Objections to that House in which it shall have originated, who shall enter the Objections at large on their Journal, and proceed to reconsider it. If after such Reconsideration two thirds of that House shall agree to pass the Bill, it shall be sent, together with the Objections, to the other House, by which it shall likewise be reconsidered, and if approved by two thirds of that House, it shall become a Law. But in all such Cases the Votes of both Houses shall be determined by Yeas and Nays, and the Names of the Persons voting for and against the Bill shall be entered on the Journal of each House respectively. If any Bill shall not be returned by the President within ten Days (Sundays excepted) after it shall have been presented to him, the Same shall be a Law, in like Manner as if he had signed it, unless the Congress by their Adjournment prevent its Return, in which Case it shall not be a Law.

Every Order, Resolution, or Vote to which the Concurrence of the Senate and House of Representatives may be necessary (except on a question of Adjournment) shall be presented to the President of the United States; and before the Same shall take Effect, shall be approved by him, or being disapproved by him, shall be repassed by two thirds of the Senate and House of Representatives, according to the Rules and Limitations prescribed in the Case of a Bill.

SECTION 8. The Congress shall have Power To lay and collect Taxes, Duties, Imposts and Excises, to pay the Debts and provide for the common Defense and general Welfare of the United States; but all Duties, Imposts and Excises shall be uniform throughout the United States;

To borrow money on the credit of the United States;

To regulate Commerce with foreign Nations, and among the several States, and with the Indian Tribes;

To establish an uniform Rule of Naturalization, and uniform Laws on the subject of Bankruptcies throughout the United States;

To coin Money, regulate the Value thereof, and of foreign Coin, and fix the Standard of Weights and Measures;

To provide for the Punishment of counterfeiting the Securities and current Coin of the United States;

To establish Post Offices and post Roads;

To promote the Progress of Science and useful Arts, by securing for limited Times to Authors and Inventors the exclusive Right to their respective Writings and Discoveries;

To constitute Tribunals inferior to the Supreme Court;

To define and punish Piracies and Felonies committed on the high Seas, and Offenses against the Law of Nations;

To declare War, grant Letters of Marque and Reprisal, and make Rules concerning Captures on Land and Water;

To raise and support Armies, but no Appropriation of Money to that Use shall be for a longer Term than two Years;

To provide and maintain a Navy;

To make Rules for the Government and Regulation of the land and naval Forces;

To provide for calling forth the Militia to execute the Laws of the Union, suppress Insurrections and repel Invasions;

To provide for organizing, arming, and disciplining the Militia, and for governing such Part of them as may be employed in the Service of the United

States, reserving to the States respectively, the Appointment of the Officers, and the Authority of training the Militia according to the discipline prescribed by Congress;

To exercise exclusive Legislation in all Cases whatsoever, over such District (not exceeding ten Miles square) as may, by Cession of particular States, and the acceptance of Congress, become the Seat of the Government of the United States, and to exercise like Authority over all Places purchased by the Consent of the Legislature of the State in which the Same shall be, for the Erection of Forts, Magazines, Arsenals, dock-Yards, and other needful Buildings; — And

To make all Laws which shall be necessary and proper for carrying into Execution the foregoing Powers, and all other Powers vested by this Constitution in the Government of the United States, or in any Department or Officer thereof.

SECTION 9. The Migration or Importation of such Persons as any of the States now existing shall think proper to admit, shall not be prohibited by the Congress prior to the Year one thousand eight hundred and eight, but a tax or duty may be imposed on such Importation, not exceeding ten dollars for each Person.

The privilege of the Writ of Habeas Corpus shall not be suspended, unless when in Cases of Rebellion or Invasion the public Safety may require it.

No Bill of Attainder or *ex post facto* Law shall be passed.

No capitation, or other direct, Tax shall be laid, unless in Proportion to the Census or Enumeration herein before directed to be taken.

No Tax or Duty shall be laid on Articles exported from any State.

No Preference shall be given by any Regulation of Commerce or Revenue to the Ports of one State over those of another: nor shall Vessels bound to, or from, one State, be obliged to enter, clear, or pay Duties in another.

No Money shall be drawn from the Treasury, but in Consequence of Appropriations made by Law; and a regular Statement and Account of the Receipts and Expenditures of all public Money shall be published from time to time.

No Title of Nobility shall be granted by the United States: And no Person holding any Office of Profit or Trust under them, shall, without the Consent of the Congress, accept of any present, Emolument, Office, or Title, of any kind whatever, from any King, Prince, or foreign State.

SECTION 10. No State shall enter into any Treaty, Alliance, or Confederation; grant Letters of Marque and Reprisal; coin Money; emit Bills of Credit; make any Thing but gold and silver Coin a Tender in Payment of Debts; pass any Bill of Attainder, *ex post facto* Law, or Law impairing the Obligation of Contracts, or grant any Title of Nobility.

No State shall, without the Consent of the Congress, lay any Imposts or Duties on Imports or Exports, except what may be absolutely necessary for executing its inspection Laws: and the net Produce of all Duties and Imposts, laid by any State on Imports or Exports, shall be for the Use of the Treasury of the United States; and all such Laws shall be subject to the Revision and Controul of the Congress.

No State shall, without the Consent of Congress, lay any duty of Tonnage, keep Troops, or Ships of War in time of Peace, enter into any Agreement or Compact with another State, or with a foreign Power, or engage in War, unless actually invaded, or in such imminent Danger as will not admit of delay.

ARTICLE II.

SECTION 1. The executive Power shall be vested in a President of the United States of America. He shall hold his Office during the Term of four Years, and, together with the Vice-President, chosen for the same Term, be elected, as follows.

Each State shall appoint, in such Manner as the Legislature thereof may direct, a Number of Electors, equal to the whole Number of Senators and Representatives to which the State may be entitled in the Congress: but no Senator or Representative, or Person holding an Office of Trust or Profit under the United States, shall be appointed an Elector.

[The Electors shall meet in their respective States, and vote by Ballot for two persons, of whom one at least shall not be an Inhabitant of the same State with themselves. And they shall make a List of all the Persons voted for, and of the Number of Votes for each; which List they shall sign and certify, and transmit sealed to the Seat of the Government of the United States, directed to the President of the Senate. The President of the Senate shall, in the Presence of the Senate and House of Representatives, open all the Certificates, and the Votes shall then be counted. The Person having the greatest Number of Votes shall be the President, if such Number be a Majority of the whole Number of Electors appointed; and if there be more than one who have such Majority, and have an equal Number of Votes, then the House of Representatives shall immediately chuse by Ballot one of them for President; and if no Person have a Majority, then from the five highest on the List the said House shall in like Manner chuse the President. But in chusing the President, the Votes shall be taken by States, the Representation from each State having one Vote; a quorum for this Purpose shall consist of a Member or Members from two thirds of the States, and a Majority of all the States shall be necessary to a Choice. In every Case, after the Choice of the President, the Person having the greatest Number of Votes of the Electors shall be the Vice President. But if there should remain two or more who have equal Votes, the Senate shall chuse from them by Ballot the Vice-President.]

The Congress may determine the Time of chusing the Electors, and the Day on which they shall give their Votes; which Day shall be the same throughout the United States.

No Person except a natural born Citizen, or a Citizen of the United States, at the time of the Adoption of this Constitution, shall be eligible to the Office of President; neither shall any Person be eligible to that Office who shall not have attained to the Age of thirty-five Years, and been fourteen Years a Resident within the United States.

[In Case of the Removal of the President from Office, or of his Death, Resignation, or Inability to discharge the Powers and Duties of the said Office, the same shall devolve on the Vice President, and the Congress may by Law, provide for the Case of Removal, Death, Resignation or Inability, both of the President and Vice President, declaring what Officer shall then act as President, and such Officer shall act accordingly, until the Disability be removed, or a President shall be elected.]

The President shall, at stated Times, receive for his Services, a Compensation, which shall neither be encreased nor diminished during the Period for which he shall have been elected, and he shall not receive within that Period any other Emolument from the United States, or any of them.

Before he enter on the Execution of his Office, he shall take the following Oath or Affirmation: — "I do solemnly swear (or affirm) that I will faithfully execute the Office of President of the United States, and will to the best of my Ability, preserve, protect and defend the Constitution of the United States."

SECTION 2. The President shall be Commander in Chief of the Army and Navy of the United States, and of the Militia of the several States, when called into the actual Service of the United States; he may require the Opinion in writing, of the principal Officer in each of the executive Departments, upon any subject relating to the Duties of their respective Offices, and he shall have Power to Grant Reprieves and Pardons for Offenses against the United States, except in Cases of Impeachment.

He shall have Power, by and with the Advice and Consent of the Senate, to make Treaties, provided two-thirds of the Senators present concur; and he shall nominate, and by and with the Advice and Consent of the Senate, shall appoint Ambassadors, other public Ministers and Consuls, Judges of the supreme Court, and all other Officers of the United States, whose Appointments are not herein otherwise provided for, and which shall be established by Law: but the Congress may by Law vest the Appointment of such inferior Officers, as they think proper, in the President alone, in the Courts of Law, or in the Heads of Departments.

The President shall have Power to fill up all Vacancies that may happen during the Recess of the Senate, by granting Commissions which shall expire at the End of their next Session.

SECTION 3. He shall from time to time give to the Congress Information of the State of the Union, and recommend to their Consideration such Measures as he shall judge necessary and expedient; he may, on extraordinary Occasions, convene both Houses, or either of them, and in Case of Disagreement between them, with Respect to the Time of

Adjournment, he may adjourn them to such Time as he shall think proper; he shall receive Ambassadors and other public Ministers; he shall take Care that the Laws be faithfully executed, and shall Commission all the Officers of the United States.

SECTION 4. The President, Vice President and all civil Officers of the United States, shall be removed from Office on Impeachment for, and Conviction of, Treason, Bribery, or other high Crimes and Misdemeanors.

ARTICLE III.

SECTION 1. The judicial Power of the United States, shall be vested in one supreme Court, and in such inferior Courts as the Congress may from time to time ordain and establish. The Judges, both of the supreme and inferior Courts, shall hold their Offices during good Behaviour, and shall, at stated Times, receive for their Services, a Compensation, which shall not be diminished during their Continuance in Office.

SECTION 2. The judicial Power shall extend to all Cases, in Law and Equity, arising under this Constitution, the Laws of the United States, and Treaties made, or which shall be made, under their Authority; — to all Cases affecting Ambassadors, other public Ministers and Consuls; — to all Cases of admiralty and maritime Jurisdiction; — to Controversies to which the United States shall be a Party; — to Controversies between two or more States; — between a State and Citizens of another State; — between Citizens of different States; — between Citizens of the same State claiming Lands under Grants of different States, and between a State, or the Citizens thereof, and foreign States, Citizens or Subjects.

In all Cases affecting Ambassadors, other public Ministers and Consuls, and those in which a State shall be Party, the supreme Court shall have original Jurisdiction. In all the other cases before mentioned, the supreme Court shall have appellate Jurisdiction, both as to Law and Fact, with such Exceptions, and under such Regulations as the Congress shall make.

The trial of all Crimes, except in Cases of Impeachment, shall be by Jury; and such Trial shall be held in the State where the said Crimes shall have been committed; but when not committed within any State, the Trial shall be at such Place or Places as the Congress may by Law have directed.

SECTION 3. Treason against the United States, shall consist only in levying War against them, or in adhering to their Enemies, giving them Aid and Comfort. No Person shall be convicted of Treason unless on the Testimony of two Witnesses to the same overt Act, or on Confession in open Court.

The Congress shall have Power to declare the Punishment of Treason, but no Attainder of Treason shall work Corruption of Blood, or Forfeiture except during the Life of the Person attainted.

ARTICLE IV.

SECTION 1. Full Faith and Credit shall be given in each State to the public Acts, Records, and judicial Proceedings of every other State. And the

Congress may by general Laws prescribe the Manner in which such Acts, Records and Proceedings shall be proved, and the Effect thereof.

SECTION 2. The Citizens of each State shall be entitled to all Privileges and Immunities of Citizens in the several States.

A Person charged in any State with Treason, Felony, or other Crime, who shall flee from Justice, and be found in another State, shall on demand of the executive Authority of the State from which he fled, be delivered up, to be removed to the State having Jurisdiction of the Crime.

[No Person held to Service or Labour in one State, under the Laws thereof, escaping into another, shall, in Consequence of any Law or Regulation therein, be discharged from such Service or Labour, but shall be delivered up on Claim of the Party to whom such Service or Labour may be due.]

SECTION 3. New States may be admitted by the Congress into this Union; but no new State shall be formed or erected within the Jurisdiction of any other State; nor any State be formed by the Junction of two or more States, or parts of States, without the Consent of the Legislatures of the States concerned as well as of the Congress.

The Congress shall have Power to dispose of and make all needful Rules and Regulations respecting the Territory or other Property belonging to the United States; and nothing in this Constitution shall be so construed as to Prejudice any Claims of the United States, or of any particular State.

SECTION 4. The United States shall guarantee to every State in this Union a Republican Form of Government, and shall protect each of them against Invasion; and on Application of the Legislature, or of the Executive (when the Legislature cannot be convened) against domestic Violence.

ARTICLE V.

The Congress, whenever two-thirds of both Houses shall deem it necessary, shall propose Amendments to this Constitution, or, on the Application of the Legislatures of two-thirds of the several States, shall call a Convention for proposing Amendments, which, in either Case, shall be valid to all Intents and Purposes, as part of this Constitution, when ratified by the Legislatures of three-fourths of the several States, or by Conventions in three-fourths thereof, as the one or the other Mode of Ratification may be proposed by the Congress: Provided that no Amendment which may be made prior to the Year One thousand eight hundred and eight shall in any Manner affect the first and fourth Clauses in the Ninth Section of the first Article; and that no State, without its Consent, shall be deprived of its equal Suffrage in the Senate.

ARTICLE VI.

All Debts contracted and Engagements entered into, before the Adoption of this Constitution, shall be as valid against the United States under this Constitution, as under the Confederation.

This Constitution, and the Laws of the United States which shall be made in Pursuance thereof; and all Treaties made, or which shall be made, under the Authority of the United States, shall be the supreme Law of the

Land; and the Judges in every State shall be bound thereby, any Thing in the Constitution or Laws of any State to the contrary notwithstanding.

The Senators and Representatives before mentioned, and the Members of the several State Legislatures, and all executive and judicial Officers, both of the United States and of the several States, shall be bound by Oath or Affirmation, to support this Constitution; but no religious Test shall ever be required as a Qualification to any Office or public Trust under the United States.

ARTICLE VII.

The Ratification of the Conventions of nine States shall be sufficient for the Establishment of this Constitution between the States so ratifying the Same.

Done in Convention by the Unanimous Consent of the States present the Seventeenth Day of September in the Year of our Lord one thousand seven hundred and Eighty seven and of the Independence of the United States of America the Twelfth.

In Witness whereof We have hereunto subscribed our Names.

Go WASHINGTON
Presidt and
deputy from Virginia

New Hampshire.
JOHN LANGDON
NICHOLAS GILMAN

Massachusetts.
NATHANIEL GORHAM
RUFUS KING

New Jersey.
WIL: LIVINGSTON
DAVID BREARLEY.
WM PATERSON.
JONA: DAYTON

Pennsylvania.
B FRANKLIN
ROBT. MORRIS
THOS. FITZSIMONS
JAMES WILSON
THOMAS MIFFLIN
GEO. CLYMER
JARED INGERSOLL
GOUV MORRIS

Delaware.
GEO: READ
JOHN DICKINSON
JACO: BROOM
GUNNING BEDFORD jun
RICHARD BASSETT

Connecticut.
WM SAML JOHNSON
ROGER SHERMAN

New York.
ALEXANDER HAMILTON

Maryland.
JAMES MCHENRY
DANL CARROL
DAN: of ST THOS JENIFER

Virginia.
JOHN BLAIR
JAMES MADISON JR.

North Carolina.
WM BLOUNT
HU WILLIAMSON
RICHD DOBBS SPAIGHT.

South Carolina.
J. RUTLEDGE
CHARLES PINCKNEY
CHARLES
COTESWORTH
PINCKNEY
PIERCE BUTLER

Georgia.
WILLIAM FEW
ABR BALDWIN

Attest:
WILLIAM JACKSON,
Secretary.

ARTICLES IN ADDITION TO, AND AMENDMENT OF, THE CONSTITUTION OF THE UNITED STATES OF AMERICA, PROPOSED BY CONGRESS, AND RATIFIED BY THE LEGISLATURES OF THE SEVERAL STATES, PURSUANT TO THE FIFTH ARTICLE OF THE ORIGINAL CONSTITUTION.

(The first 10 Amendments were ratified December 15, 1791, and form what is known as the "Bill of Rights")

AMENDMENT I

Congress shall make no law respecting an establishment of religion, or prohibiting the free exercise thereof; or abridging the freedom of speech, or of the press; or the right of the people peaceably to assemble, and to petition the Government for a redress of grievances.

AMENDMENT II

A well regulated Militia, being necessary to the security of a free State, the right of the people to keep and bear Arms, shall not be infringed.

AMENDMENT III

No Soldier shall, in time of peace be quartered in any house, without the consent of the Owner, nor in time of war, but in a manner to be prescribed by law.

AMENDMENT IV

The right of the people to be secure in their persons, houses, papers, and effects, against unreasonable searches and seizures, shall not be violated, and no Warrants shall issue, but upon probable cause, supported by Oath or affirmation, and particularly describing the place to be searched, and the persons or things to be seized.

AMENDMENT V

No person shall be held to answer for a capital, or otherwise infamous crime, unless on a presentment or indictment of a Grand Jury, except in cases arising in the land or naval forces, or in the Militia, when in actual service in time of War or public danger; nor shall any person be subject for the same offence to be twice put in jeopardy of life or limb; nor shall be compelled in any criminal case to be a witness against himself, nor be deprived of life, liberty, or property, without due process of law; nor shall private property be taken for public use, without just compensation.

AMENDMENT VI

In all criminal prosecutions, the accused shall enjoy the right to a speedy and public trial, by an impartial jury of the State and district wherein the crime shall have been committed, which district shall have been previously ascertained by law, and to be informed of the nature and cause of the accusation; to be confronted with the witnesses against him; to have compulsory process for obtaining witnesses in his favor, and to have the Assistance of Counsel for his defence.

AMENDMENT VII

In suits at common law, where the value in controversy shall exceed twenty dollars, the right of trial by jury shall be preserved, and no fact tried by a jury, shall be otherwise reexamined in any Court of the United States, than according to the rules of the common law.

AMENDMENT VIII

Excessive bail shall not be required, nor excessive fines imposed, nor cruel and unusual punishments inflicted.

AMENDMENT IX

The enumeration in the Constitution, of certain rights, shall not be construed to deny or disparage others retained by the people.

AMENDMENT X

The powers not delegated to the United States by the Constitution, nor prohibited by it to the States, are reserved to the States respectively, or to the people.

AMENDMENT XI

The Judicial power of the United States shall not be construed to extend to any suit in law or equity, commenced or prosecuted against one of the United States by Citizens of another State, or by Citizens or Subjects of any Foreign State.

AMENDMENT XII

The Electors shall meet in their respective states and vote by ballot for President and Vice-President, one of whom, at least, shall not be an inhabitant of the same state with themselves; they shall name in their ballots the person voted for as President, and in distinct ballots the person voted for as Vice-President, and they shall make distinct lists of all persons voted for as President, and of all persons voted for as Vice-President, and of the number of votes for each, which lists they shall sign and certify, and transmit sealed to the seat of the government of the United States, directed to the President of the Senate; — The President of the Senate shall, in presence of the Senate and House of Representatives, open all the certificates and the votes shall then be counted; — The person having the greatest number of votes for President, shall be the President, if such number be a majority of the whole number of Electors appointed; and if no person have such majority, then from the persons having the highest numbers not exceeding three on the list of those voted for as President, the House of Representatives shall choose immediately, by ballot, the President. But in choosing the President, the votes shall be taken by states, the representation from each state having one vote; a quorum for this purpose shall consist of a member or members from two-thirds of the states, and a majority of all the states shall be necessary to a choice. [And if the House of Representatives shall not choose a President whenever the right of choice shall devolve upon them, before the fourth day of March next following, then the Vice-President shall act as President, as in the case of the death or other constitutional disability of the President. —] The person having the greatest number of votes as Vice-President, shall be the Vice-President, if such number be a majority of the whole number of Electors appointed, and if no person have a majority, then from the two highest numbers on the list, the Senate shall choose the Vice-President; a quorum for the purpose shall consist of two-thirds of the whole number of Senators, and a majority of the whole number shall be necessary to a choice. But no person constitutionally ineligible to the office of President shall be eligible to that of Vice-President of the United States.

AMENDMENT XIII

SECTION 1. Neither slavery nor involuntary servitude, except as a punishment for crime whereof the party shall have been duly convicted, shall exist within the United States, or any place subject to their jurisdiction.

SECTION 2. Congress shall have power to enforce this article by appropriate legislation.

AMENDMENT XIV

SECTION 1. All persons born or naturalized in the United States, and subject to the jurisdiction thereof, are citizens of the United States and of the State wherein they reside. No State shall make or enforce any law which shall abridge the privileges or immunities of citizens of the United States; nor shall any State deprive any person of life, liberty, or property, without due process of law; nor deny to any person within its jurisdiction the equal protection of the laws.

SECTION 2. Representatives shall be apportioned among the several States according to their respective numbers, counting the whole number of persons in each State, excluding Indians not taxed. But when the right to vote at any election for the choice of electors for President and Vice-President of the United States, Representatives in Congress, the Executive and Judicial officers of a State, or the members of the Legislature thereof, is denied to any of the male inhabitants of such State, being twenty-one years of age, and citizens of the United States, or in any way abridged, except for participation in rebellion, or other crime, the basis of representation therein shall be reduced in the proportion which the number of such male citizens shall bear to the whole number of male citizens twenty-one years of age in such State.

SECTION 3. No person shall be a Senator or Representative in Congress, or elector of President and Vice-President, or hold any office, civil or military, under the United States, or under any State, who, having previously taken an oath, as a member of Congress, or as an officer of the United States, or as a member of any State legislature, or as an executive or judicial officer of any State, to support the Constitution of the United States, shall have engaged in insurrection or rebellion against the same, or given aid or comfort to the enemies thereof. But Congress may by a vote of two-thirds of each House, remove such disability.

SECTION 4. The validity of the public debt of the United States, authorized by law, including debts incurred for payment of pensions and bounties for services in suppressing insurrection or rebellion, shall not be questioned. But neither the United States nor any State shall assume or pay any debt or obligation incurred in aid of insurrection or rebellion against the United States, or any claim for the loss or emancipation of any slave; but all such debts, obligations and claims shall be held illegal and void.

SECTION 5. The Congress shall have power to enforce, by appropriate legislation, the provisions of this article.

AMENDMENT XV

SECTION 1. The right of citizens of the United States to vote shall not be denied or abridged by the United States or by any State on account of race, color, or previous condition of servitude —

SECTION 2. The Congress shall have power to enforce this article by appropriate legislation.

AMENDMENT XVI

The Congress shall have power to lay and collect taxes on incomes, from whatever source derived, without apportionment among the several States, and without regard to any census or enumeration.

AMENDMENT XVII

The Senate of the United States shall be composed of two Senators from each State, elected by the people thereof, for six years; and each Senator shall have one vote. The electors in each State shall have the qualifications requisite for electors of the most numerous branch of the State legislatures.

When vacancies happen in the representation of any State in the Senate, the executive authority of such State shall issue writs of election to fill such vacancies: *Provided,* That the legislature of any State may empower the executive thereof to make temporary appointments until the people fill the vacancies by election as the legislature may direct.

This amendment shall not be so construed as to affect the election or term of any Senator chosen before it becomes valid as part of the Constitution.

AMENDMENT XVIII

[SECTION 1. After one year from the ratification of this article the manufacture, sale, or transportation of intoxicating liquors within, the importation thereof into, or the exportation thereof from the United States and all territory subject to the jurisdiction thereof for beverage purposes is hereby prohibited.

[SECTION 2. The Congress and the several States shall have concurrent power to enforce this article by appropriate legislation.

[SECTION 3. This article shall be inoperative unless it shall have been ratified as an amendment to the Constitution by the legislatures of the

several States as provided in the Constitution, within seven years from the date of the submission hereof to the States by the Congress.]

AMENDMENT XIX

The right of citizens of the United States to vote shall not be denied or abridged by the United States or by any State on account of sex.

Congress shall have power to enforce this article by appropriate legislation.

AMENDMENT XX

SECTION 1. The terms of the President and Vice President shall end at noon on the 20th day of January, and the terms of Senators and Representatives at noon on the 3rd day of January, of the years in which such terms would have ended if this article had not been ratified; and the terms of their successors shall then begin.

SECTION 2. The Congress shall assemble at least once in every year, and such meeting shall begin at noon on the 3rd day of January, unless they shall by law appoint a different day.

SECTION 3. If, at the time fixed for the beginning of the term of the President, the President elect shall have died, the Vice President elect shall become President. If a President shall not have been chosen before the time fixed for the beginning of his term, or if the President elect shall have failed to qualify, then the Vice President elect shall act as President until a President shall have qualified; and the Congress may by law provide for the case wherein neither a President elect nor a Vice President elect shall have qualified, declaring who shall then act as President, or the manner in which one who is to act shall be selected, and such person shall act accordingly until a President or Vice President shall have qualified.

SECTION 4. The Congress may by law provide for the case of the death of any of the persons from whom the House of Representatives may choose a President whenever the right of choice shall have devolved upon them, and for the case of the death of any of the persons from whom the Senate may choose a Vice President whenever the right of choice shall have devolved upon them.

SECTION 5. Sections 1 and 2 shall take effect on the 15th day of October following the ratification of this article.

SECTION 6. This article shall be inoperative unless it shall have been ratified as an amendment to the Constitution by the legislatures of three-fourths of the several States within seven years from the date of its submission.

AMENDMENT XXI

SECTION 1. The eighteenth article of amendment to the Constitution of the United States is hereby repealed.

SECTION 2. The transportation or importation into any State, Territory, or possession of the United States for delivery or use therein of intoxicating liquors, in violation of the laws thereof, is hereby prohibited.

SECTION 3. This article shall be inoperative unless it shall have been ratified as an amendment to the Constitution by conventions in the several States, as provided in the Constitution, within seven years from the date of the submission hereof to the States by the Congress.

AMENDMENT XXII

No person shall be elected to the office of the President more than twice, and no person who has held the office of President, or acted as President, for more than two years of a term to which some other person was elected President shall be elected to the office of the President more than once. But this Article shall not apply to any person holding the office of President when this Article was proposed by the Congress, and shall not prevent any person who may be holding the office of President, or acting as President, during the term within which this Article becomes operative from holding the office of President or acting as President during the remainder of such term.

AMENDMENT XXIII

SECTION 1. The District constituting the seat of Government of the United States shall appoint in such manner as the Congress may direct:

A number of electors of President and Vice President equal to the whole number of Senators and Representatives in Congress to which the District would be entitled if it were a State, but in no event more than the least populous State; they shall be in addition to those appointed by the States, but they shall be considered, for the purposes of the election of President and Vice President, to be electors appointed by a State; and they shall meet in the District and perform such duties as provided by the twelfth article of amendment.

SECTION 2. The Congress shall have power to enforce this article by appropriate legislation.

AMENDMENT XXIV

SECTION 1. The right of citizens of the United States to vote in any primary or other election for President or Vice President, for electors for President or Vice President, or for Senator or Representative in Congress, shall not be denied or abridged by the United States or any State by reason of failure to pay any poll tax or other tax.

SECTION 2. The Congress shall have power to enforce this article by appropriate legislation.

AMENDMENT XXV

SECTION 1. In case of the removal of the President from office or of his death or resignation, the Vice President shall become President.

SECTION 2. Whenever there is a vacancy in the office of the Vice President, the President shall nominate a Vice President who shall take office upon confirmation by a majority vote of both Houses of Congress.

SECTION 3. Whenever the President transmits to the President pro tempore of the Senate and the Speaker of the House of Representatives his written declaration that he is unable to discharge the powers and duties of his office, and until he transmits to them a written declaration to the contrary, such powers and duties shall be discharged by the Vice President as Acting President.

SECTION 4. Whenever the Vice President and a majority of either the principal officers of the executive departments or of such other body as Congress may by law provide, transmit to the President pro tempore of the Senate and the Speaker of the House of Representatives their written declaration that the President is unable to discharge the powers and duties of his office, the Vice President shall immediately assume the powers and duties of the office as Acting President.

Thereafter, when the President transmits to the President pro tempore of the Senate and the Speaker of the House of Representatives his written declaration that no inability exists, he shall resume the powers and duties of his office unless the Vice President and a majority of either the principal officers of the executive department or of such other body as Congress may by law provide, transmit within four days to the President pro tempore of the Senate and the Speaker of the House of Representatives their written declaration that the President is unable to discharge the powers and duties of his office. Thereupon Congress shall decide the issue, assembling within forty-eight hours for that purpose if not in session. If the Congress, within twenty-one days after receipt of the latter written declaration, or, if Congress is not in session, within twenty-one days after Congress is required to assemble, determines by two-thirds vote of both Houses that the President is unable to discharge the powers and duties of his office, the Vice President shall continue to discharge the same as Acting President; otherwise, the President shall resume the powers and duties of his office.

AMENDMENT XXVI

SECTION 1. The right of citizens of the United States, who are eighteen years of age or older, to vote shall not be denied or abridged by the United States or by any State on account of age.

SECTION 2. The Congress shall have power to enforce this article by appropriate legislation.

[NOTE: The Constitution and all amendments in their original form are given above. Items which have since been amended or superseded are bracketed.]

BIBLIOGRAPHY

Alistair Cooke's America, Alfred A. Knopf, New York, 1973.

Andrews, Wayne, ed., *Concise Dictionary of American History,* Charles Scribner's Sons, New York, 1962.

Barre Foundation Book, *Philadelphia — A 300-Year History,* W. W. Norton, New York, 1982.

Bowen, Catherine Drinker, *Miracle at Philadelphia,* Little, Brown & Co., Boston, Mass., 1966.

Brown, Bernard E., *Great American Political Thinkers,* Vol. I, Avon Books, New York, 1983.

Bruckberger, R. L., *Image of America,* Viking Press, New York, 1959.

Catton, Bruce & William B. Catton, *The Bold and Magnificent Dream: America's Founding Years,* 1492–1815, Doubleday & Co., Inc., Garden City, New York, 1978.

Earle, Alice Morse, *Home Life in Colonial Days,* Jonathan David Publ. Inc., Middle Village, New York, 1975.

Farrand, Max, *The Fathers of the Constitution,* The Yale Chronicles of America Series, Yale University Press, New Haven, Conn., 1921.

Flexner, James Thomas, *George Washington & The New Nation (1783–1793),* Little, Brown & Co., Boston, Mass., 1969.

Flexner, James Thomas, *Washington The Indispensable Man,* New American Library, New York, 1969.

Garraty, John A., *Interpreting American History* — Conversations With Historians, Macmillan Co., New York, 1970.

Graebner, Norman A., Gilbert C. Fite, Philip L. White, *A History Of The American People,* McGraw-Hill Book Co., New York, 1970.

Hofstader, Richard, *The American Political Tradition & The Men Who Made It,* Alfred A. Knopf, New York, 1970.

Hogarth, Paul, *Walking Tours of Old Philadelphia,* Barre Foundation Publ., Mass., 1976.

Kammen, Michael, *The Origins of the American Constitution,* Viking Penguin, Inc., New York, 1986.

Madison, James, *Notes of Debates In The Federal Convention Of 1787,* Ohio University Press, Athens, Ohio, 1966.

Morison, Samuel Eliot, *The Oxford History of the American People,* Oxford University Press, New York, 1965.

Morison, Samuel Eliot & Henry Steele Commager, *The Growth of the American Republic,* Vol. I., Oxford University Press, New York, 1962.

Morris, Richard B., *The Framing of the Constitution,* U.S. Department of the Interior, Washington, D.C., 1986.

Neuburg, Victor E., *The Penny Histories,* Oxford University Press, New York, 1968.

Richardson, Edgar P., *Charles Willson Peale And His World,* Harry Abrams, Inc., New York, 1982.

Schlesinger, Arthur M., Jr., *The Imperial Presidency,* Houghton Mifflin Co., New York, 1973.

Shackleton, Robert, *The Book Of Philadelphia,* Penn Publ. Co., Philadelphia, Pa., 1918.

Smith, Page., *The Constitution: A Documentary & Narrative History,* Wm. Morrow & Co., New York, 1978.

Smith, Page., *The Shaping Of America,* Vol. III, McGraw-Hill Book Co., New York, 1980.

Starkey, Marion, *Lace Cuffs and Leather Aprons,* Alfred A. Knopf, New York, 1972.

Stevens, Sylvester K., *Pennsylvania, Birthplace Of A Nation,* Random House, New York, 1964.

Thorpe, Frances Newton, *The Constitutional History of the United States,* Vol. I, Callighan & Co., Chicago, Ill., 1901.

Van Doren, Carl, *The Great Rehearsal,* Penguin Books, New York, 1986.

Wood, Gordon S., *The Creation Of the American Republic, 1776–1787,* W. W. Norton & Co., New York, 1972.

Wright, Esmond, *Franklin of Philadelphia,* Harvard University Press, Mass., 1986.

INDEX OF NAMES

Book design:
DAVID MOORE
Production:
MARTHA JO CHACONAS
AND ALICE BURGESS
Picture research:
ELIZABETH JONES
Typesetting:
GENERAL TYPOGRAPHERS, INC.
WASHINGTON, D.C.
Printing:
COLLINS LITHOGRAPHING, INC.
BALTIMORE, MARYLAND
Typeface:
BERKELEY OLD STYLE
BY FREDERIC GOUDY
Paper:
LUSTRO OFFSET ENAMEL DULL
BY S. D. WARREN PAPER CO.

We the Pe

insure domestic Tranquilit

and our Posterity, do ordai

Section. 1. All legislati

of Representatives.

Section. 2. The House of

in each State shall have the Qualif

No Person shall be a

and who shall not, when elected,

Representatives and di

Numbers, which shall be determ

not taxed, three fifths of all othe